Best Of
GunDigest®

HANDGUNS & HANDGUN SHOOTING

David Maccar

Published by

Gun Digest® Books, an imprint of F+W Media, Inc.
Krause Publications • 700 East State Street • Iola, WI 54990-0001
715-445-2214 • 888-457-2873
www.krausebooks.com

To order books or other products call toll-free 1-800-258-0929
or visit us online at www.gundigeststore.com

Cover photography courtesy of Ruger and Smith & Wesson

ISBN-13: 978144024610-4
ISBN-10: 144024610-6

Cover Design by Sharon Bartsch
Designed by Kevin Ulrich
Edited by Chad Love

10 9 8 7 6 5 4 3 2 1

Dedication

For my wife Madeleine, my mother Antoinette, and my dog Hunter Stockton: constant reminders of what is worth protecting; and for my father, David Maccar, who taught me to hunt and shoot, and how to be a good man.

Table of Contents

Introduction

A pistol. It conjures up specific emotions in different individuals. To some it's the tool of the farm and ranch, a simple, unadorned revolver used to take care of dangers and nuisances and as protection while alone in the field.

To others, handguns are the iconic sidearms of the Old West--big single-action Colts and Remingtons swinging in sagging leather holsters worn by rough men in rough country. What would the image of the American cowboy be without his trusty six-shooter on his hip?

Still, to others, they represent law enforcement--from the sturdy, blued Smith & Wessons from bygone decades to today's high-capacity pistols like the Glock 17 and the SIG 226 that ride on LEO's hips and under jackets in shoulder holsters today.

Pistols have long been status symbols for military officers, and were highly sought-after arms in times when they were the only repeaters on battlefields full of single-shot muzzleloading muskets. Later, pistols like the ever reliable Luger and Colt 1911 were perfectly suited for the dark, treacherous hell of the trenches in WWI, and later served as reliable backup weapons for many a soldier in WWII, and in every war since.

They are the tools of home and personal defense for the average citizen--the great equalizer resting at the ready on the nightstand or secured in a holster inside a purse or briefcase.

At various times, handguns have been a lightning rod for the gun control debate and the scapegoat of gun violence in America. But the fact remains, six centuries after the idea for a hand-sized gun was conceived, it remains the go-to choice for self-defense for thousands of people who carry a weapon every day.

Today, handguns are just as storied and multifaceted as their history. One can find anything on the pistol landscape, depending on application. There are myriad big bore semi-autos topped with red dots or magnifiers, compensators affixed to the muzzle, perfect for hog hunting. On the other end of the spectrum, pocket pistols, like the S&W M&P Bodyguard chambered in .380 ACP, are becoming very popular as everyday carry weapons for people of all sizes.

When all is said and done, Americans have an odd but blood-deep relationship with the handgun that has been and will continue to be explored by an Internet full of people at keyboards and in front of cameras. While it has been vilified and scorned as the tool of criminals and the taker of innocent lives, it is as much the tool of the righteous and defenders of freedom.

When I was a kid, I guess about six years old, my father got me the first great gift of my life. I was too young for a .22, but not too young for the orange and black plastic knock-off Beretta 92 that paralyzed me with desire in the aisle of a KB Toys back in 1980-something. It had everything. The slide really worked, the magazine came out and you could slap it back it, there was even an orange plastic tube that screwed onto the barrel and was good enough of a suppressor for me at the time. More than that, it was a hero's gun. Even at that age, I was an action movie junkie, and I knew it immediately as the gun of Martin Riggs and John McClane. It was the gun Army guys and police carried. It was a 9mm.

I played with it until the springs that worked the slide broke, and were replaced a few times. I took it completely apart and spray painted the orange parts silver (my dad made me leave the tip orange) and made a McClane-like shoulder holster for it out of a hip holster from an old cowboy set.

It wasn't about having power or wanting to hurt people with a weapon. I would have been way too embarrassed to show any of my friends the holster I'd rigged up, and I'd never let them play with my favorite toy gun, because they just wouldn't play with it right. So it wasn't about showing off. Even at that age, though I could never have articulated it at the time, it was about having the ability to do something when evil people tried to impose their will on the innocent. It was about being John McClane.

That same feeling from all those years ago never went away. When I was a child, it was all imagination, but having a handgun became much more than that. It became a sense of security, safety, knowing that if things went truly south, I would have the ability to do something other than cower or run and hide.

And now it means even more. It's that look in a friend's eyes the first time they squeeze off a magazine at the range. It's adding something to a project gun and having it work and look just right. It's marveling at a design John Moses Browning created over a hundred years ago, newly made, the latest of millions, and sitting on my gun mat.

This collection of articles from the *Gun Digest* Annuals, spanning from the mid 1980s to the present, is an attempt to capture the depth and breadth of the handgun world and the experiences and relationships that have followed them through the past years. It also serves as a collection of milestones that show just how far pistol design and manufacturing techniques have come in a mere three decades of engineering and innovation.

David Maccar

The Good Old Days: 60 Years Of Six Guns

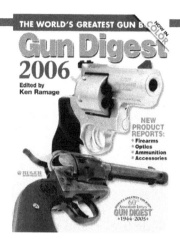

■ John Taffin

O h, for the good old days! Just about everyone, especially those on the sunset side of life, has spent time longing for the good old days. As a writer, I have often talked about the good old days and the great old six-guns of yesteryear. However, if the truth be told, when it comes to medicine, transportation, communication—and especially firearms—these are the good old days!

Consider this. When the first edition of **Gun Digest** appeared in 1944, there were only two revolver manufacturers: Colt and Smith & Wesson. The **Gun Digest** catalog section required only a couple pages to cover their offerings–and occupied that space only by using large pictures. The successful conclusion of World War II was very current history and these two manu-

A few years ago, while looking through some old papers in the Colt files an employee found a special order for a Colt .45 "peacemaker" with a 4-3/4" barrel and nickel finish. The order was from Bat Masterson and written on stationery from the Long Branch Saloon in Dodge City.

facturers were making the switch from wartime to peacetime production. The transition would not be immediate. Colt had moved their machinery for producing big-bore Single Actions and New Services to the parking lot in 1941. It does not take much imagination to realize what Connecticut weather did to the precision machinery during the war years.

Colt did not catalog anything larger than the 38 Special, while Smith & Wesson teased shooters with the 357 Magnum and the 1926 Model 44 Special. Skeeter Skelton joined the Border Patrol around 1950, and would later write about how difficult it was to acquire a 357 Magnum. These magnificent six-guns would not return to civilian production until 1948 and it would be 1952 before Skelton could come up with one.

That was then and this is now and these good days are certainly better than the good old days. The current *Gun Digest* revolver catalog section requires nearly 20 pages, with small pictures, just to cover currently produced revolvers. Those old Colt and Smith & Wesson revolvers of the 1940s have pretty much disappeared but have been replaced by many new models. We also find a large supermarket selection from Freedom Arms, Ruger, Taurus, and Wesson Firearms, and replicas of nearly every 19th-century six-gun are found. Yes, these definitely are the good old days.

Let's take a look at 60 years of great six-guns and how we got from the nostalgic good old days to today—the real good old days. Please realize this is not a complete discourse and all we can do is hit the highlights, basically of only big-bore six-guns. Several large books have been written about Colt, Ruger, and Smith & Wesson–and even these are necessarily incomplete.

During the late 1940s Smith & Wesson teased shooters with images of 357 Magnums and the 44 Special. However, it would be the 1950s before they were available.

In the mid-1960s Smith & Wesson introduced their third big-bore Magnum chambering, the 41 Magnum Model 57 in both blue and nickel, with barrel lengths of 4, 6, and 8-3/8 inches.

Smith & Wesson– Double Action Perfection

As we mentioned, after the end of World War II it took several years for Smith & Wesson to resume production of the 357 Magnum. Pre-war and early post-war six-guns from Smith & Wesson had the old long action; beginning in 1950, that action design was changed to give a shorter hammer fall. Most double-action shooters preferred the smoothness of the older long action; however, it was gone forever. The year 1950 saw several significant revolvers introduced. Though it is not a big bore, the Chiefs Special arrived as the first five-shot J-frame and would set the standard for pocket pistols. The 4th Model 44 Hand Ejector arrived as the 1950 Target Model 44 Special. These were beautifully made six-guns, mostly found with 6 1/2-inch barrels, with a few rare 4- and 5-inch versions also made. A companion six-gun was the 1950 Tar-

In the late 1980s, the new wave of Smith & Wesson six-guns arrived with rounded butts and heavy underlug barrels. Shown (counterclockwise from top left): the Model 625 45ACP, Model 625 45 Colt and theModel 686 357 Magnum.

get Model 45 ACP, also with a 6 1/2-inch barrel, with a few actually being made in 45 Colt. When Smith & Wesson went to model numbers in 1957, these two big-bore revolvers became the Models 24 and 26. The companion fixed-sight Military Model, in 44 Special *(especially rare)* and 45 ACP, was introduced in 1951 and became the Model 21 and 22, respectively.

Relatively speaking, the 357 Magnum was fairly expensive to produce, so in 1954 Smith & Wesson offered the same basic revolver, with a matte blue finish, as the Highway Patrolman. As its name suggests, it became very popular with peace officers and outdoorsmen as a no-frills heavy-duty 357 Magnum. One year later Smith & Wesson upgraded the 1950 Target 45 ACP to the 1955 Target with a heavy bull barrel, target hammer, and target trigger. Later known as the Model 25, it would also be offered in 45 Colt. The year 1955 is also especially significant for two very radical–at the time–new revolvers. The Military & Police 38 Special had been around since 1899 and was very popular

with peace officers even after the advent of the heavier 357 Magnum. Border Patrolman Bill Jordan began lobbying Smith & Wesson to build a 357 Magnum on the same size frame as the Military & Police. They listened, and the result was the 357 Combat Magnum, a Military & Police with a heavy bull barrel and an enclosed ejector rod housing. It was widely accepted as the peace officer's dream revolver. By 1957 it was known as the Model 19.

For nearly 30 years Elmer Keith had been trying to convince manufacturers such as Smith & Wesson to bring out a new revolver to house his heavy 44 Special loads. Ammunition manufacturers were afraid such a load would find its way into older, weaker revolvers so Keith suggested a 44 Special magnum with a cartridge case the same length as the 357 Magnum to preclude it fitting the chambers of 44 Special six-guns. In 1954, Smith & Wesson–in conjunction with Remington–went to work on a new 44 six-gun and cartridge. The 1950 Target Model 44 Special was specially heat-treated and re-chambered to the new,

longer 44 Magnum. Keith had asked for a 1200 fps load and received a true magnum with a 240-grain bullet at 1450 fps.

A new era in handgunning had just begun and the increasing popularity of handgun hunting coincides with the arrival of the 44 Magnum. The Smith & Wesson 44 Magnum, complete with full-length cylinder and heavy bull barrel, would become the Model 29 in 1957.

After the 44 Magnum arrived, both Elmer Keith and Bill Jordan began petitioning Smith & Wesson for another new revolver, a 41 to be used by peace officers. Smith & Wesson listened but took a different path and simply chambered the Model 29 for the new 41 Magnum cartridge. It was known as the Model 57 and was accompanied by an oversized Military & Police version, the Model 58. Both six-guns and ammunition were deemed too heavy for police use; however, they did find a special niche with hunters and outdoorsmen.

All of these six-guns are now gone. The Models 21, 22, 24, and 26 were dropped in 1966; the Models 29 and 19 in 1999; Model 25, 1991; Model 57,

1993; and even the original 357 Magnum was gone by 1994, preceded by the 1986 demise of the Highway Patrolman Model 28. It is obvious Smith & Wesson took a new direction in the 1990s.

In 1965 Smith & Wesson introduced the Chief's Special in what would become the material of the future, stainless steel. This was the first successful revolver so constructed and there was some doubt as to whether it could be used with heavier cartridges. That doubt was removed beginning in 1971 with the stainless steel version of the Model 19 Combat Magnum, the Model 66. This opened doors to the point where the majority of big-bore revolvers are now made of stainless steel. In 1979 the first truly big-bore stainless steel Smith & Wesson arrived, the 44 Magnum Model 629. A significant change had definitely been made.

The year 1980 saw a major change in 357 Magnum production as Smith & Wesson introduced the first L-frame. There were those who complained about the Model 19/66 not holding up with continued use of full-power 357 Magnum ammunition, so Smith & Wesson set about to improve matters, with the result being one of the most accurate 357 Magnums ever offered by the Springfield firm. To arrive at the L-frame, Smith & Wesson maintained the K-frame grip of the Model 66 (*as opposed to the larger N-frame grip of the Model 29 44 Magnum*), enlarged the cylinder and the front of the frame around the barrel threads. Finally they added weight and stability by using a full under-lug barrel. In stainless steel, this 357 Magnum is known as the Model 686 while the blued version was the 586. The 686, available in both six-shot and seven-shot versions, remains in production and deserves a serious look by anyone contemplating the purchase of a 357

The early 44 Magnums of 1956 are known as pre-29s. Custom stocks are by Roy Fishpaw.

Magnum.

The 44 Special had been dropped in 1966 and almost immediately people began trying to convince Smith & Wesson to bring it back. At about the same time, a freelance writer by the name of Skeeter Skelton joined the staff of *Shooting Times* magazine and soon began writing about the 44 Special, and urging its return. Smith & Wesson listened and produced a total of 7500 4-inch and 6 1/2-inch Model 24-3s in 1983, followed

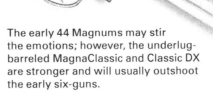

The early 44 Magnums may stir the emotions; however, the underlug-barreled MagnaClassic and Classic DX are stronger and will usually outshoot the early six-guns.

by a larger run of the same basic six-gun, the Model 624 in stainless steel, from 1985 to 1987.

By now stainless steel was firmly established as the material of the future and the 41 Magnum became the Model 657 in 1986, while the heavy under-lug Model 625 stainless steel six-guns began emerging in both 45 ACP and 45 Colt in 1989. Standard-contour barrels and square-butt grip frames had pretty much been replaced by heavy under-lug barrels and round-butt grip frames.

In the late 1980s and early 1990s Smith & Wesson made the necessary interior changes to their action, which resulted in the Endurance Package. Action parts were more tightly fitted and cylinder bolt slots were made longer. As a result, the stainless-steel heavy underlug-barreled Model 629s will endure heavier loads longer without shooting loose, as the older Model 29s were wont to do.

In 1996 Smith & Wesson took a new path with the 44 Special, offering it as a five-shot L-frame Model 696, followed three years later with the 396Ti lightweight L-frame; partially constructed of the new material for revolvers: titanium. Before the end of the century, S&W revolvers were being fitted with interior locks activated by a key in a small hole above the cylinder release latch.

Titanium was soon joined by scandium and the result, in 2001, was the seven-shot, L-framed Model 386Sc Mountain Lite, an 18 1/2-ounce 357 Magnum. Smith & Wesson did not stop there and also introduced the Chief's Special Model 360Sc and Centennial Model 340Sc, 12-ounce (!) five-shot, J-frame 357 Magnums. Considering these extremely compact 357 Magnums, it is most interesting to go back and read articles about the three pound-plus original 357 Magnum and its recoil, as perceived in the 1930s and 1940s. The 340Sc kicks to be sure; however, it is quite manageable with 125-grain JHPs and can be carried, virtually unnoticeable, in a pants pocket all day.

As this is written, the latest magnum from Smith & Wesson is the ultralight 26-ounce Model 329PD titanium/scandium 44 Magnum. If the titanium/scandium 357 Magnum kicks, then this one really kicks. Loaded with 44 Specials, it becomes an easy shooting and very portable big-bore six-gun. Two or three 44 Special rounds, followed by the same number of 44 Magnums, afford a lot of versatility. If you are in territory where a large angry beast could be encountered, load all 44 Magnums.

Smith & Wesson introduced the 357 Magnum in 1935, the 44 Magnum in 1955, the 41 Magnum in 1964, and then faded into the shadows as the 454 Casull, 480 Ruger, and 475 Linebaugh arrived from other manufacturers. However, S&W is once again the King of the Magnum Six-Guns following the introduction of the new X-frame 500 S&W Magnum capable of handling 440-grain bullets at 1600+ fps. Offered in either an 8 3/8- or 4-inch version–both with heavy under-lug ported barrels–this surely represents the ultimate, the apex, the top of the mountain—we simply cannot come up with a more powerful hand-held revolver. Of course, the same was said about the 357 Magnum, and

then the 44 Magnum.

We have covered only the high spots and I highly recommend the book *Standard Catalog of Smith & Wesson, Second Edition* by Supica and Nahas (Krause Publications 2001) for an in-depth study of all Smith & Wesson revolvers and semi-automatics going all the way back to the 1850s.

The Return of Big-Bore Colt Six-Guns

It took a while but in 1955 Colt finally reentered the 357 Magnum market. Prior to World War II, the Colt New Service was offered in 45 Colt, 44 Special, 44-40, 38-40, 45 ACP, 38 Special and 357 Magnum. Now it was gone. However, Colt took a look at their Officers Model Match, added a distinctively shaped and heavy ribbed 6-inch barrel, smoothed the action, and finished the entire six-gun in Royal Blue. It is without doubt the finest double action ever produced by Colt, and some fans will say it is the finest double action ever— period. Over the years it has been offered in blued, nickel, and stainless steel versions, as well as in three other barrel lengths: 2-1/2, 4, and 8 inches.

Never in my life did I lust for a six-gun as much as I did when Colt first started advertising the 4-inch blued Python. The Python, still in production today, is normally in very short supply.

The Python, with its action design dating to the 19th century, requires a lot

Above: In the 1980s, S&W briefly resurrected the 44 Special in both the blued Model 24-3 and stainless steel Model 624.

Right: The Smith & Wesson got smaller in the 1990s and early 2000s with the five-shot 44 Special Model 696 and Model 396Ti, and the 12-ounce 340Sc in 357 Magnum.

of hand-fitting, leading Colt, in 1986, to begin producing the King Cobra 357 Magnum with 4- and 6-inch barrels. The King Cobra was easier and cheaper to produce than the Python, and was very well known for its accuracy. However, as with so many Colt products the last quarter-century, it proved too expensive to make and so was removed from production.

For 35 years, Colt apparently considered the 44 Magnum a passing fancy. Finally in 1990 their biggest "snake," the Anaconda–sort of an over-sized King Cobra–was chambered in 44 Magnum, making it the first truly big-bore double-action revolver from Colt in 50 years. The Anaconda in stainless steel has been offered in both 44 Magnum and 45 Colt with a choice of 4-, 6- and 8-inch barrels, and 10-inch barrels are at least rumored. The 4-inch barrel version is extremely hard to find. The very early Anacondas had bad barrels; however, that was corrected quickly, and the Anaconda has proven to be a very accurate and very sturdy six-gun. It is still cataloged by Colt today.

Not only was the New Service deep-sixed by Colt in 1941, it was accompanied by the Colt Single Action Army. The New Service never returned, and Colt announced they had no plans to ever produce the Single Action Army again. However, after considering the popularity of Western movies on the relatively new medium of television in the early 1950s, coupled with the success of the Ruger Single-Six, Colt changed their mind, re-tooled, and in 1956 brought back the Colt Single Action Army as the 2nd Generation production run. These were offered in both blue/case-colored frame and nickel, and in the three standard barrel lengths of 4-3/4, 5-1/2, and 7-1/2 inches, chambered for the 45 Colt, 44 Special, 38 Special and 357 Magnum.

For some reason the 44 Special was never offered with a 4 3/4-inch barrel and the 45 Colt was also offered as a 12-inch Buntline. These 2nd Generation single actions were of excellent quality, at least until the machinery started wearing out in the 1970s.

In 1962 to celebrate or commemorate the New Frontier of John Kennedy, Colt brought out the New Frontier Single Action Army with a flattop frame, adjustable rear sight, and a ramp front sight. These are some of the finest revolvers ever offered by Colt and are mostly found in 45 Colt and 357 Magnum with the three standard Single Action barrel lengths. It is rarely found in 38 Special and 44 Special, and never found with the 4 3/4-inch barrel in the latter.

Shooting the 4-inch Model 500.

Far Right: The 4-inch Model 500 S&W dwarfs the Model 29 Mountain Gun in the background

A half-century of evolution of the Smith and Wesson 44 Magnum: a nickel-plated Model 29, stainless steel Model 629, and Model 629 with built-in muzzle brake. Custom stocks are by BluMagnum, BearHug, and Hogue.

In 1974 Colt again removed the Single Action Army from production; however, it returned two years later as the 3rd Generation model run that included a newly designed cylinder ratchet and hand, the absence of a full-length cylinder bushing *(which just recently returned)*, and different barrel threads. With all the old Colts out there going back to 1873 I cannot understand why they changed the barrel threads when they had a ready market for replacement barrels with the old-style threads. The New Frontier was also resurrected and this time the 44-40 chambering was added, but the 38 Special was dropped. By 1984 all New Frontiers were gone.

The Colt Single Action Army has been an up-and-down, in-and-out, now Custom Shop, now standard catalog item since the 1980s. It remains in production today in the standard barrel lengths, in both blue/case-hardened and nickel finishes, chambered in 45 Colt, 357 Magnum, 38 Special, 38-40, 44-40, 32-20 and finally *(at last)*—the 44 Special is back. Most shooters and collectors hold the 2nd Generation Colt

Single Actions in higher esteem than the 3rd Generation examples and they are priced accordingly. A few years ago, 3rd Generation Single Actions had a list price of $1600; however the price has dropped twice in the last five years and now they run about $1200.

Ruger Builds a Six-Gun Dynasty

The decade of the 1950s was the greatest period of six-gun development in the 20th century. Not only did Smith & Wesson introduce the Model 1950 Target and Military, the Highway Pa-

trolman, the 1955 Target, the Combat Magnum and the 44 Magnum; and Colt the 357 Python and the return of the Single Action Army; but a whole new source of six-guns arrived on the scene.

In 1949 Sturm, Ruger started business on a small scale with an inexpensive 22 semi-automatic; during the 1950s the company would become a powerful force in the industry. The 22 Mark I from Ruger had been a great success and with so many people asking for the return of a single-action six-gun, Bill Ruger built upon his success with the 22

Left: Smith & Wesson is King of the Magnums once again with the X-frame Model 500 chambered in 500 S&W Magnum.

Below: The four big-bore magnum cartridges from S&W: 357 Magnum, 1935; 44 Magnum, 1955; 41 Magnum, 1964; and the 500 Magnum, 2003.

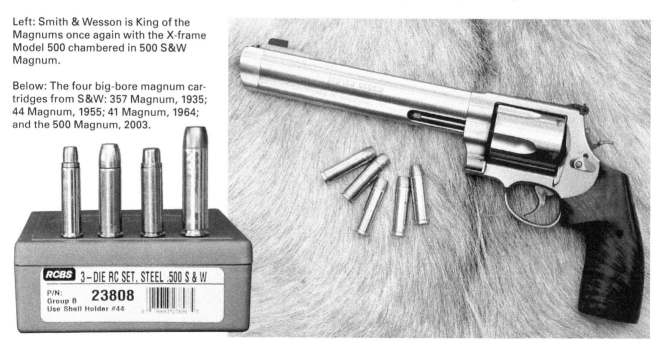

auto by offering the Single-Six in 1953.

The Single-Six maintained the same size and shape in the grip frame as the old Single Action Army, while the frame itself was downsized commensurate with the 22 Long Rifle cartridge for which the revolver was chambered. In addition to these features, Ruger modernized the action by using all coil springs. The stage was now set for Ruger's entrance into the big-bore six-gun market. In 1955, Bill Ruger took the basic Single-Six, enlarged the frame to Colt Single Action size, flat-topped the frame, added an adjustable rear sight matched with a ramp-style front sight, and the result was the 357 Blackhawk.

The 357 Blackhawk was eagerly accepted for the nearly indestructible, powerful, outdoorsman's six-gun it was. It was promised in 44 Special and 45 Colt soon, however as we related in the section on Smith & Wesson, the most powerful cartridge since 1935—the 357 Magnum—was about to be pushed aside by the advent of the 44 Magnum. Ruger's plans changed as far as chambering the Blackhawk in 44 Special, and instead the frame and cylinder were enlarged to become the 44 Magnum Blackhawk. By 1956, I had all three Ruger single actions: a 5 1/2-inch 22 Single-Six, a 4 5/8-inch 357 Blackhawk, and a 6 1/2-inch 44 Magnum Blackhawk. If neither Ruger nor I had ever advanced past this point I still would have been in pretty good shape for the balance of my six-gunnin' life. However, no gun company has the option of staying the same. They either go forward, or slide back. Ruger went forward.

In 1959, Ruger improved their 44 Flat-Top Blackhawk. The barrel length was standardized at 7-1/2 inches, an unfluted cylinder was fitted, protective ears were placed around the rear sight, and an all-steel dragoon-style grip frame with a square-back trigger guard replaced the Colt-style alloy grip frame. The extra weight and larger grip frame helped reduce felt recoil and the new Super Blackhawk was well on its way to becoming the number one six-gun among handgun hunters. The standard 44 Blackhawk would last until 1963,

when it was dropped from production. The normal barrel length on the standard 44 was 6-1/2 inches; however, approximately 1000 each were made with 7 1/2- and 10-inch barrels.

In 1963 another change was made.

The Flat-Top 357 Magnum became the Old Model following the introduction of a grip frame allowing more room between the front strap and the back of the trigger guard, and protective ears around the rear sight as found on the

An object of Taffin's Shooter's Lust, the 4-inch Colt Python.

Colt used the Officers Model Match 38 Special as the basic platform to build the 357 Magnum Python in 1955.

Super Blackhawk. During the 1960s and early 1970s the 357 Magnum, built around a Colt Single Action-sized frame and cylinder, was joined by three other Blackhawks using the same size frame as the Super Blackhawk. The 41 Magnum arrived in 1965, the 30 Carbine in 1968 and the 45 Colt in 1971. This was the first time the 30 Carbine was offered in a revolver, and for the first time shooters had a 45 Colt revolver capable of handling heavier loads than the Colt Single Action Army. It wasn't long before a 45 Colt load using a 300-grain bullet at 1200 fps became standard fodder for the 45 Colt, turning it into a true hunting handgun.

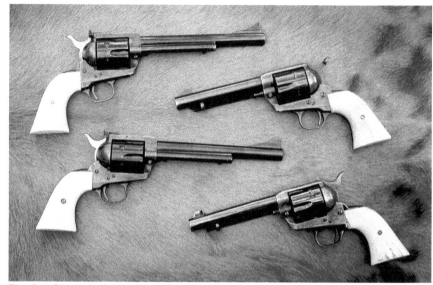

The Colt Single Action and the New Frontier were produced in both 2nd Generation runs (top), and 3rd Generation (bottom). These are chambered in 44 Special.

Since 1836 all single-action six-guns have shared the same basic action and, especially in the case of cartridge-firing revolvers beginning in the early 1870s, were only safe to carry with the hammer down on an empty chamber. This includes all Colt Single Actions, Great Westerns and Ruger three-screw models made prior to 1973. Ruger modernized the action of the single-action six-gun in 1953, and then 20 years later made it much safer. The New Model Rugers introduced the transfer bar safety that allowed safe carrying of a fully loaded single action, as the hammer did not contact the firing pin when it was in the *down* position. With the advent of the New Model, the three screws in the right side of the Ruger mainframe were replaced by two pins, the Colt Single Action-sized frame of the 357 Blackhawk was dropped, and all New Model Blackhawks and the Super Blackhawk shared the same large frame size.

By the late 1970s, long-range silhouette was the number one handgun sport, and special revolvers were offered by several companies to meet the long-range requirements of silhouette shooters. In 1979, Ruger's 44 Magnum Super Blackhawk with a 10 1/2-inch barrel was found on firing lines all over the country; my wife and I used a pair of 10 1/2-inch 44 Super Blackhawks for several years. Four years later, the Super Blackhawk, including the 10 1/2-inch version, arrived in stainless steel and, if anything, has proven to be even more accurate than the blued version. Today both blue and stainless steel Super Blackhawks are available with 4 5/8-, 5 1/2-, 7 1/2- and 10 1/2-inch barrels—and they are very popular with hunters and outdoorsmen.

In 1982, one of the finest long-range revolvers ever produced came from Ruger, designed especially for silhouette shooters. The standard 357 Magnum cartridge case was lengthened by 0.30-inch and the result was the 357 Maximum. Ruger's blued Super Blackhawk frame and cylinder were lengthened to accommodate the new cartridge and the combination proved exceptionally accurate. Unfortunately, some writers and shooters who did not understand the concept destroyed the project. The 357 Maximum was made to shoot 180- and 200-grain bullets at the same speed as the 158-grain 357 Magnum.

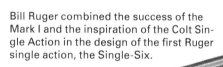

Bill Ruger combined the success of the Mark I and the inspiration of the Colt Single Action in the design of the first Ruger single action, the Single-Six.

When used this way the Maximum worked fine. However, it did not work well with lighter bullets at high speeds, with one of the problems being flame-cutting on the bottom of the top strap. This did not happen with the heavier bullets. This revolver should still be in production.

Many shooters, me included, did not care for the Super Blackhawk grip frame. For me it accentuates recoil as the angle is wrong and the square-back trigger guard raps my knuckle. Ruger looked at the Colt Bisley grip frame and Elmer Keith's #5SAA modification that combined the backstrap of the Bisley with the trigger guard of the Single Action Army and came up with their own design—which is probably better than either of the other two. The backstrap rides high in the back, and not quite as high behind the trigger guard on the Colt Bisley and does an excellent job of taming felt recoil. The Bisley Model, except for special runs ordered by Ruger distributors, has only been offered in a blued 7 1/2-inch version in 44 Magnum, 45 Colt, 357 Magnum and 41 Magnum; the latter currently out of production.

In 1959 Ruger developed the Super Blackhawk as the best six-gun for handgun hunters. In 2002 Ruger went several steps farther. The standard 7 1/2-inch stainless steel Super Blackhawk was given a heavy ribbed barrel that accepted Ruger scope rings and the back of the square-back trigger guard was rounded off, the result being the Hunter Model. With its nearly instant removal or installation of the scope it is the number one hunting handgun bargain on the market today. It was improved in 2003 with the introduction of the Bisley Hunter Model; the same six-gun with a Bisley grip frame, hammer and trigger.

By the late 1980s and early 1990s, the number one handgun shooting sport in the country was cowboy action shooting, which required firearms made prior to 1899 or replicas thereof. In 1993 Ruger took their standard Blackhawk, removed the adjustable sights, rounded off the top of the mainframe, added Colt Single Action-style sights, and cowboy action shooters had the Vaquero. Its sales have exceeded all expectations and it is now the single-action six-gun most seen at cowboy action matches.

The Vaquero has been offered in both blue and stainless steel in 45 Colt, 44 Magnum, 357 Magnum and 44-40 with 4 5/8-, 5 1/2- and 7 1/2-inch barrels, however every barrel length has

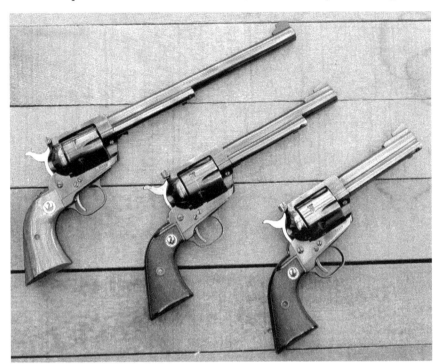

The 357 Flat-Top was offered in the standard barrel lengths of 4-5/8 and 6-1/2 inches, with the 10-inch version being very rare.

During the 2nd and 3rd Generation Colt Single Action Army production, the standard barrel lengths were/are 4-3/4, 5-1/2, and 7-1/2 inches; the 12-inch Buntline Special is no longer cataloged.

Right: The Flat-Top 357 Blackhawks (left), were produced from 1955-1962; the Old Models (right), from 1963-1972.

Below: A new era of single-action six-guns for the outdoorsman began in 1955 with the Ruger 357 Blackhawk.

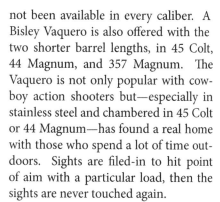

not been available in every caliber. A Bisley Vaquero is also offered with the two shorter barrel lengths, in 45 Colt, 44 Magnum, and 357 Magnum. The Vaquero is not only popular with cowboy action shooters but—especially in stainless steel and chambered in 45 Colt or 44 Magnum—has found a real home with those who spend a lot of time outdoors. Sights are filed-in to hit point of aim with a particular load, then the sights are never touched again.

In 1972 Ruger took another path with their first double-action revolver, the 357 Magnum Security-Six, and in 1985, the GP100 in 357 Magnum replaced the Security Six. Both revolvers have subsequently been made in other chamberings and other versions. The action of the GP100 differs from the Security Six, as does the grip frame, as it has none. Instead, the GP100 uses a grip frame stud, which the grip wraps around. Between the introductions of the Security Six and the GP100 came the movie *Dirty Harry*. Clint Eastwood's portrayal of the 44 Magnum-carrying San Francisco detective in the early 1970s created a tremendous demand for 44 Magnum revolvers that Smith & Wesson could not meet—even when running their factory to capacity. Ruger looked at the situation and decided to build a 44 Magnum double-action revolver.

In 1980, the extremely strong, six-shot Ruger Redhawk chambered in 44 Magnum arrived. "Extremely strong" means it will probably handle heavier loads and handle them longer than the Super Blackhawk. It has been offered in both blued and stainless steel versions with 5 1/2- and 7 1/2-inch barrels and in 357 Magnum, 41 Magnum, and 45 Colt—in addition to the original 44 Magnum. It remains today only in 45 Colt and 44 Magnum, and in scope-ready models.

Seven years later Ruger introduced their second true big-bore double-action revolver, the Super Redhawk, using the grip frame stud of the GP100. The Super Redhawk is all stainless steel and scope-ready, with the choice of either a 7 1/2- or 9 1/2-inch barrel. It is unique among revolvers in that it has an extended frame that surrounds approximately three inches of the barrel. The Super Redhawk concept is definitely "function over form" as it is not a particularly attractive revolver. It is, however, very strong and very accurate.

The original chambering in 1987 was 44 Magnum. It is now also offered in both 454 Casull and 480 Ruger. The latter two chamberings are easily distinguished from the 44 Magnum model since, instead of a satin-brush stainless steel finish, they exhibit the Target Gray finish, which is achieved by using a different grade of stainless steel to accommodate the higher-pressure cartridges.

Ruger has been offering big-bore six-guns for half a century. They are virtually indestructible when handled with reasonable care, and will last longer than a lifetime.

Dan Wesson Has a Better Six-Gun Idea

In the 1980s, the Dan Wesson six-gun was king when it came to long-range silhouette shooting. Most shooters started with Rugers and Smith & Wessons. However, as Dan Wesson listened to silhouette shooters and provided better sights and longer and heavier barrels, the silhouette crowd migrated heavily to the Dan Wesson six-guns. My first true silhouette six-gun was the Dan Wesson 357 Magnum with a heavy 10-inch barrel. It was incredibly accurate and was followed by other Dan Wesson silhouette six-guns in 44 Magnum, 357 SuperMag and the ill-fated 375 Super-Mag. The 445 came along too late for me to use in silhouette matches.

Dan Wesson's popularity with the silhouette shooters was a good news/bad news proposition. As long as there were plenty of silhouette shooters, Dan Wesson had a strong market, but once the number of handgun silhouetters started to drop, Wesson was in trouble. Dan Wesson was caught in a squeeze between two factors: the general decline in silhouette shooting clubs across the

The New Model (left) is safe to carry fully loaded with the hammer down; the Colt Single Action, Great Western, and three-screw Ruger MUST only be carried with the hammer down on an empty chamber.

country and the appearance of the Freedom Arms Silhouette Model chambered in 357 Magnum. Many of the serious shooters that remained in the game took up the Freedom Arms revolver.

Everything caught up with Dan Wesson in the early 1990s and the doors of the factory in Massachusetts closed. The company had gone through several hands, beginning with Dan Wesson; to the family when he passed on and they lost control to an outside group; then in the late 1980s the Wesson family regained control. Unfortunately, it was not to be. When I visited in the early 1990s, it was obvious the company was struggling. It was not too long before the doors were closed and the Dan Wesson revolver was no more. The passing of a truly innovative six-gun saddened many six-gunners.

Dan Wesson's great idea was unique; he planned to offer a basic revolver with interchangeable cylinders and barrels.

This concept was revised somewhat and the Wesson revolver emerged in the 1970s as a six-gun that featured interchangeable barrels only. Normally barrels must be removed using a vise and an action wrench. Wesson, by using a barrel and shroud combination with a locking nut at the front of the barrel, made it possible for anyone to change barrels by

using the special Wesson wrench supplied with every Dan Wesson six-gun.

The interchangeable barrel system delivered an unexpected bonus: Wesson six-guns were exceptionally accurate. This accuracy is normally attributed to the fact the barrel locked at the front of the shroud and the barrel/cylinder gap was set tightly by the user when the barrel was installed. Wesson was also the first to offer interchangeable front sight blades. A six-gunner could have his or her choice of black post, or ramp; red, white, or yellow inserts for the front sights–all easily changed with an Allen wrench–and the post front sights were offered in several widths and heights.

Above: Ruger's Bisley Model (top) uses a modification of the hammer, trigger, and grip frame of the original Colt Bisley.

Right: A classic single-action hunting handgun is the Ruger Super Blackhawk 44 Magnum.

19

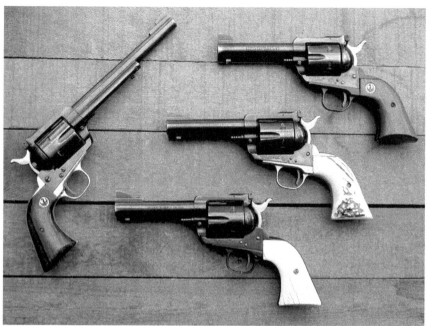

A classic single-action hunting handgun is the Ruger Super Blackhawk 44 Magnum. The Old Model Blackhawks were offered in (counterclockwise from top right) 357 Magnum, 41 Magnum, 45 Colt, and 30 Carbine. The latter was offered only with a 7 1/2-inch barrel.

414s were originally produced before the factory shut its Massachusetts doors), and even the 460 Rowland and 360 DW. The latter is on a case longer than the 357 Magnum but shorter than the 357 SuperMag case.

Editor's Note — In early February 2005, CZ-USA announced it had purchased Wesson Arms. Manufacturing will continue at the New York location, and CZ will maintain its offices in Kansas City, Kansas.

Freedom Arms Factory-Built Custom Six-Guns

Since 1983, Freedom Arms revolvers have been virtually custom-built in a small factory in Star Valley, Wyoming on the eastern Idaho border and are, in my opinion, the finest, strongest, factory-built single-action revolvers ever assembled. Every single-action six-gun from Freedom Arms is as close to perfection as it is humanly possible to build a single-action revolver. The first chambering was the 454 Casull, and the six-gun had to be specially built to withstand the tremendous pounding this cartridge affords a revolver.

Dan Wessons are being produced once again. Not in Massachusetts, but in New York. Using mostly new machinery, Bob Cerva of Wesson Firearms is turning out some beautiful six-guns, probably the best to ever wear the Dan Wesson name. The new Wesson Firearms is not only producing six-guns in the old standby 357 Magnum and 44 Magnum chamberings but also the 41 Magnum, 357 Supermag, 445 Super-Mag, 414 SuperMag *(only a very few*

Available only in stainless steel, Freedom Arms six-guns feature near-

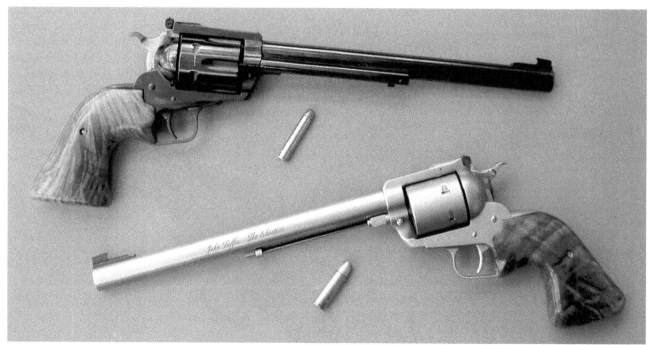

Two of the finest long-range six-guns, both with 10 1/2-inch barrels, from Ruger are the 357 Maximum and the stainless steel 44 Magnum. Custom stocks by BluMagnum.

perfect cylinder and barrel alignment, and precision fitting of all parts. Tolerances are held to a minimum. Although thoroughly modern, the Freedom Arms offering is a traditionally styled single-action revolver. The cylinders on all full-sized Freedom Arms Model 83 revolvers are chambered for five rounds, providing extra steel between the chambers *(in contrast to a six-shot revolver)* and locating the cylinder bolt slot between–instead of above–chambers. The cylinder does not have the end shake or side-to-side movement fairly common in most factory-produced revolvers—the result of tight tolerances throughout. The original 454 Casull chambering has been joined by the 44 Magnum, 357 Magnum, 50 Action Express, 41 Magnum and 475 Linebaugh. Standard barrel lengths are 4-3/4, 6, 7-1/2 and 10-1/2 inches, with other lengths—as well as octagon barrels—offered on a custom basis.

At the Shootists Holiday in 1996, I had the pleasure of test-firing two new Freedom Arms revolvers. Built to about 90 percent of the size of the 454 Casull *(slightly smaller than a Colt Single Action Army)*, one was chambered in 45 Colt, and the other—the first true six-gun from Freedom Arms—carried six chambers for the 357 Magnum. Although I was able to shoot these prototypes, I had to keep the news under wraps until they were officially unveiled at the 1997 SHOT Show in Las Vegas.

This new six-gun was first called the Mid-Frame, a temporary name until the logical name Model 1997 was applied. The first Model 97s were offered with fixed or adjustable sights, in 357 Magnum with 5 1/2- or 7 1/2-inch barrels. Other chamberings followed, including five-shot versions in 45 Colt, 41 Magnum, and 44 Special; and six-shot convertibles with extra cylinders in 22 Long Rifle/22 Magnum and 32 Magnum/32-20. The Model 97 is built to the same tolerances as its bigger brother, the Model 83, and of the same high quality materials. If one does not need the muzzle energy of the more powerful chamberings found in the Model 83, the Model 97 makes an excellent and easy-

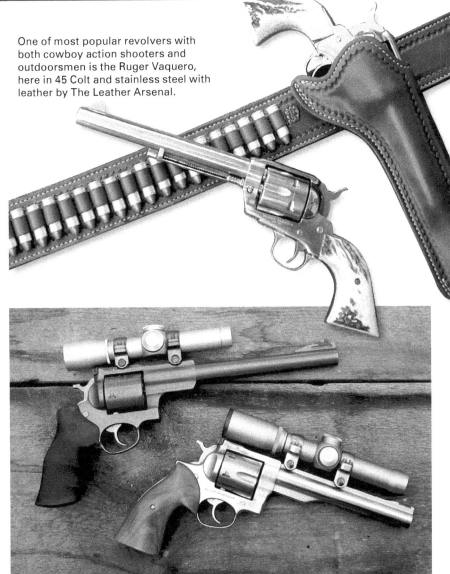

One of most popular revolvers with both cowboy action shooters and outdoorsmen is the Ruger Vaquero, here in 45 Colt and stainless steel with leather by The Leather Arsenal.

Ruger offers both the Super Redhawk and the Redhawk scope-ready for the handgun hunter.

Single-action handgun hunters now have a choice of the Bisley Model Hunter and the Super Blackhawk Hunter, both scope-ready.

Left: Dan Wesson offered a full line of SuperMag models, here shown in 357SM, 375SM, and 445SM.

Below: Two very popular six-guns with silhouette shooters in the 1980s were Dan Wesson's 10-inch Heavy Barrel 357 and 10-inch standard barrel 44 Magnum.

carrying packin' pistol. It is now also available with 4 1/4- and 10-inch barrels, and octagon barrels are a custom option. The latest chambering is the relatively new 17 HMR.

Taurus Bullish about Six-Guns

For several years Taurus was looked upon as a cheaper alternative for those who wanted a 22, 38 Special, or 357 Magnum revolver. This all changed with the coming of the Model 44 in stainless steel, chambered in 44 Magnum, which proved to be an exceptionally accurate revolver. At the 1997 SHOT Show, Taurus became the first major company—other than Freedom Arms—to chamber one of their six-guns for the 454 Casull. The prototype model shown to gunwriters did not cause much excitement; it did not even appear to have a forcing cone. As 1997 progressed, no range-test articles of this gun appeared in any of the gun magazines.

One year later, at SHOT Show 1998, a new Taurus six-gun was unveiled in 454 Casull, along with a presentation by Taurus of the first 454 Casull Raging Bull to the designer of the 454 cartridge, Dick Casull. Taurus had done their homework after SHOT Show 1997, returned to the drawing board, and delivered the best looking double-action six-gun they have ever produced—the Raging Bull Model 454.

Available in both a deep well-polished blue and a frosted matte stainless finish and in either 6 1/2- or 8 3/8-inch barrel lengths, the Raging Bull features a massive five-shot cylinder, a heavy top strap, a bull barrel with a full underlug and ventilated rib, and user-friendly rubber grips. Today it is also offered in a 5-inch version and also chambered in 44 Magnum and 480 Ruger. All models contain a built-in porting system consisting of a chamber that has four holes on each side of the front sight. This porting is approximately 1-1/4 inches long, so a 6 1/2-inch barreled model is actually slightly over 5 inches as far as the rifling in the barrel goes, while the 8 3/8-inch model is ef-

fectively a 7-inch six-gun. Triggers are wide and smooth and the hammers are the semi-target type with user-friendly checkering. The Raging Bull is a sturdy, accurate revolver and good value for the money expended.

The Rise of Replicas

Sometime after the Great Western Frontier six-shooters disappeared in 1964 and before the Colt Single Action Army really began to command high prices, replicas from Italy began to arrive in this country. Those early examples were normally poorly finished, had brass grip frames—and only at a distance resembled the original Colt Single Action Army. They were used in many spaghetti Westerns made in the late 1960s and early 1970s. I have a hard time watching these movies for many reasons including the un-authentic grip frames on the "Colts."

The situation has really changed since the 1970s. Now we have authentic replicas of virtually every percussion revolver, including the Colt Paterson, Walker, Dragoon, 1851 Navy and 1860 Army, and the Remingtons. Cartridge-firing revolvers include copies of the Colt Richards Conversion, Richards-Mason Conversion, 1871-72 Open-Top,

For easy packing and portability combined with reasonable power, Freedom Arms offers the Model 97, here shown in 45 Colt and 44 Special.

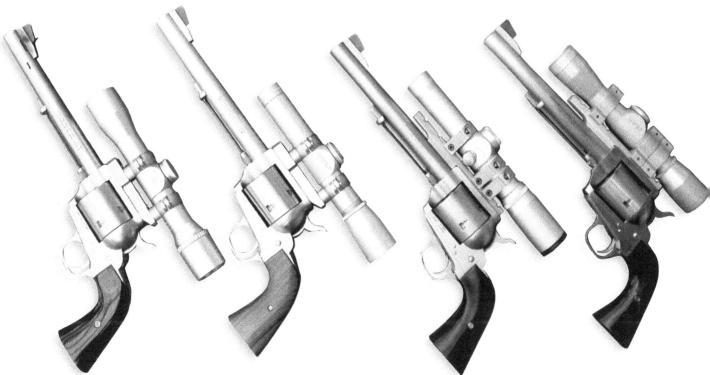

This quartet of 7 1/2-inch Model 83s from Freedom Arms covers everything when it comes to handgun hunting: for small game and turkeys, the 357 Magnum; for deer-sized game, the 44 Magnum; for Africa and Alaska, the 454 and 475. It is also available in 41 Magnum and 50 Action Express.

Two of the top candidates for the title of "Perfect Packin' Pistol," the 4 3/4-inch Freedom Arms Model 83 in 454 and 475.

1873 Single Action Army and Bisley Model; the Smith & Wesson Schofield and Model #3 Russian, as well as the 1875 and 1890 Remingtons. All of these replicas came about because increased interest in Western history, mainly due to the popularity of cowboy action shooting, created a demand for more authentically-styled replicas. Companies such as Cimarron, EMF, and Navy Arms worked with the Italian gunmakers to turn out more and better replicas. Today, these and other importers bring us truly authentic replicas.

The latest replicas are the 1875 and 1890 Remingtons from Hartford Armory. These are totally American-made revolvers and are basically exact duplicates of the early Remingtons. They are beautifully fitted and finished and chambered in 45 Colt and 44 Magnum. They are capable of handling the heavy 45 Colt loads I normally use in my Ruger 45 Colt Blackhawk.

Right: Taurus offers the Raging Bull in three serious handgun hunting chamberings: 44 Magnum, 480 Ruger and 454 Casull.

USFA's Old-Time Single-Action Six-Guns

In the early 1990s I encountered a new source for replica single actions, a source with a gimmick—actually several gimmicks—no one else was using.

The new importer was United States Patent Firearms Co. (USPFA) and they were importing Uberti parts and building the six-guns here in this country in the old Colt factory. Beautifully fitted and finished six-guns, I might add, and a cut above most imported replicas. Their goal was to eventually offer a totally American-made Single Action Army, and that took awhile.

Today, however, United States Firearms Co., now known as USFA, is offering single actions that are totally American-made, including materials sourcing. All the standard Single Action Army barrel lengths are offered, in blue/case-colored, full blue, or nickel. Available chamberings include just about any cartridge ever offered in the pre-war six-guns such as 45 Colt, 44-40, 38-40, 32-20, 41 Colt (the five top chamberings before WW II), as well as 44 Special, 44 Russian and 38 Special. Barrels can be marked the old way, such as "RUSSIAN & S&W SPECIAL 44" or "COLT FRONTIER SIX-SHOOTER" and sights may be the old, small hard-to-see style or the more modern square shape. There really is a practical limit for some of us when it comes to choosing between early authenticity and being able to see the sights. Both the blackpowder-style cyl-

inder pin screw and the more modern spring-loaded catch are offered.

One of the first things noticed about the USFA Single Action Army is the beautiful finish. The frame and the hammer are beautifully case-colored while the balance of the six-gun is finished in a deep, dark Dome Blue. Grips furnished as standard are checkered hard rubber with a "US" molded into the top part of the grip. They are perfectly fitted to the frame and feel very good in the hand.

One of the things I always look for in the fitting and finishing of a single-action six-gun is the radiusing of the lower part of the back of the hammer and the two ears formed by the backstrap where it screws into the frame on both sides of the hammer. A well-made single action will exhibit a smooth contour symmetry of all three. USFA six-guns are very nearly perfect in this respect and the same careful fitting can also be found where the top of the face of the hammer meets the top strap. The fit of the trigger guard to the bottom of the frame is so perfectly done one can run a finger over the area and not feel where one part begins and the other ends. The same is true where the backstrap meets the frame.

Colt cartridge conversion replicas are also offered by Cimarron; grips by Buffalo Brothers.

The front of both the ejector rod housing and the cylinder is beveled which not only looks good and feels good, but permits easier holstering. Markings on these six-guns include the serial number in three places: the butt, in front of the trigger guard, and on the frame in front of the trigger guard screw—exactly as the original 19th-century Single Action Armies were marked. Cylinders lock up tight both in the hammer-down and hammer-cocked position. In addition to the standard Single Action Army, USFA also offers the old 1890s Flat-Top Target Model in various chamberings and barrel lengths.

Current examples of replica single actions are shown with these 7 1/2-inch 45 single actions from Cimarron. Grips by Buffalo Brothers.

Hartford Armory is now offering very high-quality replicas of the original Model 1875 and 1890 Remingtons. These are finely finished and fitted six-guns.

Good Gone Six-Guns (GW and TLA)

One year after Ruger introduced the 22 Single-Six, another new gun company in California started building a replica of the Colt Single Action Army. Great Westerns would be pictured on the cover of the first issue of Guns magazine in January 1955. Those two six-guns were chambered in 45 Colt and, 50 years later, I had the pleasure of actually shooting them. Gunsmith Jim Martin of Arizona had to do considerable work to get them in top shooting order and they proved worthy the effort as both are very accurate.

The Great Westerns looked enough like Colts that pictures of real Colts were used in the original advertising; they also incorporated some genuine Colt parts from the Colt factory. At first they were offered with Colt-style firing-pin hammers, or a floating, frame-mounted firing pin. The standard Great Western was a 5 1/2-inch blued and case-colored 45 Colt. Also available were other barrel lengths, 4-3/4 and 7-1/2 inches, as well as other chamberings: 44 Special, 44-40, 38 Special, 357 Magnum, 357 Atomic, 44 Magnum, 44 Special and 22 Long Rifle. There was also a 12 1/2-inch Buntline Special.

Great Western supplied many six-guns to the makers of TV westerns, in fact if one watches those early programs it is easy to spot a Great Western when the hammer is cocked, as there is no firing pin to be seen. When Colt re-entered the Single Action Army market in 1956 the demise of Great Western was certain, even if the Colt sold for a 25-percent premium. By 1964, the Great Western was gone.

For both loading and unloading a Single Action Army, I always switch the six-gun to my left hand, working the ejector rod with my right hand—also using my right hand to reload—and then switch the six-gun back to my right hand for either holstering or shooting. Texas Longhorn Arms had a different way. Bill Grover's idea was to reverse everything; placing both the ejector rod housing and the loading gate on the left side of the six-gun, as well as having the cylinder rotate counterclockwise. This allows the right-handed shooter to hold the gun in his right hand while both loading and unloading operations are performed with the left hand. The six-gun never leaves the shooting hand. It makes sense; however, it does take some getting used to for one who has spent many decades doing it the other way with traditional single actions.

In the early 1980s Bill Grover began building his right-handed single actions. His first offerings were the West Texas Flattop Target and the South Texas Army. The former had a 7 1/2-inch barrel with target style sights, while the latter was a 4 3/4-inch TLA rendition of the standard Single Action Army. In 1987 Grover set out to build a salute to Elmer Keith with his Improved Number Five. Grover sent me the original Improved Number Five serial number 1 for testing in 1988. Not only was I able to test this Number Five, I also compared it to the original. Although Keith died in 1984, I was able to meet with Elmer's son, Ted, and photograph the two six-guns side-by-side and also hold one in each hand. As expected, the grips felt the same.

There's no doubt the grip frame of the #5SAA inspired Bill Ruger to build the Bisley Model Ruger. However, the Ruger Bisley grip frame is much larger

These 45 Colt Great Westerns were originally shown on the January 1955 cover of *Guns Magazine*.

Texas Longhorn Arms offered right-handed single actions as the Improved Number Five, the West Texas Flat-Top Target and the South Texas Army. Bottom six-gun has ram's horn stocks by Roy Fishpaw and the holster shown is one of the last George Lawrence #120 Keith holsters made before they close their doors.

than the Keith design as Elmer had smaller than average hands. The Texas Longhorn "right-handed" single actions were beautifully made, finished, and fitted. Unfortunately TLA closed their doors in the late 1990s and these grand six-guns are now gone the way of the Great Westerns.

BFR—Really Big, Big Bores

The BFR comes from Magnum Research and the revolver is the all-stainless steel "Biggest Finest Revolver." Actually, this revolver started elsewhere and really went nowhere until Magnum Research took it over. The BFR looks very like a Ruger Super Blackhawk; the grip frames will accept the same grips. However, unlike Ruger six-guns, the BFR has a freewheeling cylinder that rotates clockwise or counterclockwise when the loading gate is opened. This is a great advantage if a bullet jumps the crimp and protrudes from the front of the cylinder, preventing it from rotating in the normal direction.

The BFR is offered in two versions: the Short Cylinder chambered in 454 Casull and 480 Ruger/475 Linebaugh; the Long Cylinder is offered in 444 Marlin, 450 Marlin, 45-70 and a special 45 Colt that also accepts 3-inch .410-bore shotgun shells. BFR revolvers are totally American-made with cut-rifled, hand-lapped, recessed muzzle-crowned barrels; tight tolerances; soft brushed stainless steel finish; and are normally equipped with an adjustable rear sight mated with a front sight featuring interchangeable blades of differing heights. I have tested the BFR in 45-70, 475 Linebaugh and 500 S&W Magnum. They are superbly accurate and function perfectly.

Custom Six-Guns

Sixty years ago there were very few custom six-gunsmiths. The coming of the Ruger Blackhawk provided a strong platform for custom work and now gunsmiths such as Hamilton Bowen, David Clements, Brian Cosby, Ben Forkin, Andy Horvath, Ken Kelly, John Linebaugh, Milt Morrison, Gary Reeder and Jim Stroh are turning out some of the finest six-guns ever built, with standard calibers being offered in the three-screw Blackhawks and five-shot heavy-duty chamberings—45 Colt and above—on

Four great custom Ruger three-screws (clockwise from top left): 41 Special by Hamilton Bowen, and 44 Specials by David Clements, Ben Forkin and Andy Horvath. Each is a unique piece of artwork. Custom stocks on the two top six-guns are by BluMagnum and Larry Caudill.

the New Model Bisley. Both the Ruger Redhawk and Super Redhawk offer another solid platform for double-action conversions.

When the first *Gun Digest* came out in 1944, I was too young to pay any attention to six-guns; however, by the time #10 arrived I was wide-awake and shooting. I've seen a great deal of progress over the past half-century and have been able to enjoy all the grand six-guns that have been offered by the various manufacturers and many custom six-guns as well. I won't be around for all of the next 60-year period, but I hope to enjoy a sizable chunk of it.

Two custom long-range Rugers: a 445 Super-Mag built on a 357 Maximum by Ben Forkin, and a 357 Flat-Top by Gary Reeder.

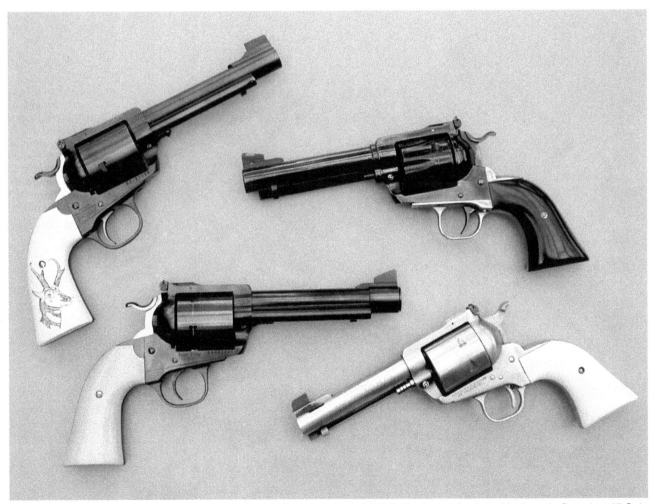

Three custom New Model Rugers (counterclockwise from bottom left): 500 Linebaugh by John Linebaugh, five-shot 45 Colt by Jim Stroh, and 357 Magnum by Milt Morrison. The latter is The Chameleon, with interchangeable barrels and cylinders also in 44 Magnum, 41 Magnum, and 45 Colt. The fourth six-gun is an Old Model Super Blackhawk by Mag-Na-Port.

A Tale of Three Outdoorsmen

THE WORLD'S GREATEST GUN BOOK NOW IN COLOR

Gun Digest 2007

61st Edition

Edited by
Ken Ramage

- Feature Reports
- New Products Reports
- Illustrated Firearms Catalog

❚ Tom Osborne

America's two oldest handgun makers have a rich tradition of assigning colorful names to many of their products. Over the years, the folks at Colt's Patent Firearms have brought us the "Lightning," "Thunderer" and "Woodsman" to cite a few examples. Smith & Wesson also applied descriptive sobriquets to a number of their handguns. Names like "Lady Smith," "Regulation Police" and "Combat Masterpiece" all suggest the purpose for which these firearms were intended, or the segment of the gun-buying public towards which they were being marketed. But of all the titles Smith & Wesson ascribed to their revolvers, the one that most captures my imagination is the "Outdoorsman." For me, the name evokes images of an independent, self-reliant individual––a man

A trio of classic Outdoorsman revolvers and contemporary ammunition repose on a reprint of a 1936 topo map, along with a World War I- vintage military compass. (Top to bottom: post-war 38/44, prewar 38/44, prewar K-22)

who is at home in the natural elements.

The term "Outdoorsman" was given to two separate Smith & Wesson handguns. One was a 22-caliber revolver with a 6-inch barrel, utilizing the medium size "Military & Police" or 'K' frame. The other was chambered in 38 Special and was built on the large "New Century" or 'N' frame, which was originally designed for the 44 Special cartridge. Standard barrel length for this gun was 6-1/2 inches. A more powerful 38 Special loading was developed for use in the 44 ('N' frame) guns and was termed the "38/44 S&W Special" cartridge, to distinguish it from the standard 38 Special round.

Both Outdoorsman revolvers were solid-frame "Hand Ejectors" with swing-out cylinders. Both were also equipped with adjustable target sights. Another trait they shared was that they were over-engineered for their chamberings. They were much more massive and rugged than any handgun Smith & Wesson had previously manufactured in either of these calibers.

Actually, the proper name for these guns has been a source of some confusion. The boxes in which both models were packaged were labeled "THE OUTDOORSMAN'S REVOLVER." Yet sales literature such as the 1938 Smith & Wesson catalog listed the larger-framed handgun as "the 38/44 Outdoorsman." Making matters even more confusing, in the first sentence of the catalog narrative the gun is referred to as the "OUTDOORSMAN'S Revolver." Regardless of which term was most correct, both firearms earned well-deserved reputations for accuracy, sturdiness and dependability.

Both models were introduced to the American public while the Nation was in the grip of the Great Depression. The first K-22 Outdoorsman revolvers were completed in late January of 1931. The first of the 38/44 Outdoorsman revolvers followed in November of the same year. The modest wages paid to factory workers of that era allowed an amount of hand labor which would be cost-prohibitive today. The guns exhibited fine polishing and high luster bluing as well

as extensive hand fitting of parts. Selecting from an assortment of sideplates, fitters matched them to frames so closely that the seams were nearly invisible. Company promotional material proclaimed there was no stoning of internal components which might compromise their case-hardened surfaces. Triggers, hammers and other moving parts were mated to each other by trial and error until the desired fit was achieved. As a result, the guns were noted for their smooth double-action cycling and crisp single-action trigger pull.

The 38/44 Outdoorsman

Pre-World War II Smith & Wesson Hand Ejectors employed what

later came to be referred to as a "long" action. When the trigger was pulled double action, the take-up had a distinctive smoothness that was praised by such noted handgunning authorities as Montana trick shot artist Ed McGivern and Idaho cowpuncher Elmer Keith. In the early 1930s both McGivern and Keith experimented extensively with the 38/44 Outdoorsman as a long-range handgun. They both found that this finely-made revolver, paired with the heavily fortified but inherently accurate 38/44 Special round, was well-suited for perforating distant targets.

The 1932 edition of *Burning Powder*, a booklet edited by Major Douglas B. Wesson, contained an article by Ed Mc-

Unconventional perhaps, but an old tree stump can make a very satisfactory platform for a Ransom Rest. Here the author prepares to touch off a round with his prewar 38/44 Outdoorsman.

A gorgeous mountain meadow—and not a bad- looking 25-yard group from the prewar 38/44 Outdoorsman.

Givern in which he discussed the new 38/44 Outdoorsman. McGivern wrote: "The new 38/44 S & W Outdoorsman revolver, with the new high speed and high velocity cartridges, opens up the field of long range revolver work with possible results that are very surprising. This particular gun, with 6 1/2-inch barrel, was the greatest and most pleasant surprise I have had since the beginning of my revolver shooting experience. The possibilities at 300 yards are surprising; at 500 yards they are more than intensely interesting, and quite successful. This new gun is, in my opinion, the finest gun ever turned out by anybody at any time."

Ed McGivern tested an Outdoorsman that had been fitted with a telescopic rifle sight by the Lyman Gunsight Company. This had to be one of the earliest 'scoped handguns ever. On page 413 of McGivern's book *Fast and Fancy Revolver Shooting* is a photo of a man-size silhouette target that he hit six out of six times at a distance of 300 yards, using his scope-sighted Outdoorsman and factory metal case 38/44 ammunition. However, McGivern eventually abandoned the Outdoorsman for long-range shooting in favor of the 357 Mag-

num revolver, which Smith & Wesson introduced in 1935.

In contrast, Elmer Keith found the 38/44 Outdoorsman superior to the 357 for long-range work, at least when factory ammunition was used. In his classic treatise *Sixguns*, Keith wrote about field-testing the then-new 357 on jackrabbits. Although he achieved hits on rabbits as far away as 180 yards with the magnum, he found that: "the factory 357 load was not as accurate beyond 125 yards as our older Smith & Wesson Outdoorsman with a 6 1/2-inch barrel and either the Remington factory 38/44 load or our handload in the same cases." The handload Keith favored in the big 38 consisted of 13-1/2 grains of 2400 behind a 160-grain hollowpoint semi-wadcutter of his own design. Elmer also considered the 38/44 to be fully the equal of his 44 Special loads for long-range accuracy, but he allowed the 44 did kick up more dirt, making bullet strikes easier to see.

In the April, 1932 issue of *American Rifleman* magazine, W. D. Frazer reviewed the new 38/44 Outdoorsman. Characterizing the Outdoorsman as "a target revolver in every sense of the word," Frazer described a long-range

test of the handgun and factory 38/44 Special ammunition. After sighting in, 20 rounds were fired at a police silhouette target some 200 yards away. Bracing his back against a car and holding the revolver in both hands, with forearms supported between his knees, the shooter achieved 17 hits on the distant target.

Development of the 38/44 S&W Special

Details surrounding the origin of the 38/44 S&W Special round have become blurred with the passage of time. The popular version holds that law enforcement agencies during the Prohibition era found that no commercial revolver round was effective against the "bulletproof" vests worn by some criminals of the day. Nor could the available revolver ammunition be depended upon to penetrate the heavier body metal of newer automobiles. The only handgun round possessing those capabilities was the 38 Super cartridge, which propelled a 130-grain jacketed bullet at a published velocity of 1300 feet per second. The only handgun chambered for the 38 Super was Colt's semi-auto Government Model. As the story goes, Smith & Wesson realized they did not have a product to compete with their rival and set out to correct the situation.

The 38 S&W Special cartridge was developed in 1899 as a blackpowder round. However, by the early 1900s, the ammunition factories had largely transitioned from blackpowder to smokeless powders. This left the 38 Special case with a much greater internal capacity than was needed for the more efficient smokeless propellant. With all this extra space, the 38 Special had the potential for greater power than it originally possessed.

Walter Roper's book *Experiments of a Handgunner* contains a letter from Major D. B. Wesson in which he recounted the development of the 38/44 S&W Special round. Major Wesson wrote: "From the time I was a kid, my one big wish was that someday I might see S&W build the finest, most powerful revolver ever made. Finally things broke so that I was really able to really think of making my dream revolver. To provide a big 38 caliber revolver, we (I was then one of the firm) had fitted a cylinder and barrel to our Military model, chambered for the 38 Special cartridge. One day Phil Sharpe brought me some high-speed handloads he had found satisfactory. After much experimenting and testing, a new cartridge, the S&W 38/44 was produced and a medium-caliber revolver, more powerful than anything made before, was a fact." Phil Sharpe was a widely recognized authority on firearms and ammunition, with an extensive knowledge of ballistics. He was an inveterate experimenter and author of *The Complete Guide to Handloading*, the definitive text of that time on the subject of making your own ammunition.

The experimenting and testing referred to by Major Wesson was a collaborative effort between Smith & Wesson and Remington-U.M.C. In the late 1920s, the two companies worked together at developing a more potent 38 Special ammunition to satisfy the needs of law enforcement. The result was the 38/44 S&W Special cartridge, which propelled a 158-grain lead, or "metal-point" bullet of the same weight, at an advertised velocity of 1125 fps. Compared to the standard 38 Special, which fired a 158-grain slug at a listed speed of 847 fps, the new round delivered about half-again the energy of the regular loading. Although dimensionally identical to the original 38 Special, the 38/44 Special cartridge was meant for use in big-frame revolvers such as the Outdoorsman, and a fixed-sight counterpart of the Outdoorsman called the 38/44 "Heavy Duty." With a standard barrel length of 5 inches, the rugged Heavy Duty was ideally suited for the demands of uniformed police work.

The K-22 Outdoorsman

Until the K-22 Outdoorsman was introduced, Smith & Wesson's only 22-caliber revolver having adjustable sights as a standard feature was their 22/32 target model, which was built on the small "I" frame. The 22/32 was accurate and had certainly won its share of competitions. However, the factory saw a potential market for a heavier, 6-inch-barreled 22 target revolver built on the M&P, or 'K' frame. They reasoned such a gun would be the perfect companion piece to their 38 M&P target revolver, duplicating the feel and handling qualities of that gun. Additionally, in 1930 Remington introduced their "Hi-Speed" 22 rimfire ammunition. Along with higher velocity, the new 22 round also generated increased pressure. The chambers of the 22/32 revolver were not recessed and did not support the rim of the cartridge. With standard velocity ammunition this was of little concern, but with the "Hi-Speed" 22 ammunition, shooters faced the risk that the unsupported rim might rupture. The K-22 Outdoorsman featured recessed chambers which surrounded and supported the rim of the ammunition, greatly reducing the hazard of a rupture.

Praised as a specimen of precision engineering, the K-22 Outdoorsman was well-received by such firearms experts as Walter Roper. In his book *Pistol and Revolver Shooting*, Roper offered this assessment of the gun: "Like all S & W guns, the K-22 is a beautiful example of fine gunmaking, the action being watch-like in workmanship and a de-

light to anyone who appreciates quality."

The K-22 Outdoorsman proved to be extremely accurate with both standard and high velocity ammunition. The Novice Pistol Match of the 1931 U.S. Revolver Association National indoor competition was won by a shooter using a K-22 Outdoorsman. The winner was shooting against competitors armed with single-shot target pistols, which dominated the rimfire events of the day. This was the first time in the history of the organization that a revolver won a national competition against the highly specialized single-shot pistols.

Extreme durability was another characteristic of the K-22 Outdoorsman. Ed McGivern fired over 200,000 rounds through a K-22 Outdoorsman he owned. At that point McGivern sent the gun back to the factory for adjustments. There the revolver was clamped into a machine rest and test-fired with several cylinders-full of ammunition before any work was done on it. Even with all the use the gun had seen, it still produced ragged one-hole groups at 20 yards. After the adjustments were made, the Outdoorsman was again clamped into the machine rest and several more groups were fired. The results of this "before & after" test, as shown on page 166 of *Fast and Fancy Revolver Shooting*, are striking. I was unable to see any appreciable difference between the two sets of groups; both are remarkably small. This is especially impressive in view of the fact that McGivern did the majority of his shooting double-action, which causes greater stress and wear on

The prewar 38/44 shot well with factory wadcutters at 25 yards.

moving parts than does single-action fire.

Personal Observations

Handguns have been a part of my life longer than I sometimes care to think about. I have owned and used a multitude of them since getting my first revolver at the age of 16. Throughout my 31 years in law enforcement, a sidearm of some type has been a regular part of my working attire. For the past 28 years I have also served as a firearms instructor for the major Southwestern department where I work. My years of handgunning have fostered a real admiration for the quality, durability and accuracy of Smith & Wesson's hand ejectors. The basic design has been around for over 100 years. There have been changes to internal parts and improvements in metallurgy, but their swing-out cylinder revolvers are still being manufactured in a variety of calibers and configurations and they still work as well as they ever did.

It is no coincidence that the majority of the handguns I have owned over the past 40 years have been Smith & Wessons, as I believe they produce a superior product. For the first 18 years of my law enforcement career I carried a 357 Magnum S&W Model 66 revolver. Even after the department for which I worked authorized the optional carry of high-capacity semi-autos, I stubbornly continued to wear that Model 66. It shot well, usually scoring "expert" at range qualification and I didn't feel particularly handicapped by its ammunition capacity. I rationalized that if I couldn't resolve matters with the first six rounds, I might as well pack up and go home. Bravado perhaps, but that gun inspired confidence and, in an armed confrontation, confidence is critical. That Model 66 served me well, but it was finally retired from duty when my department mandated the switch from revolvers to semi-autos. I never did have to test my theory about the first six rounds.

Eventually my interest in S&W hand ejectors focused on those made prior to World War II. This period has sometimes been termed the "golden age" of production, because labor was cheap, and quality was high. Also from a personal standpoint, those guns have a historical "romance" about them that I find intriguing. In pursuit of that interest, I set out to assemble a collection of prewar hand ejectors, with the ultimate goal of having a representative example of each model and caliber made by Smith & Wesson prior to the end of World War II. Over time I have been fortunate enough to acquire some nice prewar specimens. Among them are an early 38/44 Outdoorsman and a K-22 Outdoorsman, both in nearly new condition.

Part of the appeal of collecting old guns is in considering the role a firearm, or its contemporaries, might have played in history. As I examine a vintage piece, I wonder: When was it made, who might have owned it and what kind of use might it have seen? In the case of Smith & Wesson revolvers, the first question (and sometimes the second) can be answered by sending an inquiry to the factory. For a fee (presently $30.00), S&W Historian Roy Jinks will research the chronology of a piece. The requested information is documented under the old Smith & Wesson letterhead and includes a detailed outline of the model's history, the total number of that model manufactured, as well as the shipping date and destination of the particular gun in question.

Research on my 38/44 Outdoorsman revealed that it was shipped from the factory on December 31, 1931 and sent to one of their distributors in Chicago. According to S&W Factory records, the order to produce the first 500 38/44 Outdoorsman revolvers was issued by Harold Wesson on September 18, 1931 and the revolver was introduced to the public on November 21st of that year. Although the letter from Jinks didn't specifically address the subject, I strongly suspect that my 38/44 was part of that first lot of 500 revolvers. Recently I posed that very question to him at the annual Smith & Wesson Collector's Association meeting. He also was of the opinion that my 38/44 Outdoorsman probably was among the first 500 manufactured. A total of 4,761 38/44 Outdoorsman revolvers were produced over the next ten years, before Smith & Wesson discontinued commercial manufacture to concentrate on wartime production.

The K-22 Outdoorsman in my collection was shipped on June 28, 1934 to a distributor in Philadelphia. As a point of interest, Smith & Wesson regards the date of shipment from the factory as the "birthday" of their firearms. A particular gun might languish in a box at the factory for an extended period, but "life" doesn't officially begin for it until the day it is shipped. According to Roy Jinks' book *History of Smith & Wesson*, a total of 17,117 K-22 Outdoorsman revolvers were produced between 1931 and 1940.

Although my two prewar Outdoorsman revolvers are over 70 years old and have obviously seen use, they are both still in excellent condition, with 98 percent of their original bluing. They show no significant wear, other than a light "turning ring" around the cylinders. Fit and finish of both revolvers is impressive. They are sterling examples of an era when mass production methods and precise hand-fitting were combined to create high-quality firearms.

The Post-War Outdoorsman

Since the title of this article is "A Tale of Three Outdoorsmen," this seems an appropriate time to introduce the third character of this cast. This one is not a prewar hand ejector. When Smith & Wesson resumed commercial production after World War II, the first 38/44 Outdoorsman revolvers they made combined the prewar "long" action with a ribbed barrel, topped by their new micrometer sights. One deficiency of prewar target model 'Smiths was the design of the rear sight. Windage adjustments were made by turning two tiny opposing screws. This rather delicate arrangement lacked precision and was prone to loosen, which did nothing to help accuracy. With the development of the new micrometer sight, Smith & Wesson corrected this problem. It could be argued that the post-war, transitional 38/44

Outdoorsman incorporated all of the most desirable features (long action, micrometer sights and the recently introduced "magna" grips) into one package. A total of 2,326 post-war, transitional models were manufactured before the existing supply of parts was used up. Once the supply of prewar parts was exhausted, the factory began producing the 38/44 Outdoorsman with the modern "short" action.

I first saw this transitional model at a gun show some 23 years ago. At the time, I was supporting my family on a

The transitional, post-war 38/44 Outdoorsman (bottom) combined the desirable prewar "long" action with the new micrometer sights, ribbed barrel and more comfortable "magna" stocks.

patrolman's income and the $315.00 the seller was asking was beyond my immediate means. I took his business card and told him that when I saved up the money, I would give him a call. In addition to being a homemaker, my wife also contributed to the household income with part-time work, so it was only fair that a purchase of that magnitude be a mutual decision. Among my blessings I am fortunate to count an understanding, supportive spouse. Upon hearing about this latest object of my desire, she agreed that we could save the money without undue hardship on the family budget.

A few weeks later, I phoned the seller to tell him I could meet his price. He expressed his regrets as he informed me I was too late, he had recently sold the

Outdoorsman. Although disappointed, I tried to act philosophical when I told my better half about this turn of events. My disappointment was short-lived, however, as she presented me with the revolver, which she had secretly purchased because she was worried someone else might buy it first.

Upon writing to the factory for historical information on that Outdoorsman, I learned that it started life in 1947, the same year I did. At one time or another, many of us have probably thought: "If I could keep just one of my guns, which one would it be?" In my case, there is no doubt, this one is the keeper. I have other guns that are worth more money, but none of them have the personal value that this fine Smith & Wesson holds for me.

For a number of years I used that post-war Outdoorsman recreationally. It shot well, the weight of the gun contributing to its steadiness in the hand. While I didn't try to wring "magnum" performance out of it, I did shoot heavier handloads in it than I used in my K-frame 38s. Eventually, because guns like this became more sought after by collectors and their values rose, I retired that 38/44. The revolver still looks great, locks up tight and the bore is spotless. That Outdoorsman and I may be the same age, but I have to admit it

has withstood the ravages of time better than I have.

There you have my trio of Outdoorsmen, a prewar 38/44, a prewar K-22 and an early post-war 38/44. The two older guns have been around for over 70 years and the newer one is rapidly approaching 60, but all three are in excellent condition.

The Testing Process

Some time ago, I acquired a full box of 1930s-vintage Remington 38/44 Special, metalpoint ammunition. The box and the ammo were both in nice shape and would likely fetch a tidy sum from a collector. But I was curious. Several questions came to mind, including: How well does factory ammunition retain its potency over 70-plus years? Was factory ammo as accurate in the prewar Outdoorsman as claimed? And finally, did the metalpoint ammunition have the penetration power proclaimed by the manufacturer? Since I had both the gun and the ammo, some empirical testing seemed in order. A purist collector would undoubtedly cringe at the thought of shooting up rare ammunition in a pristine gun just to satisfy an idle curiosity, but I prefer to think of it as 'research to expand the sum of human knowledge.'

Having a Ransom Rest for accuracy testing and a chronograph to measure velocity, I was set. About this time it occurred to me that as long as I was going to violate the virtue of the 38/44, I might just as well include the K-22 in my "research" project. I was also curious to know how accurate the rimfire Outdoorsman might prove to be. In addition to the vintage 38/44 ammunition, I decided to purchase some modern 38 Special target ammo, along with some target-quality 22 Long Rifle ammunition, to measure the accuracy of both prewar revolvers.

Now I have to admit it had been a while since I last bought commercial centerfire handgun ammunition, as I normally use my own handloads for recreational shooting. But I wasn't prepared for what I encountered. Checking for factory-loaded 38 Special wadcutters with five local gun shops, only one had any in stock. That store had a single box of Winchester-Western Super Match, which had been ordered by mistake. Apparently no one shoots 38 wadcutters anymore, at least not in this part of the country. My search for target-quality 22 ammunition proved a little more successful and I bought a box each of CCI Pistol Match, Federal Gold Medal Target and Remington Club Extra.

A camping trip to the Coconino National Forest afforded a perfect opportunity for the accuracy trials. The stately Ponderosa pines of the northern Arizona mountains create a most appropriate setting for testing "Outdoorsman" revolvers. Fortuitously, the remote meadow we favor for our campsite is dotted with large tree stumps, remnants of a bygone logging era. Despite their age, some of these stumps are still quite sound. Experience has taught me that a tough old stump can make an entirely suitable platform upon which to mount a Ransom Rest. Unconventional as it may seem, this "stump shooting" method works very well. With the Ransom Rest secured to a sturdy plywood base, a half-dozen 5-inch lag bolts will anchor the device solidly against the recoil of any handgun.

After clamping the prewar 38/44 into the Ransom Rest, a couple of cylinders full of ammunition were run through it, to settle it into the grip inserts. The target stand was then placed a measured 25 yards out and the testing commenced. Admittedly, firing only one brand of 38 target ammunition hardly constitutes a thorough trial, but the big Outdoorsman acquitted itself well. Six test groups were fired, using all chambers. The best of them clustered under an inch center-to-center, with the overall average for all groups fired calculated at 1.289 inches.

Upon completion of the wadcutter testing, the bore of the big 38 was cleaned with several passes of a dry wire brush. The gun was then loaded with a cylinder-full of the vintage 38/44 metalpoint ammunition. With considerable anticipation, I depressed the trigger on the first round. However, when the hammer fell the only sound heard was

the "thunk" of the firing pin striking a dead primer. The second round was a repeat of the first. Then, at the third round, came the report of the stoutly-loaded 38. The process was continued, with only about half of the rounds igniting. Finally after running thirteen rounds through the Outdoorsman, I had six holes in the target. This "group" measured 2-3/4 inches center-to-center. Obviously, the past 70-plus years had not been kind to the old ammunition. In view of the ammo's erratic performance, I scrapped my plan to chronograph the 38/44 rounds.

I do not believe that the single group I shot truly represents the accuracy this 38/44 S&W Special ammunition was originally capable of delivering. If Elmer Keith said he was able to obtain minute-of-jackrabbit precision beyond 125 yards using the big Outdoorsman and factory loads, I am not about to dispute his claim based on the half-dozen rounds I fired.

Accuracy testing was not conducted with the circa-1947 38/44 Outdoorsman, as I already had a good working knowledge of its capabilities and my supply of factory wadcutters was exhausted. That post-war Outdoorsman will consistently put six rounds of its favorite handload inside an inch and a half at 25 yards. I believe that is all one could reasonably ask.

Changing out the grip inserts in the Ransom Rest, the K-22 Outdoorsman was next clamped in for accuracy testing. This revolver demonstrated some definite preferences in brands of 22 target ammo. The best results were obtained using CCI's Pistol Match, which yielded 3/4-inch groups at 25 yards.

The Ransom Rest tests of both prewar Outdoorsman revolvers proved to my satisfaction that the accuracy claims made by Smith & Wesson and contemporary gun writers were not all hyperbole. The guns did not possess any mystical abilities, but they did deliver very respectable results. To be sure, I have some more modern handguns which will equal, or exceed the accuracy of these fine old firearms, but none that exude the sense of adventure these Out-

doorsman revolvers hold for me.

While probably not very scientific by today's standards, for many years the test employed by manufacturers to measure the penetrating power of handgun ammunition was the number of 7/8-inch thick, soft pine boards a bullet would pass through. Page 50 of the 1938 Smith & Wesson catalog contains a ballistic table of the factory rounds for which S&W handguns were chambered. This table lists muzzle velocity of the 38/44 S&W Special as 1125 fps and muzzle energy as 444 fpe. According to the ballistic table, penetration of the round was 12 pine boards, 7/8-inch thick.

An obvious variable in using pine boards as a test medium is finding boards of consistent density for valid comparative testing. Also today's dimensional pine boards measure a nominal 3/4-inch thick, as opposed to the 7/8-inch thickness used by the ammunition makers. Despite these minor technicalities, I elected to conduct my own penetration test of the 38/44 metalpoint round. The ballistic table in the 1938 S&W catalog indicates the pine boards in their tests were spaced 7/8 of an inch apart. Since I would be using 3/4-inch boards, it seemed reasonable to use 3/4-inch spacing.

Accordingly, I built a wooden baffle box that allowed the boards to be replaced after each shot. The post-war Outdoorsman was drafted for the penetration test. Firing from less than one foot distance, the metalpoint bullet cleanly punched through 8 boards, breaking them in the process. The bullet dented the 9th board and was recovered un-deformed at the bottom of the box. With all the scientific fervor of a modern-day Isaac Newton, I replaced the damaged boards and the test was repeated. The results were the same. Maximum penetration was 8 boards and other than rifling marks, the bullet was undamaged.

In addition to the recovered bullets, I also pulled the bullets from some of the faulty 38/44 rounds. Unlike modern jacketed handgun bullets which typically have gilding material to the base of the projectile, the "metalpoint" of the 38/44 covers only the exposed portion of the bullet. The bullet's shank is either pure lead or a very soft alloy, with a single, narrow lube groove. Bullet diameter measured exactly .357-inch, using a micrometer. Weighing several of the slugs, they averaged 156.6 grains, with a deviation of +/- .3 grain. The powder charges were also weighed, averaging 7 grains of a disc-type propellant. Visually comparing the powder to two that were available in the 1930s and are still around today, the flakes were smaller than Unique and larger than 2400. A fired case was cross-sectioned to examine its construction. The cases are of solid head design, and other than lacking the shallow rebate found just above the rim on cases of current manufacture, the 38/44 cases appear very similar to modern 38 Specials.

At the conclusion of the tests, the revolvers were given a thorough cleaning. They suffered no harm from the shooting sessions and looked as good as before. A collector's reluctance to fire––or even cycle a rare, mint condition gun is certainly understandable. However, with guns that are in less than perfect condition, being able to use them as was intended only adds to the pleasure of ownership. This doesn't mean that I routinely shoot with my collectibles, but there is a certain satisfaction in knowing that I can. The informal tests I conducted with the Outdoorsman revolvers were both enjoyable and enlightening. The experience left me with an even greater appreciation for the quality and craftsmanship of these handsome pieces of American handgun history.

Conclusion

Gun writers today usually regard the 38/44 Special and the companion Outdoorsman revolver as an evolutionary step in the creation of the 357 Magnum, which was introduced in 1935. It is generally accepted that the 357 Magnum was developed not only to give shooters the most powerful handgun of the time, but also out of concern that the high performance 38/44 Special cartridge might be used in old or small-

The post-war 38/44 Outdoorsman was used in the two penetration tests. Each time, the maximum number of 3/4-inch pine boards penetrated was eight. Both bullets were recovered virtually undamaged.

frame 38 Special revolvers that were not designed to handle the pressure of the round. Despite this, I consider the 38/44 Outdoorsman an end in itself in terms of handgun development. The revolver was a magnificent example of American gunmaking and the 38/44 round achieved substantially more power than the standard 38 Special, while retaining all of its accuracy.

In addition to being a beautifully-crafted firearm, the K-22 Outdoorsman was significant because it legitimized the full-size 22 revolver as a sporting handgun. Use of the 22 revolver for target competition was diminishing, as semi-automatic 22 pistols gained increasing acceptance among competitors. The semi-auto's advantage wasn't necessarily greater intrinsic accuracy, but they did allow the shooter to maintain a consistent grip on the gun from shot to shot. Firing a revolver in the single-action mode required the shooter to alter his grip each time the gun was cocked, cre-

ating a distinct handicap in timed and rapid fire. However, for casual shooting or small-game hunting, the K-frame 22 revolver proved to be an ideal sidearm.

Although Smith & Wesson continued to offer the 38-44 Outdoorsman when commercial production resumed following World War II, demand for the big 38 was fading. The gun-buying public now wanted the 357 Magnum. Revolvers like my post-war Outdoorsman found their niche with knowledgeable shooters who had no need for the roar and thunder of the 357, but who desired a supremely well-made, rugged and accurate 38 Special.

The Outdoorsman revolvers were state of the art firearms in their day and the craftsmanship that went into their manufacture was unexcelled by any other production handgun. This venerable trio of Outdoorsmen has definitely earned a permanent, prominent place in my gun collection.

About Dueling & Dueling Pistols

Throwing Down a Gauntlet ∎ by Norm Flayderman

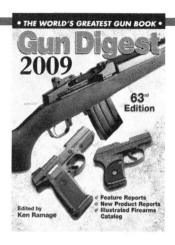

What constitutes an American dueling pistol…or, for that matter, any "dueling pistol?" How might it differ from a large "holster pistol," "horse pistol," "target pistol" or "officer's pistol?" It's a cloudy subject, at best, and a question that may not be easily resolved to everyone's satisfaction.

The conclusions drawn from the following discussion are likely numbered among the earliest attempts (if not the initial salvo!) to question and provide a logical rationale to understand "dueling" and "dueling pistols." Ostensibly, both subjects have been taken for granted by historians, collectors and the public at large as historical fact. These remarks venture to step into that breach and approach the subjects from a rational and questioning viewpoint. In offering this alternate perception of dueling,

Right: Pair of large flintlock "dueling pistols" by Middletown, Conn. Maker Simeon North. Stylistically somewhat different (especially shape of handles) from the pair presented by the state of Connecticut to Macdonough. Ten and a half-inch octagon barrels. Fifty two-caliber smoothbore. Checkered walnut stocks; single set triggers (a.k.a. "hair triggers") engraved iron mountings. From the collection of William R. Orbelo.

it clearly becomes subject to challenge. For an energetic researcher it affords potential for a sensible resolution to what has unmistakably been a long-standing enigma. Resolving that inaccuracy will add substantially to the literature of firearms and American folklore. It's a topic overdue for serious, unemotional inquiry… just waiting to be tapped. Optimistically, these remarks will offer incentive for that investigation.

The Practice of Dueling In America (…and the casual approach to the facts)

A much-abused subject, dueling in 19th century America has spawned a vast treasury of legend and folklore, all too often contradictory and aggrandized. The wide gap between perception and reality has been further magnified, often altered, by time and re-telling. Dueling is undeniably a subject that fascinates our collective imagination and clamors for attention! Before probing the essentials requisite of "dueling pistols," it is relevant to offer introductory comment about the time-honored "gentlemanly" practice itself.

It is regrettable there has been such a great propensity to accept, unquestioned, most dueling accounts (almost

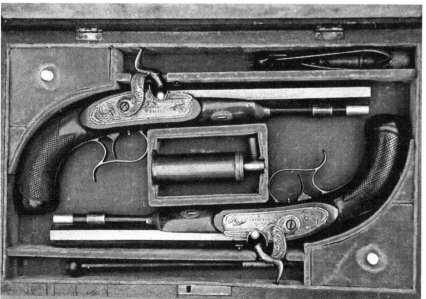

Cased pair of American percussion dueling pistols circa late 1830s – 1850 with their locks and 8-inch octagon barrels marked "S. HALL NEW YORK" .44-caliber with deep rifled bores. Black walnut halfstocks with checkered handles, each gun fitted with single set trigger (a.k.a. "hair triggers").

without exception), merely because they appeared in print over a century and half ago. There is an obvious willingness to believe that newspapers and other literature of earlier centuries must be accurate and more honest than any published in more recent eras; the reverse is likely true. The subject is rife with fictitious reports, distortions and spurious quotations. For many who chose to write about dueling, the subject proved too tempting not to embellish…especially so as there was little likelihood of contradiction.

The practice of dueling to defend one's honor or take revenge for a real or imagined slight, was a somber part of the American scene, particularly in the pre-Civil War years. Although observed in all sections of America and by officers of various branches of the military, the vast majority of such contests took place in the South and Southwest and by mid-century, in California. Duels in America, that is, those conducted under a formalized set of rules, were fought almost exclusively with firearms. Handguns were the usual weapon of choice; infrequent encounters are noted with rifles or shotguns, or an occasional motley assortment of less conventional weapons (many of them merely fabrication and magnified by time). Most duels arranged under such precepts were customarily fought between men of equal standing, those who would have considered themselves the upper strata of society.

The most cursory examination of dueling reveals how remarkably widespread was its practice; enough so that laws were almost universally passed against the custom. Many states, as well as the federal government, administered oaths to elected and public officials to affirm that they had never engaged in, would not engage in, nor would be party to such contests.

To the Public.

Whereas MARCUS GILLIAM, has by means the most base and false, tryed to destroy my reputation; and would not concede to any efforts that have been made by my friends to have the matter investigated; and at the same time declined to say that he was of opinion that I was guilty of the act, which has according to report, been laid to my charge; he has also refused to give me the satisfaction that an injured person has a right to require. I therefore pronounce him a *liar*, a *base slanderer* and a *coward*.

WM. NOBLE.

Petersburg, March 12, 1825.

To the Public.

The circumstances attending the loss of my Pocket Book were so strong, and so fully warranted my suspicions, as to convince me and every friend with whom I advised, that I could not, with propriety, accept the invitation contained in the note of William Noble. The ground of my refusal was, that I did not believe him to be a gentleman, which was distinctly stated to his friend who handed me the note. A regard to public opinion alone induces me to take this notice of an unprincipled vagabond & scoundrel.

Marius Gilliam.

MARCH 14th, 1825.

RIGHT: Public Challenge to a Duel (popularly referred to as "posting" an individual for a real or imagined slur, misbehavior, or other wrongdoing, etc.). Publicly posting printed broadsides or posters such as these was a conveniently proper and customary manner to challenge a transgressor to a duel. The act of bringing the accusation to public notice could hardly be ignored by the party thus disgraced. In Petersburg, Virginia, on March 12, 1825 William Noble publicly challenged Marius Gilliam to a duel for the reasons so-described here. Two days later Gilliam made public his refusal to the duel (highly unusual) naming, in turn his adversary William Noble "… an unprincipled vagabond and scoundrel." These mementos of that altercation may suggest a duel dodged… or perhaps a more bitter one in the offing?

Lorenzo Sabine (1803-1877), a highly regarded American historian, in his *"Notes on Duels and Duelling...With Preliminary Historical Essay"* (1855), possibly the very first credible study of dueling and rational examination of the subject, placed it neatly in perspective:

"In the United States, as in England, killing in a duel is murder; but here, as there, opinion is superior to law. Bennett,1 as far as I have been able to ascertain, is the only person who has been executed for taking the life of a fellow-man in single combat since we became a free people. In some States, the parties have seldom been held even to answer; in others the inquiry in the courts has been confined to the single question of "...the fairness of the fight;" and this point determined in favor of the survivor, acquittal has followed as a matter of course. In one State, we find the judge of a court on the dueling ground as a principal; and another, the ex-governor is there as a second; in a third, we read of principals and seconds, attended by an immense concourse in carriages, on horseback, and on foot...on their way to the appointed spot, without hindrance...[in other cases] the judicial records show the mockery of a sentence against the parties who had completed their arrangements for a mortal strike, of a fine of one dollar and an imprisonment of one minute. Yet in these states there are not only statute laws, but constitutional provisions in the book adverse to this relic of the Dark Ages."

Sabine's Notes on Duels and Duelling should be required reading for any student of the subject. Of the many American duels cited, some were merely named, while others were described in protracted detail. Immediately apparent is the frequency that such recourse was taken by U.S. senators, congressmen and legislators of all states; the very same that passed laws prohibiting dueling!

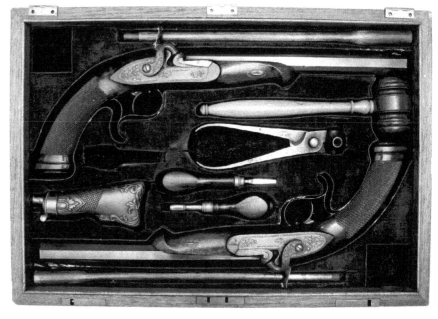

Defining "Duel" And "Dueling"

It is essential that the term duel be defined and distinguished from merely a fight or encounter between two individuals. Primary definitions of duel: "...a prearranged combat between two persons fought with deadly weapons according to an accepted code of procedure" or "a formal fight between two persons armed with deadly weapons; prearranged and witnessed by two others called seconds, one for each combatant" (from Random House and Webster's dictionaries, respectively).

The secondary definition of duel covers its broadest possible interpretation: "any contest between two persons or parties" or "any contest or encounter suggesting such a fight, usually between two persons." Hence, that might indicate a wide host of contests, such as a "verbal duel...judicial duel...a scholarly duel." It is in its secondary connotation that the terminology is most often employed, and where much illogical and distorted (often fictitious) dueling stories are hatched.

Overworking The Code Duello

Repeatedly encountered in dueling literature is the phrase code duello. It is a generalized or generic term to indicate the adoption of some established or negotiated rules, along general principles, that two duelists and their seconds agree upon to conduct a formalized duel in America. It is noted that on occasion, duels were never fought because the principals or their seconds were unable to agree on the very rules by which they were to be conducted.

Thoroughbreds Only, Please

In Europe, dueling, in its earlier eras, was almost exclusively the practice of the landed gentry. The bourgeoisie and the proletariat were generally not considered qualified (but that was soon to be modified). In the British social system, where (prior to the Industrial Revolution) one's blood counted more than his bank account, rules governing duels were apparently more closely observed. In some of its codes, even the seriousness of the offense and the acceptance of an apology to avert a duel

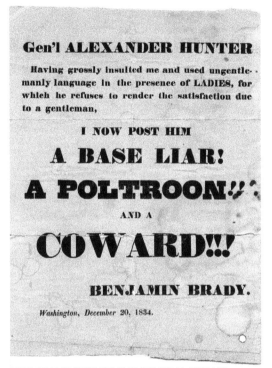

PUBLICLY "POSTING" THE GENERAL FOR HIS UNGENTLEMANLY BEHAVIOR. Tantamount to an open challenge to a duel, and to be read by his fellow citizens in Washington D.C. No self-respecting gentleman (or military officer) could ignore this base insult and have his honor remain unblemished.

had a ranking and a protocol. Countless breaches of behavior and deportment could precipitate a duel. Physical blows and questioning one's parentage, as serious as they were, did not appear to be as base or amoral as bedding down a lady of high birth.

With the passage of time it is clear that in England and likely much of Europe, the exclusivity of dueling and confining the practice only to the "landed gentry" became subject to considerable modification. The widespread development and advance of the Industrial Revolution, along with a simultaneous growth of an increasingly important and wealthy middle-class, accompanied a corresponding change in attitude towards what constituted the very terminology of "gentleman."

Some writers have maintained that few men participated in a duel seeking satisfaction from the death of their opponent; rather, the duel itself offered the opportunity to risk one's life by proving one's honor and enhanced reputation. That may have had validity in some duels, but could hardly be accurate as a generalization. As D. D. Bruce in Violence and Culture in the Antebellum South (1979) observed, dueling made men careful, compelling them to be thoughtful and respectful of their choice of words. The duel acted as a strong deterrent to impugning another gentleman's reputation; its mere threat was preventative. A decided distinction was made between authentic duels and common physical violence.

A "Code Duello" Custom-Made For Americans

South Carolina Governor John Lyde Wilson's Code of Honor; or Rules for the Government of Principals and Seconds in Dueling, first published in 1838 and reissued at various times to 1883 (and possibly later), contrast the American view of dueling to that of Europe. It is significant that it is the most often mentioned of the two American codes yet to surface with even a modicum of frequency.* Invariably it is accorded the status of the American counterpart to the widely known British codes; an importance clearly overemphasized by one and all. Circulation and recognition of American Codes were significantly less than credited. The most telling observation attesting to that fact was made by Sabine in his 1855 landmark reference *Notes on Duel and Duelling* where he asserted (italics added):

"I am not aware that American duellists have ever adopted a written code or that rules among them are entirely uniform. Certain points, however, are well established. I suppose for example, that in a duel upon a mere question of honor, and

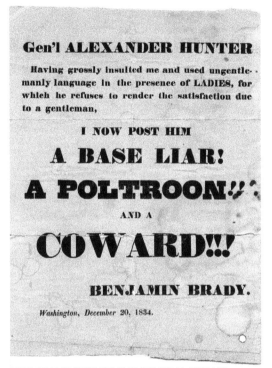

Text within the posted notice image:

Gen'l ALEXANDER HUNTER

Having grossly insulted me and used ungentlemanly language in the presence of LADIES, for which he refuses to render the satisfaction due to a gentleman,

I NOW POST HIM

A BASE LIAR!

A POLTROON!!

AND A

COWARD!!!

BENJAMIN BRADY.

Washington, December 20, 1834.

exchange of shots, whether with or without effect, is sufficient; while a combat of positive wrong or deep injury may be and ordinarily should be, continued until the aggressor offers satisfactory explanation or apology, or until the fall or disability of one of the parties...it seems well settled that the challenged, in the matters of weapon, time and distance, shall be governed by usage between gentlemen; and that propositions to sit across a cask of powder, to jump from a precipice or a building, to meet at midnight, at a lone or distant spot, without friend or surgeons, may be rejected by the challenger."

Governor Wilson, a man who had engaged in numerous duels, specifically stated in the preface to his "Code": "I believe that nine duels out of ten, if not ninety-nine out of one hundred originate in the want of experience of the seconds." That clearly implied that any code duello observed for an American duel was most likely improvised at the whim of the participants or their seconds; if followed at all.

*The other code (unknown to Sabine in 1855) was "The Code of Honor; or The 39 Articles... Showing the Whole Manner in Which the Duel is to Conducted; with Amusing Anecdotes by a Southron".

Thus, it becomes apparent that formalized dueling codes, i.e. the code duello in the United States, were improvised and tailored by the combatants for the individual duel, taking into account some generally understood precepts of "gentlemanly" behavior and conventional, local customs.

And, those improvised, impromptu rules obviously made for an unmitigated miscellany of dueling formats. Their vagueness and ambiguity ceded a virtually bottomless supply of fresh fuel for the creative writing talents of the host of reporters, dueling aficionados, dilettantes and devotees possessing literary talents and a ready pen-in-hand... through the ages.

Pistols "Sanctioned" For Duels

Bearing in mind the foregoing commentary on the American conception of a code duello, it becomes readily understandable that the specifics of firearms that might be chosen for weapons were likely to be generalized, if not dubious... and they were!

Nowhere in the "British Code of Duel" (1824), that widely known and obviously well-circulated work, are specifics revealed for the firearms that might be used other than alluding to the general type of ignition of the pistol in its instructions for the seconds "...To examine the pistols and see that they are

THE BRITISH

CODE OF DUEL:

A REFERENCE TO

THE LAWS OF HONOUR,

AND

THE CHARACTER OF GENTLEMAN.

Honesta mors turpi vita potior.   TACITUS.
Ex abusu, non arguitur ad usum.   AX. LEG.

AN APPENDIX,

IN WHICH IS STRICTLY EXAMINED,
THE CASE BETWEEN THE TENTH HUSSARS AND
MR. BATTIER;
CAPT. CALLA'N, MR. FINCH, &c. NOTED.

LONDON:

KNIGHT AND LACEY, PATERNOSTER ROW,

1824.

Photographs of the title pages of the two most often mentioned dueling codes of Great Britain (right) and America (opposite page).

perfect even to the flint, that preclude mis-fire; and then to load them equally in the presence of each other." From practical experience in personally viewing and handling antique English handguns customarily considered as "dueling pistols," they are invariably fitted with long (approximate 8-inch to 10-inch) smoothbore barrels with a wide range of calibers. Rifled bores were not prohibited, although they apparently were occasionally utilized (as was often the case on the continent).

Governor Wilson's 1838 Code of Honor or Rules for the Government of Principals and Seconds in Duelling specifically dealt with the subject. Its section "Arms and the Manner of Loading and Presenting Them" states: "The arms used should be smooth-bore pistols, not exceeding 9 inches in length with flint and steel. Percussion pistols may be mutually used if agreed on, but to object on that account is lawful." The "Code" continued with instructions for loading, the manner of presenting pistols to participants and fighting positions with the pistols. Regardless of the suggestion for the use of "smooth-bore pistols" it is well recorded that many with rifled bores of varying calibers were chosen by a wide cross-section of duelists... as were others with set triggers (often termed "hair triggers").

Defining "Dueling Pistol"

In much the same manner as they embroidered the practice of dueling...a wealth of misconception, myth and unverified vague tradition flourished alongside the characterization and history of the "dueling pistol." It is apparently customary for collectors, historians and authors to believe there is a "hard and fast" authoritative definition of exactly what constitutes a dueling pistol. It became evident upon examining the subject that no such generally sanctioned rendering, contemporary to the era of their usage, or concurrent with modern arms collecting literature, was or has been arrived at by a general consensus. Other than the single, broad qualifying feature of a "smooth-bore barrel" (i.e. without rifling) neither the recorded American code...nor the more widely recognized British code, contained further qualifying features for the pistol. It is obvious that there was, indeed, broad latitude as to the type handgun British or American duelists might choose to employ.

Thus, the enigma: Did many well-known American and British gunmakers devote some of their manufacturing and sales energies to the development of a style of handgun whose features were peculiar to and designed specifically for the practice of dueling, as many authors have proclaimed or would have you believe? Or, was the handgun that emerged to be "traditionally" accepted by arms historians and collectors as the "classic" dueling pistol merely the result of normal evolutionary innovations and improvements in all firearms and advances in industrial and manufacturing techniques... the result of numerous influences, dueling merely being one among many? Those questions have apparently never been posed. They are deserving of deeper investigation and resolution. Resorting to the threadbare analogy of "which came first, the chicken or the egg?" reduces the dilemma to its essentials and likely best expresses the quandary.

On reviewing the subjects "dueling pistols" and "dueling" in a generous cross-section of antique arms literature, it becomes apparent that most treatises and discourses describing the development and evolution of "dueling pistols" are ostensibly predicated on theory and assumption, if not outright conjecture. Many writers, including those of the nineteenth century, reached plausible, reasoned conclusions that almost every innovation introduced on a particular style of large, non-military handguns was designed specifically as a result of...and for the sole benefit and use by those engaged in the practice of dueling. However, there does not appear to be solid documentary evidence to substantiate such common and deep-rooted beliefs. Those conclusions and explanations appear to be based more on the allure, imagery and the romanticized aura surrounding dueling, and are often in contention with one another. The assumption that they were designed solely for dueling...

and therefore should be made more accurate, possess better balance and be easier to handle than any normal handgun of those respective eras, appears tenuous at best...merely presumptions taken on faith from some earlier writer, news reporter or weapons specialist's article which, by virtue of time, became deep-rooted in arms lore. There is no doubting those same handguns commonly termed "dueling pistols" were

THE CODE OF HONOR;

OR

RULES FOR THE GOVERNMENT

OF

PRINCIPALS AND SECONDS

IN

DUELLING

BY JOHN LYDE WILSON.

CHARLESTON, S. C,:
PRINTED BY JAMES PHINNEY,
In the rear of 48 Broad-st,
1858.

The American Edition of 1858 shown here was merely a later reprint of the original 1838 Edition... written by the Governor of South Carolina John Lyde Wilson. Although often accorded the status of being well-known and recognized by American duellists (and the myriad of authors, reporters and dueling aficionados/disciples that followed), this American code had but very minor circulation or recognition of its existence!

used in such contests...or that some innovations popularly attributed to their development may be feasibly and reasonably granted them. Lest I be castigated for demeaning the widely admired, if not awe-inspiring dueling pistol, it cannot remain unsaid (and reiterated here) that the subject of dueling did decidedly play a role in the early development of some of these pistols...and was obviously instrumental in naming the

entire genre. Printed and documentary evidence exists that well-known, widely recognized British gunmakers (notably Rigby, Wogdon and Manton) recommended, developed and adopted certain innovations they asserted were designed specifically for dueling pistols.

The actual term "dueling pistol" was apparently in common usage, although used sparingly for an advertisement or printed label of a British gunmaker or merchant in the early 19th century. The same use of those words "dueling pistol" is rarely observed in advertisements by an American firearms merchant or gunmaker. Should a concerted effort be made, it is likely that other indication of use of the terminology will surface. However, the very fact that the practice of dueling was frowned upon by society in general (even though widely practiced) and that it was generally prohibited by legislative statute and a miscellany of (governmental) ordinances, would ostensibly preclude gunmakers from devoting their special talents to fabricating weapons designed expressly for such purpose. Nor would it be thought prudent to be noted for promoting and trafficking in weapons exclusively intended for their clientele to use for unlawful purposes; all the foregoing to the detriment of other "common" handguns (excepting specific target types) that were more likely to be employed in potentially life-threatening situations. And further: it is seemingly inconsistent to infer that a dueling pistol, by virtue of its implied use, required greater accuracy (or as some have implied, less accuracy!) or ease of handling than any other form of large handgun. Improvements, changes and innovations on all types of firearms are more reasonably attributed to normal technical and manufacturing innovations, fashion trends, cost of production and selling price. Thus, the origins and accuracy and very definition of "true dueling weapon" are dubious.

It is justly logical to conclude that

there is no fundamental difference to large size, single shot, flintlock or percussion handguns that may have been sold in their day as officer's pistols... holster pistols...target pistols...or dueling pistols! The vagueness of terminology has the earmarks of belonging solely in the eye of the beholder... or the gunmaker...or arms scholar... or just as plausibly, the creative writer of both earlier and current eras. Of all those various named handgun categories, none has aroused as much interest nor bequeathed such a legacy of disputable and uncertain arms lore as those said to have been specifically designed and purchased for...or actually used in a formalized duel. There is an obvious aura and wide range of fascination... from the valorous to the macabre, surrounding the practice of dueling and those handguns generally considered to have been specifically designed for that deliberate intent. With the passage of time and the many early and repeated usages of the terminology in the general literature of America and Britain, (especially firearms treatises) the "dueling pistol" has become a unique, yet indeterminate entity. An examination of firearms literature specifically dealing with dueling pistols clearly reflects a wide disparity among authors as to the attribution and development of innovations, modifications and technical improvements in handguns said to be specifically designed for, and unique to dueling. Risking redundancy: A significant flaw, apparently inherent with such studies is the almost complete lack of documentation in the form of footnotes alluding to valid sources. Also lacking are direct quotations from gunmakers, merchants, duelists or others contemporary to the fabrication of those same dueling firearms. All too often such treatises, laboring under the guise of accuracy, do not include even a sparse bibliography of published references utilized by the writer for their sources.

In view of preliminary rational study and personal experience in handling many of these same pistols, accompanied with an awareness of the diverse personalities that originally owned...

or were presented with them, it is reasonably concluded that the term "dueling pistol" is fundamentally generic, to include handguns of varying configurations, designed for a variety of roles and functions...in similar manner to the collective terminology "pepperbox", "deringer", "bootleg pistol" or even the unseemly "Saturday Night Special". It is suitably comparable to other eponymous names embodied early in the formal and informal history of firearms... and subsequently the jargon of firearms collecting. The significant, and most notable, dissimilarity was the mystique and sense of fearlessness, if not chivalry, that accompanied the "dueling" pistol. Its very name carried with it a certain poignancy and aggressive spirit...much as the legendary terminology "Bowie Knife" is all-embracing and entered the language in a similar manner. And that subject, too, has proven equally contentious as to the origins of its name! Thus it becomes evident that this genre of handgun had captured the imagination and fascination (if not morbid curiosity) of the gunmaker, arms merchant and the consumer (who was not necessarily a duelist!) of their day... and the popular writer and collector of present day, allowing the terminology permanent residency in the language.

Further demonstration of the incongruity of the terminology "dueling pistol" and confirmation that the nomenclature was generic and merely a term of convenience is apparent when viewing the below illustrated cased and matched pair of fine quality American percussion pistols of the type normally considered and classified as "duelers:"

Made by, and fully marked, "G.B. EVANS – PHILADELPHIA" and representative of the best of the American arms maker's craftsmanship, each pistol bears a large, silver plaque inset on its left side engraved with the lengthy

Cased set of percussion "dueling pistols" by one of America and Philadelphia's most noted makers HENRY DERINGER. Known almost exclusively for his small, pocket-sized, single-shot percussion pistols (of which there were many imitators during their period of manufacture) he is also known to have produced a few pistols similar to these large "duelers" this pair with 9 1/2-inch barrels and also marked with name of the Louisiana dealer for whom they were made by Deringer: "MAN'D FOR A. MILLSPAUGH / WASHINGTON, LA." Fitted in their original leather-covered wooden case, red velvet lined, accompanied by their original accessories.

inscription: "Presented to General Edward S. Salomon. Declared by the vote of his fellow citizens as the most popular Soldier of Cook County [Illinois] at the Fair of the Chicago [Military Training League], September, 1867." Each is 17 inches overall with 10-inch octagon barrels; caliber 48 smooth-bores. Breech of barrels, barrel tangs, sidelocks and hammers are profusely scroll engraved. Walnut halfstocks with checkered handles. Guns are fitted with single set triggers (i.e. "hair triggers"). General Salomon had earlier led the 82nd Illinois Infantry Regiment through many heated battles of the Civil War including Gettysburg.

In 1870 he was appointed by President Grant as the governor of the Territory of Washington.

Should that fine set not prove the point, this spectacular pair by one of America's best known early arms makers, Simeon North of Connecticut further supports the contention that the terminology "dueling pistol" is merely generic: In the collections of the Smithsonian Institution in Washington D.C. is this historical matched pair of elegantly embellished, gold mounted and engraved flintlock, half-stock 54-caliber smoothbore pistols; locks marked "S.NORTH/MIDDLETOWN/CONN." Their 10-inch barrels each engraved: "VOTED BY THE GENERAL ASSEMBLY OF THE STATE OF CONNECTICUT TO COMMODORE THOMAS MACDONOUGH [sic]". The pistols were presented by the governor and legislature of the state of Connecticut circa 1817 to honor a native son, U.S. Naval Commodore Macdonough's capture of an English squadron on Lake Champlain on Sept. 11th 1814.

Also on record is a near-identical Simeon North set of flintlock pistols, made on order of the General Assembly of Connecticut and presented by the governor to U.S. Naval Commodore Isaac Hull to commemorate the escape of the U.S.S. Constitution from a British squadron while on her passage from Chesapeake Bay to Boston during the War of 1812.

And... if those above misnamed "dueling pistols" do not prove the point that such terminology is generic to include a broad cross-section of other handgun types, here are two more that firmly buttress that contention. Well illustrated and described in the often quoted "The British Duelling Pistol" (by John Atkinson, 1978) are two pairs of classically designed British flintlock "duelling pistols" (styled similarly to the same genre of American manufacture). One set by the noted London maker H. W. Mortimer was made for no less than King George III... a fellow hardly likely to be engaged in single combat! The second pair of fine "saw handle" duelers, circa 1815-1820, were made for and

Made by noted Baton Rouge, Louisiana firearms and Bowie knife makers. Large percussion halfstock "dueling pistol" marked "SEARLES & F'PATRICK [sic]" on the back action lock. Nine-inch octagon barrel; large caliber. Daniel Searles and Rees Fitzpatrick were well-known gunsmiths whose shops were located near each other. Although the most of their work was independent, this pistol is evidence of a short-lived partnership. Both makers are also known (and played a role) in the legend of the American Bowie knife.

presented to the Duke of Wellington by the East India Co. They are considered by the author to be representative of the classic dueling type.

Other so-called "duelers" are known and recorded having belonged to, being presented to or purchased by citizens and officers with no known record of having engaged in a duel or any proclivity for doing so. Were such pistols as those illustrated and described here (or many others similarly owned and presented), all of which are categorized under the general terminology "dueling pistols," to have been specifically designed (and in the public's concept, uniquely adapted) for dueling, they would hardly have been found suitable for an organizational, governmental (or other) presentation to a public figure, reigning monarch, distinguished personage or national hero! Nor would they have been wielded only incidentally by ordinary citizenry for the more conventional roles of a handgun.

Having ventured into relatively unexamined territory (and possibly belabored the subjects to the dueling devotee's vexation) it is essential to recognize that these large single shot, non-military flintlock and percussion handguns are invariably representative of the best of the American gunmaker's craftsmanship and artistry. The mere fact that "dueling pistol" has been the traditional, generically applied nomenclature to describe and classify a broad range of styles and types...to the detriment of their other, possibly more urgent functions...is imperative to cite and recognize. There is but slightest likelihood (if any) that there were the multitudes of "gentlemen" (English or American) seeking uniquely designed handguns

with which to engage in duels, as might appear to have been indicated in dueling (and firearms) literature. Consequently, the marketplace for such narrowly specialized "dueling pistols" was relatively small. Judging from the great many gunmakers on both sides of the Atlantic known to have produced "dueling pistols" and the specimens yet surviving of those same type handguns, it becomes further obvious that the purposes for which they were actually designed were multifold...and their generic name merely being all-embracing. There is no doubting that the inspiration for some innovations or improvements in these handguns was influenced by dueling. However, there is every reason to believe that the trade for which they were sold was generalized and that the great majority of buyers were men who were neither duelists nor preparing for the eventuality of a duel. Thus, the conclusion, that the wide spectrum of uses for which these handguns were designed, purchased and put to use (dueling included) lends them considerably greater significance than the narrowly confined designation "dueling pistol" to which they have been confined.

Perhaps the entire subject and foregoing may have been placed in its clearest perspective by Colonel William Orbelo, well-known arms author and collector of American dueling pistols. When asked what was the difference between a target pistol and a dueling pistol, he candidly answered: "....The target!"

Smith & Wesson's M&P Pistol For USPSA

Practical Plastic for Production ▮ Paul Scarlata
▮ Photos by Nathan Reynolds

As I finished the stage, the RO instructed me to "Show clear...slide forward...hammer down...and holster." He then, somewhat grudgingly, added, "That's the best run I've seen on this stage so far today." By exerting supreme self-control I was able to keep a straight face while I muttered "thanks," although as I walked back to join my squad, to everyone's delight, I did a little victory dance!

Readers familiar with my crude efforts at journalism are aware that I am an avid (note, I said "avid" not "skillful") action pistol shooter. I first became involved in the sport about thirty years ago when it bore the politically incor-

rect moniker of "Combat Shooting." My enthusiasm for it grew until, nowadays, most weekends will find me wasting ammunition at various USPSA, IDPA, steel plate and bowling pin matches.

Of the various action pistol disciplines, the one I find most enjoyable are those matches held under the auspices of the USPSA (United States Practical Shooting Association), the U.S. affiliate of the International Practical Shooting Confederation (IPSC).

Over the years two forces have led to both IPSC and USPSA creating new divisions. First we had the so-called "Technology Race" that saw the development of recoil reducing devices (compensators, ported barrels, etc.),

electronic dot sights, and high capacity pistols. Shooters who did not wish to, or could not afford to, utilize these mechanical marvels became disenchanted when they had to compete against those who did. The result was the creation of Open and Limited (IPSC - Standard) divisions. The former permitted just about any modification to your handgun that the shooter's bank account could handle while the latter sought to encourage the use of "practical" pistols by forbidding recoil reducing devices, electronic sights, and imposing caliber restrictions. This two tiered system worked well for several years, until......

As competitors are wont to do, Limited shooters began trying to gain an edge and it wasn't long before they were modifying their pistols to the point where they barely – and I mean just barely! – stayed within the limits set down for the division. Once again the hardcore "practical" crowd began crying foul.

The second influence on the sport were firearms laws such as the Clintonista high-capacity magazine ban in the United States – and similar laws in other countries – which restricted shooters to 10-round cartridge containers. It was feared that new shooters would be turned off if they had to use an 11-round pistol when competing against those Limited shooter who were lucky enough to possess a stockpile of (very expensive) hi-cap magazines. Accordingly, USPSA instituted Limited 10

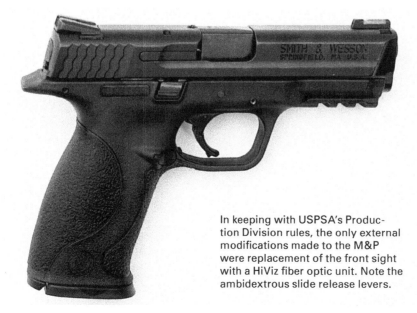

In keeping with USPSA's Production Division rules, the only external modifications made to the M&P were replacement of the front sight with a HiViz fiber optic unit. Note the ambidextrous slide release levers.

Division which restricted the shooter to ten rounds loaded in the pistol's magazine, but otherwise the rules are identical the Limited. It proved most popular with owners of single-stack 1911 pistols.

OK, so much for background. As I said at the beginning of this report, I am an avid USPSA shooter. I was turned off by the technology race and began shooting Limited – and ended up spending a lot of money building Limited pistols! In recent years, such mundane matters as putting my daughter through college and graduate school, needing a new car and – groan! – buying a house, have put a severe crimp in my "fun funds." Because of this I began looking for a less expensive means of pursuing my favorite sport. Enter Production Division.........

USPSA created Production Division for those persons who wanted to compete with basically factory, stock (read, "inexpensive") pistols. Besides restricting magazine capacity to 10 rounds, there are strict limitations as to what modifications can be made to the pistol (e.g.: internal polishing and detailing of parts, changing the sights, etc.) and the rules mandated that only pistols using DA/SA, DAO or Safe Action type triggers were permitted.

Unlike Open, Limited and Limited Ten divisions, Production did away with the Major/Minor power factor (P.F.) controversy for ammunition by specifying that only Minor P.F. was needed to compete.[1] This had the result of making the readily available, and inexpensive, 9mm Parabellum cartridge the overwhelming choice among Production shooters.

Over the past few years I have used several different pistols in Production division and, while all have proven suitable for the sport, most lacked that "something" that I considered necessary for competition. Last year I obtained a 9mm Smith & Wesson M&P pistol which, until recently, spent most of its time as my "night stand" gun.

The M&P is Smith's newest addition to their extensive line of semi-auto pistols and, IMHO, possibly the best one they have produced so far. Since its in-

troduction, the M&P has been examined extensively in gun magazines and I don't feel it is necessary to repeat the technical nitty-gritty here. Suffice it to say that the M&P is a polymer-framed pistol that uses integral steel rails to strengthen the frame and provide rigidity that improves accuracy and functional reliability. It features a double-action-only (DAO) type trigger, multiple internal safety devices, accepts high-capacity magazines and features an ergonomically-shaped grip with interchangeable inserts (S&W calls them "palm swells") that allow the shooter to fit the pistol to their particular hand size.[2] It is available in 9mm Para, 357 SIG, 40 S&W and 45 ACP, in both standard and compact versions.

I found my M&P a very shootable pistol and, as these things tend to happen, began ruminating upon the idea of using it in competition. With this I mind, I approached my good friend, fellow action pistol shooter, and part-time gunsmith, Lin Webb. Lin has built several competition pistols for me and when I asked him if he could work his magic on the M&P he responded rather guardedly "Well...I haven't done a trigger job on one of them before and, as far as I know, neither has anyone else. I guess someone has to be the first? Leave

ABOVE: Team S&W shooter Julie Golowski using a 9mm M&P at the 2006 Production Nationals. (Photo courtesy of S&W)

it with me." I did.

After some time had passed, Lin called and told me "I think I've figured out how to smooth out the trigger and get the let-off a bit lighter." The following month, a rather cryptic e-mail arrived from my erstwhile 'smith informing me that "....I believe it will work. I'm almost done." A few weeks later a follow-up message arrived "Yup, it works. I've taken first place Production with it in two matches so far. You're not going

My gunsmith, Lin Webb, used my M&P to compete in several matches before I ever had a chance to try it!

to believe the trigger!" Needless to say, my anxiety level was steadily rising and I could not wait to get my hands on my M&P.

I asked Lin if he would tell the readers in his own words how he accomplished this. No one has ever been able to accuse him of being the taciturn type, so he elaborated thus:

1 Make sure the pistol is unloaded and remove any and all ammo from the same area as the pistol you are working on.

1.1 Make dad-gum sure the gun is unloaded, with no ammo in the same area you are working in.

2 The M&P, like any other semiauto on the market today, has 'way too much take-up and over-travel as it comes from the factory. Remove the slide, and pull the trigger to the rear and note where the trigger bar engages the sear. If your pistol has the magazine safety, you must hold the mag safety lever up to see this function, so you may as well insert an empty magazine so you'll only need two hands instead of three. If your gun does not have the mag safety lever, you must pull the sear deactivation lever back up in order to see the trigger bar move in its normal operating position. Just be sure to return the deactivation lever to the 'down' position before reassembly.

3 Once you've got it in your head where and how the trigger bar contacts the sear, proceed to remove the sear housing block. Use the correct size pin punch or roll pin punch and remove the pin from the frame. Be sure to support the frame from the bottom so the pin can clear the frame as it is driven out. The pin can be removed from either direction. Then lift the sear housing out of the frame. You can use the same punch you used to remove the pin to pry the sear housing block out of the frame. When you get the sear housing about half-way up, pull the trigger to the rear to take tension off the trigger bar. Continue to lift up on the sear housing, and then it will slide right off the rear of the trigger bar. On older model M&Ps, the ejector will practically fall off the side of the sear housing. This is OK, but on newer models, it will be staked on pretty tightly, so don't bother to remove it.

4 Locate the sear pin, and push it out. It will come out easily and from either direction. Be sure to keep the sear housing in the upright position as you remove the pin, and then remove the sear itself. Again, be sure to keep the housing upright so the sear spring and plunger stay in place because if they fall out, they are a pain in the ass to get back in. Use a small piece of leather or wood to clamp the sear in a small vise. Make sure the contact point with the trigger bar is facing up. Using a small fine cut mill file, start cutting the rounded portion of the sear where the trigger

My newest Production pistol is a customized Smith & Wesson M&P in 9mm. While a number of internal modifications were made, except for one spring all factory parts were used.

The M&P features interchangeable "palm swells" that allow the shooter to fit the pistol to his particular hand size.

bar makes contact. Cut SLOWLY at a 45-degree angle, and remove about 20 percent of this contact point. Finish with a fine cut stone to polish the surface, and then finish by slightly rounding the edges for a smooth "compound" type finish. Then polish the trigger bar where it contacts the sear to a fine mirror-like finish. Remember to go slowly, and don't remove any metal from the trigger bar, just polish only. You might want to put the gun back together at this point to test it out to see where you are. Just this little bit of work will greatly improve the pull.

5 For a further reduced trigger pull weight, remove the sear again and look at the rear of the sear. You'll see a hump where the sear engages the striker and pulls it to the rear during trigger pull. Polish the rear of the sear with a polishing wheel, and also the top flat portion of the sear where the tang of the striker rides across during re-set. Be sure to keep the two surfaces at right angles to each other. In other words, don't round off this edge. Keep it at 90 degrees to each other. Polishing with an aggressive jeweler's polishing compound works quite well. You can also use a Dremel polishing wheel to speed this process, but go slowly. This will remove metal faster than you think. You can remove the striker now and polish the tang of the striker where it makes contact with the sear. Polish only here, DO NOT remove any metal. To remove the striker, push down on the striker sleeve, just like brand "G" and push the end cap off, while holding your thumb over the striker to keep it from flying into the next room, and remove the striker.

6 To remove the "crunchiness" from the trigger pull, now is the time to do this while the striker is removed. Wrap the slide in several wraps of cloth or use a large piece of leather, and clamp it in a vise with just the rear sight area clear of the vise jaws. Loosen the set screw in the rear sight. Using a brass drift punch, tap the rear sight out from left to right. Don't be afraid to whack it, as some rear sights are tough to remove. Nylon punches give too much, and steel punches will mar the sight. Use a brass punch with nice square edges. If yours is not, straighten it up with a file first. When the sight is almost out, look for the firing pin safety block spring cap and spring underneath the rear sight. Hold your finger over this cap as you continue to tap the sight out. Hold onto to the cap to keep it from flying into the next county. Remember, the striker must be OUT of the gun to be able to do this. Remove the firing pin safety block from the frame.

7 Using a 3/32" pin punch, place the firing pin safety block on the end of the punch. Hold the firing pin block at a 45-degree angle to a 3M polishing wheel and polish the head of the safety block until you have a

The HiViz front sight has the fiber optic rod encased in high-impact polymer to protect it from damage. Its brightness greatly enhances fast target acquisition and accuracy.

The only change I made to the rear sight was to use a marker pen to blacken the dual white dots.

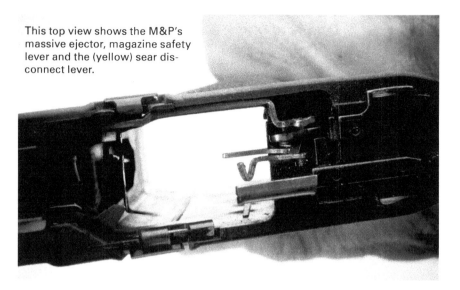

This top view shows the M&P's massive ejector, magazine safety lever and the (yellow) sear disconnect lever.

nice rounded edge all the way around the firing pin block. It will rotate on it's own as you do this. Make sure the polishing wheel rotates downward so as to keep downward pressure on the firing pin block. This will keep it from flying off the pin punch. Do not remove any metal from the top of the firing pin block, just the outer edge only. Be sure to polish the area of the trigger bar that contacts the firing pin block, too. Just polish the trigger bar contact points for the sear and the firing pin safety block contacts to a mirror finish, do not remove any metal from these two areas of the trigger bar. Clean the hole where the firing pin block goes and lube it with a good quality gun lube. Put the firing pin block back in, along with the small spring. Start the rear sight into the dovetail from right to left. Place the spring cap on top of the spring and press it into place. While holding it there, tap the rear sight back over this assembly to hold it in place. Don't let go until the rear sight has almost covered the cap or it will fly out. NOTE: This procedure is very tricky, but go slow and you can do it. Some rear sights are easier to get out and back

in than others on the same model gun, so don't be afraid to whack the hell out of it with a brass punch to get it to move. Brass marks can be easily removed with 0000 steel wool.

8 There is one last thing you can do for the ultimate M&P trigger job. Obtain a Glock trigger return spring and replace the stock M&P trigger spring with this spring. Be sure to place the open end of the spring on the trigger bar in the UP position. The end that goes on the trigger pin must

For competition I used a Comp-Tac Belt Holster and Beltfeed staggered magazine pouches (opposite page).

be slightly enlarged to fit over the M&P trigger pin, but it can be done. Use a pin punch of the proper size as a guide to align the pin hole and spring as you tap the trigger pin back in. If you have done everything as I have described it, you will have a much improved trigger pull over the stock configuration. If you shoot a lot of USPSA or IDPA matches, your scores will definitely improve. There are several M&P triggers jobs described on the Internet now, and they are very much like I have described it here, however, you must have some familiarity with the M&P to perform these modifications correctly. It isn't as easy as some would have you believe.

I have found out that the 45-caliber M&P differs slightly from the 9mm, 40 S&W, and the 357 SIG calibers. The firing pin is different, the angles on the trigger and sear are different, and pretty much everything as far as a trigger job goes is different, so take your time on the 45s. Again, go slow, and don't remove too much. If you don't feel comfortable doing it yourself, then you will be way ahead of the game to send your gun out to some of the shops that advertise M&P trigger jobs on the Internet.

Since working on Paul's pistol, I've done about two dozen M&P trigger jobs without any failure, and no safety parts violations, but they were T&E guns and they were not returned to the general shooting public. Most all of these guns broke the trigger pull gauge at around 3 pounds, and were smooth as silk. If you feel like it, and have the confidence, give it a try. You might want to purchase a spare sear, safety block, and trigger bar from Smith & Wesson just in case you mess something up. That way you can put stock parts back in and get the gun back up and shooting again.

As I make no pretense whatsoever to being technically minded, I will have to

Smith & Wesson M&P
Specifications:

Caliber: 9mm, 357 SIG & 40 S&W
OAL: 7.5 inches
Barrel length: 4.25 inches
Height: 5.5 inches
Width: 1.2 inches
Weight (unlocked): 27.45 ounces
Magazine: 17 rounds (9mm)
              15 rounds (.357 & .40)
Construction:
   frame: Zytel Polymer
   slide: Stainless steel with
   Melonite finish
Sights:
   front: Steel Ramp
   rear: Novak Lo-Mount

take what Lin said at face value. But I can tell you this: once I finally retrieved my M&P from Mr. Webb's clutches, and got a chance to try it, I was most impressed. The trigger take-up was so light and smooth as to be almost unnoticeable; the let-off was a crisp 2.5 pounds while reset distance was less than a half-inch. During rapid fire drills it almost felt as if I was shooting a single-action pistol.

In fact, after getting my M&P back the only changes I made to it were to install a HiViz fiber optic front sight and use a marker pen to blacken out the white dots on the rear sight. Aside from the trigger return spring and front sight replacement it remains a100-percent stock pistol and thus abides by USPSA rules to the letter! [3]

Being the M&P has fixed sights I experimented with various brands of factory and handloaded ammo and eventually settled on Cor-Bon's 9mm 147-grain Performance Match ammunition for serious competition shooting. I have used this ammo in several pistols over the years and it has proven to be the most accurate 9mm load I have ever shot. My handload consists of a Berry's 147-grain plated bullet over 3.6 grains of TiteGroup. Both provide 100-percent functioning, shoot close enough to point out to 25 yards to keep me happy, produce low levels of recoil and make Minor P.F. with a bit to spare.

I also experimented with a number of holsters and mag pouches and settled on a Comp-Tac Belt Holster and Beltfeed magazine pouches. The former holds the M&P at just the right height and angle for a fast acquisition and smooth draw while the latter rig holds four spare magazines in a staggered row allowing a fast, secure grip on each to ensure fast and smooth reloads.

Unfortunately, I did not have an opportunity to practice very much with my M&P before the next match but, despite the trepidation I felt at competing with a pistol I had little experience with, I finished 2nd Place overall in Limited Division and 1st Place in B Class. And while I like to think that my personal skill (?) had a little something to do with it, a good measure of the credit must go to Lin's excellent trigger job and the accuracy, reliability and ergonomics that were built into the M&P at the factory.

The M&P has served as my regular Production pistol for several months now and my positive opinion of it continues to grow. As Humphrey Bogart said at the end of his classic film Casablanca, "....I think this is the beginning of a beautiful friendship."

For further information:
Berry's Manufacturing - *401 North 3050 East St. George, Utah 84790. http://www.berrysmfg.com*
   Cor-Bon Ammunition - *1311 Industry Rd., Sturgis, SC 57785. www.dakotaammo.net*
   Comp-Tac - *P.O. Box 1809 Spring, Texas 77373. http://www.comp-tac.com*
   Smith & Wesson - *2100 Roosevelt Ave, Springfield, MA 01104. www.smith-wesson.com*

Test firing results:	Group Size	Velocity
Cor-Bon 147 gr. Performance Match	1.75"	878 fps
Berry's 147 gr. Plated/3.6 TiteGroup	2"	865 fps

3. I inquired of USPSA as to the legality of changing trigger return spring and received the following e-mail: Item 21.4 of the Production rules, allows for action work to enhance reliability, throating, trigger work, etc., this would mean that while doing the action work, springs may be replaced.
John Amidon, VP USPSA, Director NROI

The Double Action Revolver For Concealed Carry

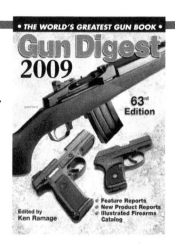

After 157 Years, Does It Still Measure Up? ▌ Jerry Ahern
▌ Photos by Sharon Ahern

In 1851, inventor Robert Adams obtained a British patent for the first successful double-action revolver. Although hardly the epitome of mechanical perfection, the Adams revolver and its subsequent improvements effectively started a revolution in personal defense. The double-action revolver came along slowly in the United States, starting to truly gain ground in America only in the waning years of the 19th century, although some British double actions saw service as private purchase firearms during the American Civil War years. By the turn of the 20th century, however, the double-action re-

volver had even penetrated the ranks of the American military, despite a rather dubious caliber choice (an underpowered .38) in a swing-out cylinder Colt. The double-action revolver's popularity would not erode until the late 1970s and early 1980s, when the double-action semi-automatic at last came into its own, this flatter, faster loading, higher-capacity handgun — at least temporarily — largely supplanting the double-action revolver as the arm of choice for lawmen and civilians alike. During the first seven and one-half decades of the 20th century, however, the double-action revolver was the most commonly encoun-

The Colt in 41 Long Colt, a formidable weapon then as now, and not too large for concealed carry. This is an 1895 New Army and Navy, precursor of the Official Police and dates from 1904.

tered concealed weapon in the United States, perhaps only discounting the ever ubiquitous 25 automatic.

Although the American armed forces returned to the 45 caliber after their unsuccessful flirtation with 38-caliber revolvers and had, for the first time, adopted a semi-automatic pistol, the exigencies of World War I brought double-action revolvers from Smith & Wesson and Colt back into the U.S. military as substitute standard weapons, a situation which would recur during World War II. Privately purchased snub-nosed 38 Special revolvers were in use during the Viet Nam War as "sleeping bag" guns. In actuality, revolvers were still issued in the U.S. military as special purpose weapons well into the end of the 20th century, signed out to plain-clothes military intelligence and law enforcement personnel as well as uniformed security officers, pilots and others, certain of these applications involving concealed carry.

In Europe, the double-action semi-automatic took serious hold in the late 1920s with the success of the Walther PP and PPK, the double-action auto rising to prominence as a military weapon with the Walther P-38. The question of reliability concerning the automatic generally — whether a traditional single-action style such as the 1911A1 or the more modern European double actions — was off-putting to most of American law enforcement, the civilian population following suit. When the Illinois State Police adopted the Smith & Wesson Model 39 in 1967-68, they were all alone among major departments and remained that way for some years

The sights of these service-style revolvers are rudimentary and quite similar, whether a Colt, as is this specimen, or a Smith & Wesson.

to come. One of the reasons for Illinois switching to the Model 39 was the belief that the gun would be carried both on-duty and off-duty, taking snubby off-duty double-action revolvers out of the picture entirely.

The double-action revolver's principal claim to fame was quickness from the holster or pocket. It certainly wasn't accuracy. In appropriate hands, a traditional single-action revolver was much more accurate than even the best double action, a condition largely unchanged despite a century and one-half's strides in double-action lockwork designs. This accuracy question only has merit as regards target accuracy, however, not practical accuracy in combat. Single-action revolvers are vastly simpler affairs, the amount of moving parts required to raise a hammer from full rest and subsequently trip it, all in one double-action cycling of the trigger, considerably more complicated.

The terms "double action" and "single action" are a point of confusion to many people. By double action, what is meant is that two functions are performed with one action: the hammer is raised and released with the operator merely working the trigger. A single action requires two separate actions to be performed by the operator: cock the hammer, thus setting the sear, and pulling the trigger, thus terminating hammer/sear engagement. Two actions are needed to fire a single action, one to fire a double action, unless, of course, one chooses to fire the double action in the more deliberate and usually more accu-

The diminutive Colt 32 was an ideal size for concealed carry in the days of woolen sportcoats and heavy outerwear, and it's still quite practical today, if one can live with the caliber. 32s were often the issue guns for policewomen well past the mid-point of the 20th century. This Colt 32 is interesting in that it is one of a batch of Colt New Police revolvers made with frames still marked New Pocket, a practice which continued for about four years. Various barrel lengths were offered. This gun was made in 1905-06.

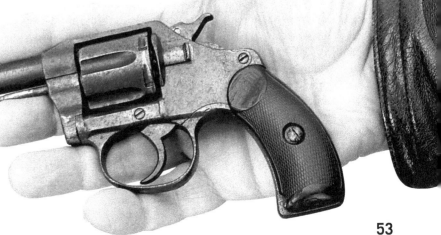

At top, a heavily customized Smith & Wesson Model 686 by Mahovsky's Metalife, the barrel slab-sided and engraved, custom round butted, fitted with a crane lock and treated to a buttery smooth action job. Only a six-gun! At center a stock 6-inch blue Model 586. At bottom, a Model 681, action tuned and crane lock fitted and round-butted by Mahovsky, this is a fixed sight L-Frame, very early on discontinued. The gun is extremely accurate and durable in the extreme, the Metalife SS Chromium M treatment applied over the stainless steel. The wooden grips on both stainless revolvers are Smith & Wesson Goncalo Alves Combat Stocks, both good looking and functional.

rate single-action mode, which applies to most double-action revolvers, but not all. One can easily grasp the confusion suffered by the tyro!

The first American double-action revolvers were developed by Smith & Wesson. Colt entered the lists later. Smith & Wesson's initial double-action offering premiered in 1880, a top-break, the 38 Double Action. Colt's Lightning, also a 38, but utilizing a loading gate rather than a swing-out cylinder, appeared in 1877. The Thunderer was Colt's Lightning Model produced in the heavier 41 caliber. In 1899, Smith & Wesson introduced what indisputably can be considered the most enduringly popular double-action revolver ever designed, a true benchmark, the Smith & Wesson Military & Police. Original calibers were 38 S&W and 32 Winchester Centerfire. As this is written, this revolver is still available as the Model 10 in blued carbon steel and as the Model 64 in stainless steel, both with four-inch barrels, both for 38 Special +P.

When Teddy Roosevelt was Police Commissioner of New York City, he was sent serial number "1" of the Colt New Police 32. He must have liked the revolver, acquiring over four thousand of them for the New York City police department in 1896. This double-action revolver eventually morphed into the Colt Police Positive, the Hartford version of a benchmark modern double action. Teddy Roosevelt liked his Colts.

The double-action revolver has been associated with some rather interesting people over the years, most of them real, a few fictional, at least two of them having crossed the line from fiction into reality for many. By this latter reference, I could mean no other personages than Dr. John H. Watson and the world's first consulting detective, Mr. Sherlock Holmes, both gentlemen of 221B Baker Street, London.

Although various arms entered into Holmes' exploits — even an extremely lethal airgun — both the Great Detective and his Boswell usually relied on 450-caliber double-action revolvers — it was the British service round, after all — Holmes' Webley Metropolitan Police a snub-nosed model, Watson's Second Model Adams, a full-sized weapon. Holmes and Watson count among the first of a long list of detectives — in fiction and reality — to rely on the double-action revolver. But, so did bad guys.

For example, in 1895, John Wesley Hardin got into a crap game in El Paso, Texas, only to discover -- at least to his way of thinking — that the game was rigged! Wes Hardin jerked his 41-caliber double-action Colt Thunderer smokewagon and took back only what he had lost. Later, he was arrested and fined $25 for carrying a concealed weapon, the Colt confiscated. On other occasions, Hardin was also known to carry a shorter barreled Lightning with ivory grips, a gift from his cousin.

Pat Garrett, the inordinately tall (standing well over six feet, he was often referred to as "Long John") lawman who took down Billy The Kid, as history relates, had a Colt 1877 double action engraved on the backstrap as a gift from his friends in El Paso. But, Billy The Kid, not in that most famous of flipped photos where he carried a Colt Single Action Army, was known to use the 41-caliber double-action Colt as well. And, when Emilio Estevez portrayed Billy in "Young Guns II," in some scenes he actually used a genuine Colt Model 1877 Thunderer double action.

Miss Bonnie Parker and Mr. Clyde Barrow were serious Colt users and, among the guns in their car when Texas Ranger Frank Hamer got them, was a 45 Colt New Service. Until the advent of the 500 Smith & Wesson revolver, the New Service was the largest double-action revolver ever produced.

Although some of the Old West lawmen who survived into the modern era of the 20th century — men like Wyatt Earp and Bat Masterson — may have used double actions at times, one of the most famous of 20th century lawmen relied on a double-action revolver. That was Eliot Ness. In the well-respected television series starring the late Robert Stack, Ness carried a four-inch double action. If memory serves, it was a Colt. In the film with Kevin Costner, Ness carries a 45 automatic. In real life, Eliot Ness carried a two-inch ba rreled Colt Detective Special 38 Special. According to Ness himself in The Untouchables and Four Against The Mob, both written with Oscar Fraley, he never drew his gun in the line of duty. Sadly, Eliot Ness died before The Untouchables was turned into a television series and he was turned into the most storied lawman of the 20th century.

A 20th century lawman who drew his gun quite a lot in the line of duty and survived many gunfights, Bill Jordan was, quite possibly, the most passionate supporter of the double-action revolver one could imagine. When the Smith & Wesson Model 59 came out, Bill Jordan got one, a gift from the factory, if memory serves. He thought the large-capacity 9mm made a nice backup gun, but stuck with his four-inch Model 19 357 Magnum double-action revolver as primary ordnance. Bill Jordan was a gunfighting United States Border Patrol officer back in the days when gunfights with smugglers were so hot and heavy along the Mexican Border that horse-backing officers would carry a flour sack filled with spare ammo lashed to their saddle horns. Jordan authored the classic book on modern gunfighting, No Second Place Winner, as well as numer-

This mysteriously marked Spanish revolver is formidable in appearance and chambered for the 455 cartridge, it wouldn't be much fun to be shot with, either!

ous gun articles.

Bill Jordan was always a very pleasant guy — unless you were a crook — and even appeared on television doing quick draw with a double-action revolver. He could place an aspirin tablet on the back of his gunhand, draw and drill the tablet before it hit the floor. Another trick was to place a cocked single-action revolver in a volunteer's hand, then outdraw the person with his double-action revolver before the single-action's hammer could fall. It is because of Jordan that the Model 19 357 Magnum came to exist.

A fan of fast gunplay when required, Jordan wanted the power of the 357

Magnum cartridge in the handier package of a K-Frame revolver. The 357 S&W Magnum, as introduced on April 8, 1935 (the first example was presented to then-FBI Director J. Edgar Hoover) in what was to become the Model 27 was a truly custom revolver of the first rank. The caliber was indeed handy for law/anti-law encounters as well as being a fine big game-getter. After World War II, production of civilian firearms resumed; Smith & Wesson introduced several new models of double-action revolvers, among these in 1954 the Model 28 Highway Patrolman. This was a plainer, less pricey, law enforcement-oriented version of the Model 27, available with a 4-inch or 6-inch barrel, the shorter barrel more comfortable when the gun was worn behind the wheel of a patrol car.

The revolver that Jordan pushed for — essentially a 38 Special Model 15 Combat Masterpiece, but in 357 Magnum and with more hand-filling stocks — became known as the Model 19 Combat Magnum. Initially offered in two barrel lengths with a choice of blue or nickel finish, the gun debuted on November 15, 1955. Bill Jordan was the recipient of this soon-to-be-legendary revolver. He promptly thereafter appeared on national television as a guest on the popular "You Asked For It" program. He held up his brand new Model 19 and proclaimed, "The answer to a peace officer's dream!"

Originally available in four-inch and six-inch lengths, it was offered not long

The 4-inch Model 686.

Ahern wearing a Hip-Gripped original Smith & Wesson Model 60 38 Special, the revolver acquired a quarter-century ago.

Galco's Miami Classic for an L-Frame revolver is extremely concealable when properly adjusted and properly worn. And, it is comfortable.

afterward with skinnier grips and a 2 1/2-inch barrel for concealed carry. All three barrel length options were eventually available on the Model 66, the Stainless Combat Magnum. The first of these guns debuted in 1971, 4-inch versions only, the other two lengths arriving on the scene by the middle of the decade. The Model 66 2-1/2 was possibly the hottest selling double-action revolver on the planet, except, of course, for the double-action revolver worn as a con-

cealed weapon by the movies' favorite cop, "Dirty Harry."

The Model 29 6-1/2 was sought after long before Clint Eastwood first played the role in 1972. Afterward, finding one of these 44 Magnum double-action revolvers sitting unclaimed on a dealer's shelf was almost less likely than finding the proverbial money tree growing in your backyard. The concept for the 44 Magnum cartridge was the brainchild of noted firearms authority and pundit Elmer Keith. Smith & Wesson completed the first Model 29, sending it to Remington for the ammunition-maker to use in load development. Elmer Keith received the third Model 29 made. "The world's most powerful handgun," as Clint Eastwood's character would describe it, premiered in 1956. With the Model 29, prolific screenwriter Harry Julian Fink took an aficionado's double-action hunting handgun and turned it into a full-fledged movie star.

A major problem, of course, with larger handguns of any operating system, double-action revolvers included, is concealment. Despite Bill Jordan's devotion to the Model 19 357 Combat Magnum with 4-inch barrel, the gun that he carried in the muff pocket of his

sweats when he went jogging was a J-Frame snub-nose 38 Special; if memory serves, a Bodyguard Airweight.

The "...peace officer's dream..." of 1955 was about to endure a rude awakening.

On April 11, 1986 the death knell rang on the double-action revolver as an issue weapon for America's most high-profile law enforcement agency, the FBI. It started a trend. For some time, FBI personnel and Metro-Dade police had been in pursuit of a violent two-man crew wanted in association with bank and armored car robberies. It wasn't quite ten in the morning when one of the cars associated with the fugitive duo was spotted. To employ an egregiously overused expression, it was then that "all hell broke loose." The two bad guys were armed with shoulder-holstered 357 Magnum revolvers, only one of these loaded with Magnum rounds. Michael Lee Platt, who would prove to be the most methodically deadly of the duo, had a folding stock semi-auto 223 equipped with 30-round magazines. And, he seemed to enjoy using it, especially with head and groin shots on men already wounded. Platt's partner, William Russell Matix, had a 12-gauge folding-stock shotgun fitted with an 8-round extended length magazine loaded with #6 shot. The FBI Special Agents just had handguns and a shotgun which was only successfully deployed after the shootout

The DeSantis fabric Patriot Shoulder Rig works quite well and has the advantage of being ambidextrous and able to function with various versions of K-Frame and L-Frame size revolvers.

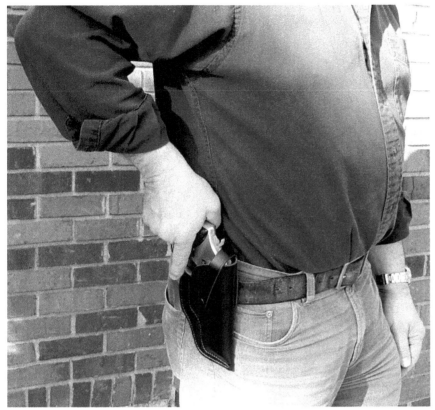

A typical field holster for belt carry shown with a 4-inch revolver. This is not concealable; but, when worn while tramping the woods, it usually doesn't have to be.

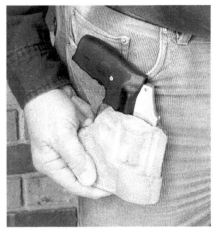

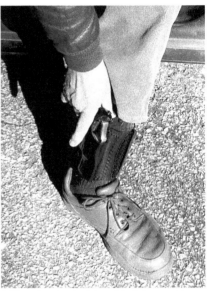

TOP: A Model 640 38 with Crimson Trace Lasergrips shown in an Ahern Pocket Natural front pocket holster. Front pocket carry for revolvers of this general size is quite common and can be quite concealable.

ABOVE: Galco's ankle glove is a superior ankle holster. It is worn properly here, the gun on the inside of the off ankle, i.e., a right-handed man carrying on the inside of the left ankle.

was well underway.

Special Agent Edmundo Mireles, badly wounded, revealed himself as an iron-willed hero. He ended the bloody firefight by emptying the six shots from the cylinder of his Smith & Wesson Model 13 (I have read an account giving the revolver a 4-inch barrel, but the issue weapons had 3-inch barrels), all but one round entering into Platt and Matix. Matix died before medical personnel arrived. Platt died very quickly after their arrival.

Two FBI agents lay dead in the line of duty: Special Agent Jerry Dove and Special Agent Benjamin Grogan.

The shootout eventually led to the FBI switching to 10mm S&W semi-automatics, eschewing revolvers because of limited firepower and the +P 38 Special round they'd used for something with greater penetration. These 10mm autos manifested problems and, while such issues were being addressed, the FBI switched to 9mm autos. The double-action revolver was made the "fall guy" in this excessively bloody

gun battle, the most intense in FBI history. Curiously, two FBI personnel in the gunfight had been allowed to carry high-capacity 9mm semi-automatics. Nobody blamed these, although close to 30 shots were fired at the killers from the two pistols. The actual FBI issue load in the 357 Magnum caliber Model 13s was the .38 Special +P 158-grain lead semi-wadcutter hollow point, not a 357 Magnum round. Although the FBI revolvers were given a great deal of the blame, issues ranging from ammunition choice to tactics to planning were of much greater import. In the end, the double-action revolver was out. The 10mm auto the FBI chose in its stead was itself replaced. The "10mm Lite" became the 40 S&W, the caliber of choice for platoons of today's American law enforcement personnel.

A perusal of current Smith & Wesson offerings reveals that only three basic K-Frame Models remain in the line, all 4-inchers, all 38 Specials. The 3-inch Model 13, along with the once highly prized Model 66 2-1/2 and its blued

Model 19 counterpart, also 357 Magnums, are no longer made.

The most popular of all double-action revolvers these days are J-Frame-sized, whether from Smith & Wesson itself or from Taurus or Charter Arms. So many of these revolvers, of course, are no longer offered in 38 Special, but instead in 357 Magnum. Compounding the caliber issue in so small a revolver are metallurgical concerns. Only five

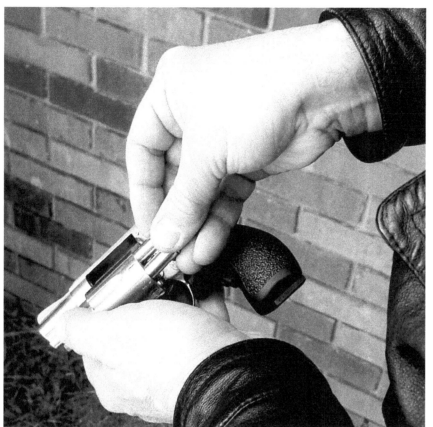

Supposedly, British officers were taught to load their Webley service revolvers this way. Be that as it may, absent speed loaders, this two-at-a-time loading technique is reliable and faster than single loading.

basic models of J-Frame Smith & Wesson exist in 38 Special, including the original Model 36. Even the Model 60 has been morphed into a 357! If you want a Model 640 in 38 Special, you can't get it. One can, however, obtain a current production "Classic" Model 40 in 38 Special, complete with its original grip safety.

The first handgun I ever purchased was a 2-inch barrel 38 Special S&W J-Frame, a blued Model 36. That was forty years ago, as this is written. One can understand that I have a certain fondness for the things. Be that as it may, the combination of 357 Magnum recoil in guns as light as 12 ounces, rubber grips notwithstanding, will discourage practice. The key to successful service from a small double-action revolver is to shoot it. People used to complain about +P 38 Special rounds from an alloy-framed Smith & Wesson Airweight. Can it be that today's shooters are so much tougher and stronger than pistoleros of yester-

year? I think not.

The typical steel-framed J-Frame Smith & Wesson double action of yore weighed 21 ounces. That is over a half-pound difference between the steel gun in 38 and the Scandium/Titanium/Stainless combination found in the 357 Magnum Model 360PD weighing 12 ounces. Twelve and one-half ounces to 13-1/2 ounces was typical weight for the "punishing" 38 Special Airweights. Then, why does anyone want a 12-ounce 357 Magnum? Certainly not to shoot it! My opinion, of course, for what it's worth.

Whatever one's choice in a double-action revolver — whether the firearm is the size of the N-Frame Model 29 or the original Model 36, whether a 6-inch Colt Python or a 2-inch Detective Special, Cobra or Agent — the guns can be effectively concealed. What is said here is just as true, of course, for Taurus, Charter Arms and Ruger revolvers. Movies place an inordinate emphasis on

shoulder holsters, for example. Almost as well-known as "Dirty Harry's" Model 29 was the shoulder holster in which he carried it in most of the films, the shoulder holster itself marketed as "The Dirty Harry Shoulder Holster." For a double-action revolver that size, a shoulder rig was practical. However, larger guns can be carried at waist level if one knows how. Over the years, when I've done seminars on how to carry and spot concealed weapons, I've taken a 6-inch barrel revolver and positioned it inside the waistband of my trousers, behind my left hip bone, butt forward, the entire weapon positioned so that the muzzle is angled toward the front. This keeps even a 6-inch double-action Colt or Smith & Wesson or Ruger or Taurus within the average man's body plane, thus effectively concealed under a normal covering garment.

Most double-action revolvers that will be carried concealed are not 6-inch barrel models or longer. Most, instead, are a nominal 2-, 3- or 4-inches in barrel length.

With a 4-inch barrel, the most practical on-body carries are with a holster worn inside the waistband, with an actual belt-mounted holster or with a shoulder holster. In most cases, however, the straight up and down vertical shoulder holster is usually the least concealable when serious concealment — rather than just covering up the gun — is at issue.

For a shoulder holster for the double-action revolver with a nominal 4-inch or even 3-inch barrel — or, for that matter one of the no longer produced Smith & Wesson Model 19 2-1/2 or Model 66 2-1/2 or the long-gone Colt 357 Magnum Lawman MK III 2-inch or short-barreled Diamondback or Python — the diagonal/horizontal shoulder holster is usually best. Some people refer to these shoulder systems as "horizontal" and wear them that way. They are most concealable and faster when worn as a "diagonal." Although most full-line and custom holster makers offer such shoulder rigs, three of the best are from Galco (which really pioneered with these rigs and popularized them), DeSantis and custom maker Sam Andrews. The Galco Miami Classic is probably the most well-known shoulder holster in the world because of the "Miami Vice" television series. Similarly, the DeSantis diagonal rig is what is worn by Bruce Willis in the "Die Hard" films. Currently, DeSantis only offers a fabric diagonal rig for double-action revolvers. Galco still offers the Miami Classic for "wheelguns," as double-action revolvers are sometimes called. As a custom maker, Sam Andrews will likely be able to make whatever the customer requires.

In belt holsters, the single tunnel loop variety is to be avoided for strong-side carry except when the gun is worn more or less openly. This style allows the butt of the gun to swing away from the body, thus profiling or outlining under clothing, disallowing any true concealment. Select either a holster utilizing two (or more, for different carry angles) belt slots, sometimes called generically a "pancake" style holster, since this type of slot arrangement was popularized by Roy Baker with his "Pancake" holsters. Or, choose a holster combining a single tunnel loop on the body side of the holster with a belt slot at the rear of the holster. This is a very effective system, one well-known example of this type developed years ago by Bianchi International and dubbed the "Askins Avenger" after the famous firearms authority and writer Col. Charles Askins.

Double-action revolvers were/are often carried crossdraw, wherein the operator reaches to the opposite side of his body rather than his hip for the weapon, and these types of holsters may indeed be adequate with merely a single tunnel loop.

Whereas a snap closure safety strap is essential to the operation of most diagonal shoulder holsters, and even though all of these waist-level style holsters, of course, can be had with or without various types of safety strap arrangements, in the belt holster and, even more so, with inside-waistband holsters, the safety strap is largely unnecessary.

When it come to the smaller revolvers with their nominal 2-inch barrels and usually fixed sights (meaning less

The Null "Vam" holster was developed for police and security personnel who needed fast access to an inconspicuous gun while seated behind the wheel. Unlike many such holsters, the Vam is perfectly acceptable when up and moving about. It is also, when practiced with, quite possibly the fastest crossdraw rig Ahern has ever seen or tried. This one is from horsehide, which wears like iron.

chance of snagging on clothing), concealment options grow. What was said about shoulder- and waist-level holsters for the longer barreled guns certainly applies; but, other factors — useful ones — enter in. For one thing, a great many double-action snubby revolvers are five-shooters. This imparts a narrower cylinder to the gun, aiding somewhat in concealment, closer to the flatness of a semi-automatic pistol.

Aside from all the carries mentioned above, these smaller guns can be worn in ankle holsters and even crotch holsters. The Galco Ankle Glove is an excellent example of the ankle holster and the K.L. Null Holsters crotch holster (Ken Null may be the only source in the U.S.A. still offering such a holster for a snubby revolver) is truly well-designed and well-made. Although Bianchi International and Safariland used to offer upside-down shoulder rigs for these double-action small revolvers, Null alone offers upside-down holsters for this or any revolver, to the best of my knowledge. Null's shoulder holsters

of this type are excellent, by the way, whether one chooses the horsehide or plastic version.

For decades, my favorite way to carry a J-Frame snubby 38 double action was with the excellent Barami Hip Grip. These are still available in limited quantity, even more limited for double-action revolvers besides the J-Frame S&Ws, including Taurus, Charter Arms, Colt and Rossi models. The Hip Grip incorporates a shelf extension rising from the upper most portion of the right grip panel from behind the recoil shield. Slip the revolver inside the waistband, sans holster, and the shelf hooks over the waistband or waistband and belt. This keeps the revolver from sliding down into the wearer's pants and out the bottom of the trouser leg. The Hip Grip can work well for women, also. If one finds the comparatively skinny Hip Grip too skinny for comfortable shooting — I never did — you can acquire a Tyler T-Grip which fills in on the grip front strap, enlarging the grip surface.

These smaller double-action revolvers can even be carried in front pocket holsters. Indeed, J. Henry Fitzgerald, Colt's consummate ballistician/shooter/gunsmith/showman during the early decades of the 20th century, carried two Colt New Service double-action revolvers with barrels cut down to 2-inch length, the fronts of the trigger guards removed, the hammer spurs excised and new front sights attached. These 6-shot 45 Colt revolvers would be drawn with lightning speed from his leather-lined trouser pockets. The "Fitz Specials," as they came to be known, were adopted by Captains W.E. Fairbairn and E.A. Sykes as recommended arms in their landmark book Shooting To Live, detailing their police training techniques used in the embattled streets of Shanghai. Later, during World War II, these men went on to work with the British special forces and the American OSS. The well-respected Col. Rex Applegate was no stranger to these admittedly odd but quite effective double-action revolvers. After the tragic kidnapping of the Lindbergh baby, America's favorite aviator had Fitz make one of these for him. On his earlier world-famous trans-Atlantic flight, Charles Lindbergh had a Detective Special along.

The modern double-action revolver has other useful accessories beside Hip Grips, Tyler T-Grips and the like. There are speedloaders which, when trained with, can allow terribly rapid reloading of the double-action revolver, one of its principal shortcomings where compared to the speed and ease with which a semi-automatic pistol can be refreshed with an already loaded spare magazine. I have always favored my quite old Safariland loaders, but there are other brands, HKS having a fine reputation.

Quite possibly, the most terrific revolver accessory on the market is the laser grip device from Crimson Trace. Crimson Trace Laser Grips are made for a wide range of semi-autos, of course, but the firm's most popular seller out of all the models it makes for revolvers and semi-autos is for the J-Frame. Actually,

Ahern holds a 4-inch revolver in his right hand, a 2-inch snubby in his left, the two extremes of practical double-action revolver concealables, both serious weapons in good hands.

there are several different models for the J-Frame Smith & Wessons and, I would hazard a guess that, if Colt had not abandoned its small D-Frame revolvers — the Detective Special, Cobra, Agent and Diamondback — Crimson Trace would be making hot-selling Lasergrips for these as well.

Note to entrepreneurs out there: I would imagine that the Detective Special is totally public domain, by now, all patents likely expired. Just a thought!

The Crimson Trace Laser Grips almost never affect holstering, the batteries are easily and cheaply found, service life for the laser component terrific (the unit our daughter uses on her J-Frame is well over five years old), and, the laser itself not withstanding, the grips are comfortable and concealable. The laser unit is built into the right grip plate and zeroed at fifty feet from the factory. Zero is

adjustable, of course, both for windage and elevation. I've been involved with experimenting with lasers since about 1974. I've never seen a better one than Crimson Trace Lasergrips and I use these on several handguns.

Perhaps, consideration of the laser as a sighting device for a design the first commercially successful example of which debuted in 1851 encourages the right perspective for the double-action revolver. With Smith & Wesson back in good hands, one can actually purchase the updated version of a "modern" revolver which debuted in 1899 from the original manufacturer — the Military & Police Model 10. The J-Frame Smith & Wesson, which first appeared as the Model 36 in 1950, inspired a host of other guns, many from Smith & Wesson itself, but from other fine firms as well, both foreign and domestic. One can still buy a 2-inch blue Model 36 in 38 Special from Smith & Wesson.

My maternal grandfather, Hunting Colfax Morrell, carried a revolver from time to time, one can presume, since he was quite the "gunny" guy, an expert rifleman, yet, the only handgun he owned was a nickel-plated Hopkins & Allen 32 top-break. It cost just a few dollars in the Montgomery Ward catalogue of 1896; but, it still works. The Hopkins & Allen was a short-barreled double action of overall diminutive proportions, even fitted with a quite innovative folding hammer spur to facilitate smoother draws from the trouser or jacket pocket. In those days, the double-action revolver, although mechanically more complicated than single-action revolvers and the new single-action autoloaders, was the simplest defensive arm to operate quickly and reliably from concealment when one's life was on the line.

Some things just never change.

The conclusion which will be drawn is that the double-action revolver, when sensibly considered for its weight and size, is still viable for concealed carry, if one takes the time and effort to do it right.

The Return of the Krieghoff Luger

■ By Jim Dickson

2006 marked the return of the Krieghoff Luger to production after a lapse of over 60 years. A limited edition of 200 guns was begun, built by hand to the Best Quality standards of a Dickson, Purdey, or Holland & Holland double, with the sole exception that the WWII finish is applied instead of the finish of a Best Quality double. The parts were all hand-fitted and finished by one man, master gunsmith Frank Kaltenpoth, the same way a Best Quality double is made. The enormous hours of handwork are reflected in the Best Quality price of $17,545 and the fact that production is still underway as I write this in 2009.

This is the only Best Quality production run of a pistol in history. It is fitting that this tribute to the Luger is being made by Krieghoff because they made the finest Lugers of all time during WWII. Krieghoff was the only Luger manufacturer to achieve 100% interchangeability of parts without any hand-fitting: a monumental achievement and a milestone in the history of mass production.

Krieghoff is no stranger to Best Quality guns. Their Essencia is a hand-made traditional Best Quality sidelock shotgun built to be the equal of anything made by the best British makers. The Luger is the only pistol worthy of this level of treatment simply because it is the only pistol that has a service life measured in the millions of rounds. This is because it is a miniature pistol version of the Maxim machinegun, the only machinegun design that can fire 10 million rounds and still be good to go. Of course we are talking about regular barrel changes along the way here. The Luger also is one of the designs that works better if precisely fitted. The higher the quality of the fit of the parts, the better it works – just like a Best Quality double. Some designs work best with lots of slop in the parts, while others like just a !ittle and some like everything as tight as possible for the best reliability under all conditions. The Luger is one of the latter.

Krieghoff 1-of-200 Luger, action open. Note the exquisite finish and straw coloring on the trigger and safety.

A Little Background

The pistol popularly known as the Luger began to take shape in 1893 when Hugo Borchardt, inspired by the success of the Maxim machinegun, built his toggle action automatic pistol. But this was not Maxim's heavy, robust, virtually jam-proof design with plenty of places for dirt to hide. The Borchardt featured a toggle that was very lightweight and bottomed out on the bottom of the pistol, where enough dirt can jam the gun. It's an overcentered, toggle-leveraged action, which

The quality of the Krieghoff Essencia hand-made Best Quality sidelock shotgun rivals that of the finest British doubles. The Krieghoff Lugers are made to precisely the same standards.

means the toggle lock was over the centerline of the cartridge. This mechanism is an inclined plane so the action doesn't open on itself.

The longer the cartridge and the greater the mass of the gun, the better the Borchardt worked. In a lightweight gun with a short cartridge, you get too fast a cycle time for proper feeding. The slower burning the powder, the slower the breechblock goes back, thus partially offsetting a fast action cycle. Therefore Hugo Borchardt decided to put a 7.63 bullet of 85 grains in a bottlenecked case with slow burning powders for a velocity of 1,280 fps. Mauser would later take this cartridge and increase the velocity to 1,410 fps for his M1896 Mauser military pistol. The Borchardt had a vertical grip, so there was virtually no drag on the cartridges as they were fed through the magazine, which contributed greatly to its reliability.

Reliable or not, the Borchardt was a clumsy, strange-looking gun. If it were ever to sell, something had to be done. The rights to the Borchardt pistol were owned by Ludwig Loewe of DWM (Deutsche Waffen und Munitionsfabriken). Ignoring the original designer, he turned the redesign over to Georg Luger. It was time for the ugly duckling to turn into a beautiful swan, a swan that combined ergonomic and esthetic perfection in a remarkably lightweight all-steel gun of just 30 ounces.

Georg Luger had considered well the needs of a combat shooter: the beautiful new gun had the fastest possible toggle release. The toggle stayed open on the last shot; you changed the magazine and gave the toggle a quick tap with the hand that inserted the magazine and you resumed firing. The bulge at the bottom of the front of the frame was hollowed out to facilitate loading a magazine that might be jammed in at the wrong angle by a soldier under fire with his eyes on the enemy instead of the gun. The lanyard loop is in the perfect position above the hand to steady the gun in firing. In addition, the maga-

zine release was so perfectly designed and positioned that it was copied on the M1911 .45 automatic.

The new gun was a beauty, the belle of the ball. Everywhere people were entranced by its striking appearance and the new-found ease of hitting the target with a pistol that it offered. The Luger's legendary handling qualities took the shooting world by storm. Switzerland was first to adopt it in 1900, with Germany adopting it in 1908 (hence the

Like all Lugers, the Krieghoff has an immediately-identifiable profile.

P08, or Pistole 08, nomenclature). Many more nations adopted it and still more bought large qualities. At last there was a pistol that seemed to accurately aim itself!

The transition of Borchardt to Luger without the input of Hugo Borchardt was not perfect, though. The Borchardt lock was carefully balanced to the recoil impulse of the 7.63 Borchardt cartridge. Luger used the same lock with shorter, higher-intensity rounds without adding the mass to the lock to compensate for them, which resulted in excessively fast action cycling times. This became a critical problem when the grip angle was changed from the vertical Borchardt grip to the steeply angled Luger grip, where the drag on the cartridge reduced the magazine spring's efficiency to only 60%. A powerful magazine spring that is strong enough to require the use of a loading tool was needed on the Luger to be sure that the magazine could feed the cartridge up to the proper position before the breech closes prematurely, jamming the gun. This is the cause of almost all Luger malfunctions.

You really can't have a Luger's magazine spring too strong. American gun designer Max Atchisson once managed to get a spring in a Luger magazine so powerful that even with a loading tool he could only load five rounds. That gun was unjammable, cycling the hottest loads effortlessly. British Best Quality gunmaker Giles Whittome once put one coil spring inside another in a Luger magazine, resulting in a magazine that was a beast to load but effortlessly cycled the hot "For Submachinegun Use Only" British Sterling SMG ammo at over 1400 fps. The need for a powerful magazine spring is the reason that the WWI Luger magazines with their wooden bottoms were later replaced with extruded magazines with aluminum bottoms that could accomodate stronger springs for greater reliability. Overall cartridge length is important also. The steep angle of the magazine is only 1.070 inches front to back, which dictates a maximum overall cartridge length of 1.180 inches with very little under that acceptable.

While the Luger likes a slow push recoil, the Browning-design pistols of today like a hot primer and a sharp recoil. Consequently most of today's ammo is made for their functioning needs, which are the exact opposite of the Luger's. Also, their overall length does not always lie within the Luger's operating lengths. Like the M16, the Luger is sensitve about the ammo used in it.

To keep the lock from cycling too fast, the WWI German Army Luger load was a 115-grain bullet at 1,025 fps. A slow-burning, single-base nitrocellulose powder with a high silica content that slowed ignition coupled with slightly underpowered low-flame primers gave a slower burning curve and a slower push, resulting in a slower cyclic time to allow proper feeding and reliability. WWII ammo was also slower burning but with a 124-grain bullet and, later, a 130-grain bullet. Mauser Werke altered the spring strength of the German Army's Lugers for this ammunition. Ammunition marked for machinepistol use (MP-38, MP-40) was loaded with extra-hot primers that make the Luger cycle too fast for reliability. The best American powder for Lugers is Red Dot shotgun powder as it most closely equals the WWI powder's burning and acceleration rate. 4.1 grains of Red Dot and a 115-grain bullet will give 997 FPS and 3.9 grains of Red Dot and a 124-grain bullet will give 1,025 FPS. Winchester primers are the best American primers for Lugers because they are the least likely to be pierced by the Luger's long firing pin. When that happens, gas can go back through the firing pin hole, pushing the firing pin and spring back and ripping the back out of the breechblock. The extractor may also be forced up and torn out of the breechblock.

Prior to WWII, Germany put three relief grooves in the firing pin to let the pressure from a pierced primer go past the firing pin instead of driving it as a piston backwards. The Finns drilled a hole in the bottom of the breechblock into the firing pin area to bleed gas off in their guns.

The 9mm Parabellum cartridge has always presented problems for gun designers because its tapered case can give uneven pressures in an automatic. The tapered case grips the chamber and if there is dirt in the vicinity, the tapered

case wedges in it and jams instead of pushing it forward into the chamber as a straight case does. As a result, no 9mm Parabellum can function reliably with a rough or dirty chamber. The 9mm Parabellum also has a high chamber pressure of 36,000 psi, which can rise into the low 40,000 psi range if a bullet is bumped and set back into the case. This is not the sort of pressure the light Borchardt toggle liked and, remember, it was not

beefed up in mass when it became the Luger.

The tapered 9mm cases also gave feeding problems in the Luger's sharply-inclined magazine where they tend to tilt and create extra drag in addition to the side drag, resulting in a magazine that has difficulty feeding cartridges to the super-fast toggle action before the bolt rides into the top side of the cartridge instead of the cartridge base because the

A grouping of unfinished Krieghoff Luger parts from the bench of master gunsmith Frank Kaltenpoth.

Precision machining
at its finest.

cartridge hasn't had time to rise up to full feeding position. The problem was compounded by the Luger's incredibly light weight of 30 ounces, which lets the muzzle flip up more in recoil as the cartridges in the magazine are simultaneously driven down by that flip – this on a magazine whose angle of feed dictates that it be so precisely positioned that a worn magazine catch or a magazine that hangs too low will cause feeding jams.

Georg Luger had originally designed his gun for the .30 Luger cartridge, which was well balanced to the design. Someone took the case and opened it up to 9mm for a bolt action "garden gun" cartridge, in which role its tapered case was an aid to extraction. About this time, the German police experienced several failures of the 93-grain .30 Luger to stop a determined assailant, so DWM or-

dered Georg Luger to chamber the Luger for the new 9mm cartridge as this would only require rebarreling. Georg pointed out the aforementioned objections plus the fact that the heavier bullet would have a larger recoil impulse than the lightweight toggle had sufficient mass to resist. Bottom line: business cost-cutting overruled the designer and Georg's protests fell on deaf ears.

To his credit, Georg Luger made the

gun work with a less than perfect cartridge for it. When you consider the initial strikes against it and the final outcome, you realize that this is one of the finest triumphs of German firearms engineering.

The Luger was inspired by the Maxim Machinegun and indeed Hiram Maxim referred to it as a Maxim machinegun in pistol form. (He also considered it a patent infringement.) Like the Maxim, the Luger is an incredibly long-lived gun. According to Alfred Gallifent, a Swiss Federal Certified Armorer who was qualified to work on the Swiss Army's Lugers, the five most common Luger repairs in order of frequency were 1) the grip screws were buggered up by someone with an ill-fitting screwdriver; 2) the L-shaped spring that retains the takedown lever would break; 3) the leaf spring on the M1900 would break; 4) the receiver forks would break when some idiot dropped it on concrete; and 5) the transfer bar from the trigger to the sear was buggered up by people tinkering with it and bending it in an attempt to get a better trigger pull.

When these are the most common repairs on guns in continuous service since 1900, you have a most excellent design.

The New Krieghoff

An enormous amount of research went into ensuring that the new Krieghoff Lugers were absolutely perfect continuations of the WWII production run. Krieghoff's production drawings did not all survive the war intact but the Bavarian Main State Archives, Department 4, War Archives in Munich had the "Dimension Tables" for the P08. Original Krieghoff P-code pistols were carefully studied to ensure exact duplication of the technical details unique to the Krieghoff Luger. Precise duplicates of the original marking stamps such as the Krieghoff "sword/anchor logo" were made. Molds were made to produce duplicates of the original military brown bakelite grips and tooling produced to once more make the WWII Krieghoff PO8 magazine and aluminum magazine bottom. Original gun barrels were copied to make the correct land and groove pattern on the new barrels. This is unheard-of attention to technical detail in a recreation.

Great attention was given to getting the precise bluing colors of the original, a job complicated by new environmental laws banning some of the original ingredients in the blueing formulas. However, Krieghoff succeeded with true Teutonic precision. Every color is absolutely the same. The full attention of this German industrial giant was devoted to getting every detail exactly right. The finish has no tool marks except for the obligatory milling machine swirls in

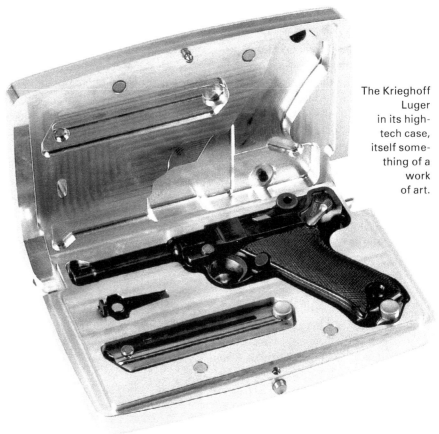

The Krieghoff Luger in its high-tech case, itself something of a work of art.

the safety area which also had to be exactly reproduced. A Luger without these would just not be an authentic Luger.

The parts all begin as precision forgings for maximum strength. The original alloys are used where they are still available and when new ones had to be substituted, careful chemical experimentation was done to be sure the bluing was exactly the same as the originals on the new alloys. Most people would not be able to tell the difference, but Krieghoff could, and only perfection was acceptable. The forgings were then sent to a modern five-axis CNC milling center to make the pieces that will be hand fitted together. The machine requires custom tools and contoured cutters.

The Krieghoff Luger's frame has more than 600 points where measurements are taken. A 13-pound forging is milled and broached down to a half-pound semi-finished frame. It takes 7.5 hours to reduce 20 to 25 pistol frames to this stage with the most modern production equipment. The rear cuts to hold the trigger sear flat spring proved

a difficult problem to solve, as did many others in the 100-year-old design. This gun was not intended for easy modern production. Specialized broaches like the one used to cut the slide guides in the side of the frame had to be made. It should be noted that it is a huge financial undertaking to tool up to make the Luger or any other gun, and Krieghoff has not done that – nor could anyone – for a mere 200 guns. What they could do was machine it to a point that a master gunsmith could take over with his hand files and hand-make it the rest of the way in the same manner that Best Quality doubles are hand-filed from forgings provided by a blacksmith. Believe me, it is a long way to go. You are paying one of the world's greatest gunsmiths to hand-make you a pistol just as he would hand-make a Best Quality double shotgun or rifle. You are getting every cent's worth of the price. Indeed, Krieghoff cut profits to the bone on this tribute to their old friend the Luger. The guns are only sold direct to the customer without a middleman to keep the price below $20,000.

65

This is a true labor of love by Krieghoff.

The artist doing all the hand work on the Krieghoff Luger is Frank Kaltenpoth. While the English gun trade has tended to keep their gunmakers at the bench and away from the fame they are due as individual artists, this attitude has actually worked against them, as today most people imagine "Best Quality" guns to be mostly machine-made. Nothing could be further from the truth, and that mistake is not to be repeated with the Krieghoff P08.

Frank Kaltenpoth was born on October 20, 1963, the son of a lockmaker. He started his apprenticeship as a gunsmith at Ferlach in 1980, graduating with honors in 1984. He then spent four years in military service as armorer in charge of all hand-held weapons and the main gun of the Leopard 1 tank in Panzer Battalion 134 of the German Army stationed in Wetzlar, Germany. He began working as a gunsmith at Kettner in Augsberg in October of 1988. After four years, he was eligible for the two-year master gunsmith course in Ulm, where he graduated with honors in June of 1993. He then worked for Kirstein, remodeling and custom-building M1911-A1 pistols. There he learned to use CNC machines to rough out a part to a point where he could hand-file and hand-fit a gun to Best Quality standards. Combining the latest machining techniques with traditional Best Quality handwork is a great skill and one that few men have. As befitting a great master, Kaltenpoth is technically self-employed but since 1999 has done work only for Krieghoff.

Krieghoff's production of the Luger pistol dates back to 1934, when they were awarded a Luftwaffe contract for 10,000 pistols. The last of these were delivered in 1937. Most significantly, they delivered on the Luftwaffe's contract clause that required interchangeability of parts. Previously all Lugers were hand-fitted. Furthermore, they did this with a massive reduction in rejected parts during production, reducing Mauser's 40% rejection rate to a more acceptable 10% rejection rate. This heightened standard of machine production raised the bar for Mauser and the other German firms.

For Krieghoff, it resulted in lucrative contracts to make the MG 15 and other weapons.

Both Mauser and Krieghoff remedied a problem found in the 1920s-vintage Lugers made by Simson. The top rear of the ear on either side of the Luger's frame must be of sufficient thickness to prevent the head of the rear toggle link axle being completely exposed as the toggle cycles. If fully exposed, the axle (or pin, if you prefer) can drift out during recoil and prevent

The Luger is a natural pointer. Fully extend your arm, lock your eyes on the target, nestle your chin on your shoulder, and squeeze. Chances are you'll hit what you're aiming at.

the toggle from returning to battery. This was found to occur only on Simson Lugers, which had the most metal removed from this area. Mauser and Krieghoff both increased the thickness here beyond even that of the DWM Lugers to make sure this would not happen to a German soldier in combat. To draw attention to their fix, Mauser added an extra machining cut to produce a slight bulge over the area needing more thickness, a sight that many former Simson users found comforting.

The Luger is a gun well worthy of such attention to detail. It is the easiest pistol of all to hit with; nothing points faster or more accurately. It is the most accurate service pistol ever issued. Most Lugers will shoot 10mm groups or less at 25 meters, and the only repeating pistols that I know of that have shot a 1-inch minute of angle group at 100 yards are the Luger and the 8-3/4-inch-barreled S&W .44 Magnum, although the latter hardly qualifies as a service pistol because of its huge size, recoil, and inability to fire rapid fire. Despite the many slanders leaped on it by gun writers over the years, when given the correct ammo and a magazine with a powerful spring, the Luger is also one of the most reliable pistols in the world – the number one spot being held, of course, by the M1911-A1 .45 automatic.

These virtues enabled the Luger to become one of the top three gunfighting pistols of all time based on the number of kills made. The other two are the M1873 Colt Single Action Army revolver and the sainted M1911-A1. The latter is the gun I carry but the fact remains that the Luger points better and is more accurate. It's the pistol I use for varmints and trick and fancy shooting.

The Luger was one of the most popular military pistols in the world in the first part of the 20th century. Many nations adopted it and used it in far-flung corners of the world, but its greatest combat use was by the German Army. The German soldier was not a pistoleer and did not know about instinct shooting without sights. In the rough and tumble brawl of trench raiding and close-quarters fighting, the P08's handling qualities gave him all the lessons he needed. It was quickly found that if you looked at the target and pointed the Luger at it, you usually hit exactly where you were looking. In the close confines of a trench, the Luger was a far more deadly weapon than the bolt action rifle and bayonet of his adversaries. The Luger continued to rack up its score through WWII, where German officers who intended to actually shoot someone with their pistol went for the Luger and those who wanted a pistol as a badge of rank opted for .32s. A good example was the SS officer who, as legend has it, was presented one of the first Walther P38s but continued to carry his Luger because he could hit better with it.

The Luger was often slandered by contemporary American gunwriters, perhaps out of an admirable sense of national pride or perhaps because they could do so without offending an advertiser. They attacked "the enemy's gun," the Luger, calling it unreliable and saying things such as, "If your Luger jams, use hot ammo. Lugers like hot ammo" and "The Luger's magazine spring is unnecessarily strong and makes it too hard to load. Clip a few coils off to make it easier." The truth is that Lugers don't like hot loads and they won't work with a weak magazine spring. Today, perhaps as many as nine out of 10 Luger magazines in the country have been shortened, causing jams.

As previously noted, the Luger is very ammo-sensitive and requires the strongest magazine spring possible. Give it this and it is reliable. As for its not working in the dirt, it performed perfectly in the maelstrom of flying mud and dirt of WWI while the vaunted S&W Triple Lock revolvers jammed in the mud. So much for revolver vs. automatic reliability! WWI settled that issue quite nicely. After WWI, the Luger was

Holsters for the Luger, left to right: Strong Leather pancake with thumb-break snap, post-war East German military, and fast-draw pancake without safety strap from El Paso Saddlery.

rather popular with the American cowboys. It perfectly fit the chaps pocket, a notorious dirt and sand trap infamous for tying up revolvers with sand in their guts. When WWII came along, the Luger continued to shine.

The Luger was always carried in a holster designed for maximum protection from the elements. The German officer was expected to have the pistol in prime operating condition instead of trying to do a fast draw every time an enemy popped up. For modern civilian carry, I have never found anything better than the pancake holster design. It offers the best combination of concealability, comfort, and fast draw available. I have used this design ever since it first appeared many years ago. Here are two companies' versions:

Strong Leather Co. makes a classic molded thumb break pancake holster of the very highest quality for the Luger pistol that will meet any civilian or police needs. I have never been able to find fault with their work. Contact Strong Leather Co., P.O. Box 1195, 39 Grove St., Gloucester, Massachusetts, 01930.

A quick-draw pancake holster without a retaining strap is offered by El Paso Saddlery Co., 2025 East Yandell Dr., El Paso, Texas, 79903. This company began

in the days of the Wild West and made holsters for the deadliest old West gunfighter of them all, John Wesley Hardin. They have the longest history of making fast-draw holsters of anyone. This is the holster to wear when action is imminent. It may not have a securing top strap for normal duty use, but, man, it is fast!

As we have seen, the Luger is one of the finest pistols ever made, and the new Krieghoff is the finest Luger ever made. As the late great Col. George Chinn, whose monumental five-volume series The Machinegun is the definitive work on machinegun mechanisms, once told me, "As long as nitrocellulose is our propellent, all possible mechanisms have already been invented. All that remains is to reconfigure existing systems into different guns." Pistols don't offer as many different tactical design configuration possibilities as shoulder arms, so the pistol got perfected early. Once you reach the summit, all roads lead downhill regardless of how new they are. So if you want the ultimate pistol, you get a M1911-A1 .45 automatic. If you want the best pointing, easiest to hit with, and most accurate pistol, you get a Luger.

And if you want the finest Luger, you get a new Krieghoff.

The .357 Magnum

A Twentieth Century Handgun and Cartridge ▮ By Frank W. James

Forty years ago, one handgun caliber dominated all others, regardless the intended application. It didn't matter whether it was used by law enforcement, for self-defense, the relatively new sport of handgun hunting for whitetail deer, or for just plain fun and plinking—the most popular handgun at the time was a revolver chambered for the .357 Magnum.

The adoption by the United States military of the 9mm Beretta, in 1985, changed things dramatically for both revolver shooters and devotees of the beloved 1911 .45, as both law enforcement agencies and civilian consumers stampeded to a variety of semi-auto pistols in 9x19mm caliber. These guns held far more rounds in reserve than did the six-shot .357 Magnum or the 7+1 1911 .45, but, for a major part of the 20th century, the .357 Magnum held sway. Many experts feel that, even today, if the firearms world had not witnessed the tidal surge move to semi-autos during the 1980s, the .357 Magnum would still be the most popular handgun caliber out there.

Origins

The .357 Magnum cartridge was introduced, in 1935, by Smith & Wesson, but Winchester Ammunition worked directly with S&W to bring it to market. Major Douglas B. Wesson and Phil Sharp were responsible for much of the final developmental work, although it is noted in several historical records that both authorities consulted with Elmer Keith, because of his experience in developing heavy bullet loads with higher than normal muzzle velocities for the .38-44 cartridge. The .38-44 had been an attempt to develop a more powerful cartridge than the standard police .38 Special. Smith & Wesson, prior to the introduction of the .357 Magnum, even made a heavy-frame revolver that was nominally a .38 Special revolver, but it

In 1955, Colt's Firearms introduced what many believe to be the most elegant .357 Magnum revolver ever created—the Python. This example is an Ultimate Python in stainless steel and has the best features found with any Python, plus the bonus of custom grips to make it one of the nicest .357 Magnum revolvers one can find.

was referred to as the ".38-44."

At the time of its introduction, the .357 Magnum was, in fact, the most powerful handgun round in production. The original load chronographed 1,510 fps with a 158-grain bullet out of an 8¾-inch barrel. It certainly wasn't the first attempt to create a powerful handgun cartridge. Other startups had come before it. The most notable was that by an Englishman, H. W. Gabbet-Fairfax, who'd developed, around 1900, a self-loading pistol employing a cartridge called the 9mm Mars. It had a reported muzzle velocity of 1,607 fps with a bullet weight of 156 grains. But the British military rejected it after trials, and neither the gun nor that cartridge ever achieved commercial success.

Smith & Wesson chambered its heaviest revolver frame (later known as the N-frame) for it. The revolver was a special order item introduced during the height of the Great Depression. Each revolver was registered with the factory and came with a certificate designating this registration. The Smith & Wesson "Registered Magnum" and its cartridge soon acquired a mystique that created a following among legendary lawmen (J. Edgar Hoover received Registration No. 1), military generals (one of General George S. Patton, Jr.'s famous ivory revolvers was Registered Magnum No. 506), and high-profile Hollywood movie actors (a Registered Magnum supposedly belonging to Clark Gable sold at a high-end gun auction in 2012).

Originally, Smith & Wesson felt the round should be fired through the 8¾-inch barrel, but because the early .357 Magnum Registered revolvers were all custom orders, they had been made with a wide variety of individual characteristics. These revolvers have been found with 23 different barrel lengths, as well as a number of non-cataloged sight and grip combinations.

.357 Advantages

The designation ".357" refers to the bore diameter, which is also the bore diameter of the less powerful and older .38 Special cartridge. The .38 Special was introduced in 1902, also by Smith &

The Smith & Wesson Model 386 utilized a lightweight frame with a six-inch barrel to create a .357 Magnum revolver that employed some of the most advanced technology available in the twenty-first century.

A steel spring shield is positioned above the barrel on the Smith & Wesson Model 386, to prevent damage to the top strap of this revolver from the gas escaping through the barrel/cylinder gap.

It's been a standard for more than five decades, but the fully adjustable rear sight found on Smith & Wesson's .357 Magnum revolvers remains a standard of the industry and did much to enhance the shootability of the gun and round.

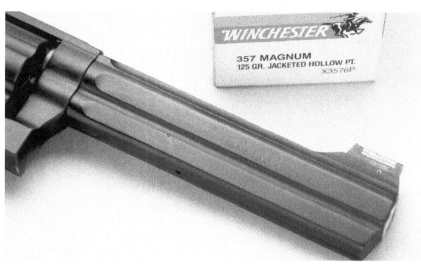

It was the lightweight bullet loads in the .357 Magnum that really established the round's reputation as a stopper in lethal-force encounters between law enforcement officers and armed criminals. This success carried over to the civilian self-defense market and made the .357 one of the popular cartridges of the twentieth century.

Wesson, to provide a .38-caliber handgun cartridge that was more powerful and effective than any of the previously seen .38-caliber rounds such as the .38 S&W, the .38 Short Colt, and the .38 Long Colt. The latter had served briefly as the standard service handgun round of the military services and was blamed, in large part, for its many failures to stop antagonists during the Spanish-American War and the insurrection in the Philippines.

The .38 Special was initially loaded with a 158-grain round-nose lead bullet and it had a muzzle velocity of 855 fps out of a standard service-length revolver barrel. While proving extremely popular with American law enforcement, the .38 Special also experienced criticisms for failures to stop armed bad guys, particularly during the more violent episodes of the 1930s. These criticisms are what lead to, first, the development of .38-44 rounds (.38-caliber loads meant for use in a .44-sized revolver frame), and then, ultimately, to the .357 Magnum.

Still, by the late 1940s and early 1950s, the .38 Special was the dominant handgun service round in American law enforcement. This popularity was due to its inherent accuracy and relatively easy recoil ,and, with its straight-walled case, it was an easy round for the recreational shooter to reload.

When the designers created the .357 Magnum, they took the existing .38 Special case and simply lengthened it by 1/10-inch, mostly to prevent chambering of this new, more powerful, far higher chamber pressured round from being loaded in the older, weaker guns of .38 Special design. The bullet diameter, naturally, is the same for both the .38 Special and the .357 Magnum. For training or practice purposes, this meant the .38 Special round could be safely loaded and fired in any cylinder chambered for the .357 Magnum; that was and is probably the greatest asset of any .357 Magnum handgun, its versatility across both rounds.

My First .357

I acquired my first .357 Magnum while I was a lowly college student. Money was extremely scarce. It was during the mid-1960s, the Vietnam War was on, and finding a brand new .357 Magnum Smith & Wesson was virtually a search for the Holy Grail, because so many of the guns being made during that time were committed to law enforcement agencies. Having worked every extra hour I could get during a summer between semesters, I was determined to reward myself with the purchase of a new and powerful handgun. It would be the fourth handgun I would ever own, the first two being .22 rimfires the third a like-new Smith & Wesson Model 10 in .38 Special.

I wanted a .357 Magnum because I knew I wouldn't have to buy new ammo. I could use the ammo I already had, the .38 Special ammunition, and keep reloading the same cases, using the same projectiles and, after readjustment, the same reloading dies. For a college kid counting his pennies, this caliber and gun combination made a whole lot of sense.

Just before I had to return to school, I put out the word that I was looking for

Smith & Wesson has produced a wide range of .357 Magnum revolvers in stainless steel. First introduced in the mid-1960s, the use of corrosion-resistant material, together with the caliber, helped make this one of the more popular self-defense cartridges in history.

Even though it has a large frame, it doesn't mean it can't have a short barrel and extra-capacity cylinder. This Model 327 from Smith & Wesson sports a short barrel and an eight-shot cylinder in .357 Magnum.

On the left, a .357 Magnum handload employing the Keith 168-grain cast SWC. On the right, the round many believe is its equal, the factory .357 SIG round with a 125-grain bullet. The author feels the .357 SIG round is a good one with light-weight bullets, but lacks the case capacity to work well with heavier bullets.

This L-frame Mountain Gun from Smith & Wesson features a four-inch barrel and a seven-shot cylinder, and is chambered for the .357 Magnum cartridge. It represents an advancement, in terms of construction and size, over the original .357 Magnum revolvers.

The Mateba is a twenty-first century design chambered for the .357 Magnum round. Unlike most conventional designs, this revolver fires the bottom chamber on the cylinder, so as to provide the shooter with a lower bore axis and increased control.

a .357. I was working as a meat cutter at a large supermarket, and the night security consisted of city cops. A couple of these cops asked around and, finally, they told me to head down to a big sporting goods store outside the city of Indianapolis, as that was the only one known to have anything such as I wanted in stock.

I walked up to the counter after finding the place, and the older gentleman behind the counter asked what he could do for me?

"I would like to buy a Smith & Wesson .357," I stated flatly.

He paused and looked to his right, then slowly to his left. Without saying a word, he reached under the counter and pulled out a blue box with silver lettering on top that said "SMITH & WESSON." It was the only one he had.

The clerk's name was Sherm, and he explained the store kept the Smith & Wesson .357s out of sight because they didn't want police officers to spot them. If an officer did, then the store had to sell them at a police discount and, with the demand so high, they wanted to sell to law enforcement only on an agency order, with everything else sold at full retail.

I had wanted a Model 19 with a four-inch barrel, but, after weeks of searching, I knew that wasn't going to happen. So, when Sherm opened the box and I saw the deep blue finish of that six-inch barrel Model 27, I knew I was in love. It cost me $143 plus $2.86 tax. I still have this gun!

Later on, a last minute trip out west to visit a cousin in San Francisco that same summer, I stopped at P.O. Ackley's shop, in Utah, and purchased a set of diamond centered-checkered goncalo alves target grips to replace the Magna-style grips that had come with it. A few years later, I would trade with an acquaintance the narrow hammer and trigger on my Model 27 for the wide hammer and trigger that were on his Model 29, and that is pretty much the way the gun has remained for the 45 years I've owned it.

Shooting the .357

Over the years since that first purchase, I've owned a large number of .357 Magnum revolvers, and if there is one characteristic of this gun and caliber combination that can be universally said, it is the fact that they are accurate. I think I may have scrounged up enough loose change to purchase one 50-round box of .357 Magnum cartridges when I got that first one, but, by and large, most rounds I fired that first year were heavy .38 Special handloads.

I started casting my own bullets, because I was always looking for a way to shoot more for less. At the time, Elmer Keith was one of the foremost handgun writers in print, and he constantly promoted a cast bullet of his design every time he mentioned the .357 Magnum. It was made by Lyman, and the mould was No. 358429. I ordered a two-cavity mould and was soon producing my own cast bullets that I sized at .358-inch. Depending upon the mixture and ratio of tin to lead, this bullet normally casts up at 168 grains in the typical Keith-style bullet having a relatively long nose, flat meplat, and wide grease groove. Later, I would obtain a four-cavity mould for this bullet and, over the decades since, I have shot literally thousands upon thousands of these bullets through .357 Magnum handguns. I still say this bullet, loaded in either a .38 Special case or a .357 Magnum case, with just about any decent charge and corresponding .357 Magnum revolver, will yield one of the most satisfying and accurate handgun/ammo combinations available—even today in this age of plastic frame pistols and enhanced magazine capacities.

I should mention I discovered that Elmer must have used this load and caliber on larger stuff than I did initially, mostly, I suspect, because it would really

In a way, this particular .357 Magnum is something of a nostalgic revolver, one like those seen back in the 1930s, where the barrels were cut back and the grips shortened so they could be carried comfortably in a pants pocket. The difference here is the enhanced capacity of the cylinder and its chambering—.357 Magnum!

penetrate. I've shot raccoons, red foxes, coyotes, and a number of whitetail deer, and I have to say that only on the deer did I feel this load worked as Elmer advertised. Everything else it just flat sailed through as if each of the creatures were a sheet of paper. That was fine if the bullet hit vital organs in its passage through, but, if it didn't, then I wound up looking rather foolish in front of my friends.

It was the introduction of lightweight jacketed hollowpoint bullets (125- to 140-grain) and high-velocity loads that really gained the .357 Magnum the respect it so richly deserved in law enforcement and self-defense circles during the 1970s. It has that same respect today. I discovered these same loads worked far better at stopping varmints on our farms than had the previous loads that employed Elmer's cast bullets. I know that sounds like heresy to some, but it was an observation I learned through experience on our farm fields and not the square target-shooting range.

The .357 Expands

In the 1950s, the cartridge's popularity grew when manufacturers other

Part of Smith & Wesson's Night Guard series of self-defense revolvers, this Model 386 sports a short barrel, a seven-shot cylinder, and a .357 Magnum chambering.

This retired police-duty Smith & Wesson Model 66 with a four-inch barrel in .357 Magnum is representative of what many in law enforcement thought was the ideal service revolver during the 1960s and 1970s.

than Smith & Wesson began chambering revolvers for it. Colt's started the ball rolling, when it introduced the Colt .357 Magnum, in 1953, a heavy-frame, double-action, swing-out cylinder revolver with either a four- or six-inch barrel length. Later, the large New Service revolver was chambered for the round, but, then, in 1955, Colt's started producing what many feel is the most elegant .357 Magnum ever made—the Python.

Smith & Wesson would continue promotion of the round, but the next thing it introduced was a medium-frame gun (the K-frame) that was known far and wide as the Combat Magnum or, simply, the Model 19. Add another decade or more, and a host of other manufacturers would come out with their own service-style .357 Magnum revolvers, including the Ruger GP-100 that proved to be a popular alternative for those seeking a .357 Magnum from someone other than S&W or Colt's.

The author's Model 27, with an 8³/₈-inch barrel and custom grips, is an expression of his appreciation for this gun and cartridge. The original Registered .357 Magnums from Smith & Wesson were supposed to have 8¾-inch barrels, but 23 different barrel lengths have been documented as shipped by the factory prior to World War II.

The rounds represented here are three of the author's favorites. From left is a .41 Magnum with a cast truncated cone gas check bullet. Next is the .357 Magnum with the Keith 168-grain Lyman No. 358429 SWC bullet and, on the right, a typical, 158-grain lead round-nose bullet for the .38 Special case.

A Lasting Legacy

Perhaps the greatest legacy this cartridge established was its legendary reputation for ending a gunfight with its first solid hit. With relatively lightweight projectiles loaded above 1,250 fps, the round achieved a reputation that remains even to this day. Of course, the downside to these same effective loads was a fearsome muzzle blast and, if the gun was light enough, considerable felt recoil. Just about any .357 Magnum revolver with full-power loads requires a dedicated individual to master it and, for some, that simply wasn't in the cards. This certainly was a factor in the move, now more three decades ago, away from revolvers and toward semi-auto pistols.

The .357 SIG round that is chambered in many law enforcement semi-auto pistols capitalizes on the success of the .357 Magnum, if for no other reason than the use of ".357" in its name. In reality, the .357 SIG employs bullets of .355-inch diameter. It is a good self-defense/law enforcement round, when loaded with bullets weighing 125 grains or less, but it lacks the case capacity to duplicate the performance and terminal ballistics that so characterized the .357

Magnum over the decades, when it was loaded with heavier bullets. This is true even though the .357 SIG is offered in a modern pistol with more than twice the ammunition capacity of a six-shot revolver.

The .357 Magnum and its revolvers are not as popular today as they were

40 years ago, but the inherent traits of power, penetration, accuracy, and simple economics remain for those willing to explore one of the twentieth century's greatest handgun rounds. It certainly has proven itself in many different endeavors, and still holds potential for those willing to work with it.

The .357 Magnum and its associated revolvers have garnered a fearsome reputation in law enforcement history. The H&K pistol below the author's Model 27 is chambered for the .357 SIG round, which attempts to capitalize on that same reputation, albeit in a modern semi-auto pistol format.

Fill Your Hand!

The Best of the Biggest Revolvers Ever Made ▮ Wayne Van Zwoll

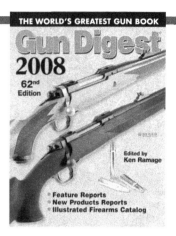

Ruger's Alaskan offers
454 punch in a short
barrel. The Freedom
Arms 83 legitimized
the Casull.

During the mid-1950s, other handgunners were busy boosting horsepower in Colt's iconic 1873. Dick Casull loaded the 45 Colt to pressures higher than were safe in early SAs, and from his shop came the 454 Casull (acknowledged by P.O. Ackley in 1959). That year Ruger announced its Super Blackhawk in 44 Magnum and Blackhawks in 45 Colt. The stout Blackhawk was perfect for the 454 Casull. Dick replaced its six-shot cylinder with a five-round version to increase chamber wall thickness. Meanwhile, the 44 Magnum went to Hollywood. When Clint Eastwood raised his Model 29 and rasped, "Go ahead, make my day," he sold more 44 Magnum pistols than Smith and Wesson could have by including a trip to Tahiti with each one. Dirty Harry reminded people who'd never heard of Elmer Keith that the raw-boned bronc-buster's brainchild was still, after four decades, the most powerful handgun in the world.

A 400-grain bullet at 1250 fps leaves with some violence, but drills tight groups.

"With improvements, I think they can be rendered the most perfect weapon in the world for light mounted troops...." In 1846 Texas Ranger Captain Samuel H. Walker praised Colt's Paterson revolver but suggested changes. Pushed by the Ordnance Department's order for 1000 of the new pistols, Walker and Sam Colt collaborated on a massive 44-caliber revolver. The prototype, from the New York City gunshop Blunt & Syms, weighed 4 pounds, 9 ounces. Eli Whitney, Jr. won the production contract, including a run of 100 revolvers for public sale.

Just a few months later, at the battle of Juamantla, Captain Walker was killed by a Mexican lance.

Impressive in the hand and lethal on target, the Walker Colt did not ignite a trend to bigger pistols. Colt's 1873 Single Action Army, a smaller gun in 45 Colt, struck fear into bandits and lawmen alike. Development of smokeless powder in the 1890s made these revolvers even more effective; but not until 1955 would a pistol round hit significantly harder than the 45 and its contemporary heavy-weight, the 44-40. Their 255-grain and 200-grain bullets clocked

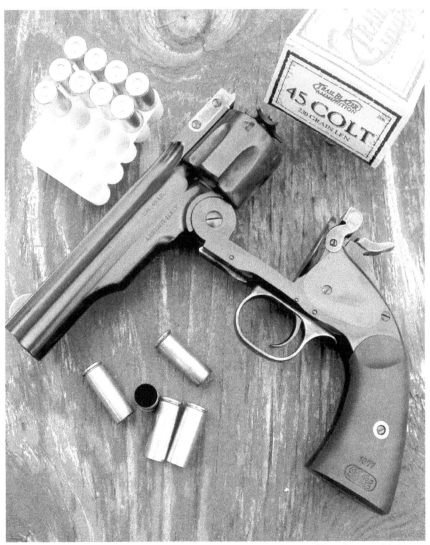

Top-break revolvers of the 19th century could handle big cartridge, but not high pressures.

900 fps and 1100 fps, respectively.

Ironically, the modern hunting revolver has rimfire roots. During the late 1920s, Smith & Wesson designed a beautiful 22 double-action. In 1930 the six-shot, 35-ounce K-22 Outdoorsman featured a 6-inch barrel, checkered grips of Circassian walnut and target sights. Shortly a centerfire counterpart appeared, a 38 Special with the heavy "N" frame used on 44-caliber revolvers. Like its smallbore sibling, the 38/44 Outdoorsman had a fine trigger. Gun writer Phil Sharpe urged Smith & Wesson to develop a more potent round for the pistol. Winchester Repeating Arms assisted with that project, coming up with a case 1/8 inch longer than the 38 Special's. It debuted as the 357 Magnum, spitting 158-grain bullets at over 1500 fps. The first N-frame revolvers so chambered appeared during the Depression at $60, roughly $15 more than S&W charged for any other revolver. The company's own market gurus predicted limited demand, so they advertised the first 357 Magnums as custom guns, available with many sight and barrel options. Each gun would be zeroed by the factory at 200 yards, and each owner would get a registration certificate.

Demand for the powerful new gun far exceeded expectations. In 1938, after 5,500 revolvers, S&W dropped the registration certificate. At 120 guns a month, it could barely keep up with orders! Exhibition shooter Ed McGivern had demonstrated the round's great

Bill Booth examines a revolver from the S&W Performance Center. Here, anything is possible!

reach by hitting deer-size targets at 600 yards. If shooters hadn't thought of the K-22 Masterpiece or 38/44 Outdoorsman as hunting guns, many now saw the 357 Magnum as having potential beyond law enforcement, defense and target shooting.

In 1946, under the stewardship of Carl Hellstrom, Smith & Wesson began a vigorous push to hike civilian sales. Four years later they paid for a new 270,000-square-foot plant. About this time Elmer Keith appeared; a short cowboy in a tall Stetson, complete with tales of life in Idaho's wild canyons. But despite his rough-hewn demeanor, he had extraordinary gun-savvy. Keith's 44 Special handloads in the 1950 N-frame Target revolver made factory ammunition look anemic. He advocated a super-velocity 44 cartridge in a longer case. Remington's R.H. Coleman took Keith's notion to heart and in 1954 brought to Smith & Wesson a new 44 (the hull 1/8-inch taller than the 44 Special) chambered in a modified Model 1950. The S&W Model 29 revolver weighed 7 ounces more than its forebear – and became an immediate hit. More than 3,100 Model 29s sold the first year. An obvious sequel: single-action revolvers bored for this powerful round. But Smith & Wesson wasn't in the single-action business.

During the mid-1950s, other handgunners were busy boosting horsepower in Colt's iconic 1873. Dick Casull loaded the 45 Colt to pressures higher than were safe in early SAs, and from his shop came the 454 Casull (acknowledged by P.O. Ackley in 1959). That year Ruger announced its Super Blackhawk in 44 Magnum and Blackhawks in 45 Colt. The stout Blackhawk was perfect for the 454 Casull. Dick replaced its six-shot cylinder with a five-round version to increase chamber wall thickness. Meanwhile, the 44 Magnum went to Hollywood. When Clint Eastwood raised his Model 29 and rasped, "Go ahead, make my day," he sold more 44 Magnum pistols than Smith and Wesson could have by including a trip to Tahiti with each one. Dirty Harry reminded people who'd never heard of Elmer Keith that the raw-boned bronc-buster's brainchild was still, after four decades, the most powerful handgun in the world.

But in the early 1980s the mighty 29 lost that title to a tightly fitted single-action revolver built in the small town of Freedom, Wyoming, and chambered to the 454 Casull. The 454 uses a Small Rifle primer to light the fire under its .451-inch bullet, which was bigger than the 44 Magnum's .429-inch bullet. The Casull pushes a 260-grain bullet at 1800 fps, and a 300-grain at 1625. Pressures can exceed 50,000 CUP. Loaded by Winchester with 260-grain Partition Golds and Platinum Tips, a 250-grain JHP and a 300-grain JFP, the Casull was once listed with 300-grain Core-Lokt Ultra bullets by Remington. Federal still loads a 250-grain Barnes Expander, Hornady 240- and 300-grain XTPs.

Ruger's first handgun round, the 480 Ruger, appeared in the company's revolvers about 20 years after the Casull. The 480's 325-grain bullet (.476-inch in diameter) is heavier than any commonly loaded in the Casull; but factory loads develop less pressure, so muzzle energy won't match the 454's.

Arguably, hunters didn't need more power than provided by the Casull and company. But they got more in the 475 Linebaugh, initially a handloading proposition but chambered in Freedom Arms revolvers. It came about in 1988, when Missouri shooter John Linebaugh trimmed a 45-70 case and installed a five-round cylinder and a 5 1/2-inch .475 barrel on a Ruger Bisley. With a 370-grain bullet at nearly 1500 fps, a 400-grain at 1400 and a 440-grain at 1360, the Linebaugh develops 1800 foot-pounds at the muzzle.

Of course, no revolver can equal the performance of stout, fixed-breech handguns chambered for rifle rounds – like the Thompson/Center Contender. In 1965, shortly after Warren Center joined the K.W. Thompson Tool Company of Rochester, New Hampshire, Thompson agreed to manufacture an odd pistol that Center had designed in his basement. The Contender appeared in 1967, with switchable barrels and a good trigger. It fired proven deer rounds like the 30-30, accommodating pointed

Hornady's pointed bullets extend the effective range of S&W's potent 460 cartridge.

Grizzly-loaded 370-grain cast bullets shot very well; so did the others Wayne tried in his M83.

bullets and scopes. It sold briskly and still does. Barrels on new G2 pistols interchange with old Contender barrels, but not with those of the beefier Encore. Bolt-action pistols from Remington, Weatherby and H-S Precision, and the recent 5-pound Savage Striker with muzzle brake and magnum chamberings, have nothing on the Contender. But neither a hinged breech nor a bolt action delivers the heft, lines, balance and fast repeat shots of a revolver. Con-

sequently, Smith & Wesson never felt threatened by them. But it chafed under the growing popularity of the 454 Casull in Freedom Arms revolvers. Not that either could compete with the Model 29 in sales, but Eastwood's iron was no longer heralded as the world's most powerful. S&W Product Manager Herb Belin wanted to trump the Casull. In early 2002, he and engineer Brett Curry started work on a super-size handgun, while engaging Cor-Bon's Peter Pi and Terry Murback to design its cartridge. The Cor-Bon team came up with a 50-caliber bullet in a case 1.625 inches long, with three loads under a pressure lid of 48,000 psi (20 percent lower than the Casull's). A 275-grain Barnes X launched at 1675 fps, a 400-grain Hawk JSP at 1650, and a 440-grain hard cast bullet from Cast Performance at 1625. The Barnes X, though lighter than the other bullets, is also harder and has a long bearing surface. So at any pressure, velocity can lag what's possible with lead bullets of similar heft. But it does not lack for penetration! Smith & Wesson's 500 develops 700 foot-pounds more energy than a 454 Casull and twice as much as a 44 Magnum.

The "X-Frame" revolver for the 500 S&W has a five-shot cylinder 2-1/4 inches long. Its sleeved barrel has a frame-to-yoke cylinder latch and a muzzle cap with top porting to reduce climb. At

72 ounces, the S&W 500 is more than a pound heavier than a Model 629 44 Magnum with the same-length (8 3⁄8-inch) barrel.

"Seventy years ago the 357 Magnum made headlines with a 158-grain bullet at 1200 fps," mused Bill Booth, as he thumbed the hammer slowly to ready his 500 S&W for the shot. The big revolver stayed under control as it lifted from the sandbag. Not a jump or a hop; this was a muscular launch that not even veteran handgunners with ham-size hands could deny. Thin white smoke swirled as the big Smith's thunder echoed through the canyon. Double ear protection had been a good idea.

I peered through the spotting scope. A hundred yards downrange, Bill's second bullet had landed an inch and a half from the first. Many shooters cannot milk that consistency from rifles!

"We had trouble with your gun," said Bill. A career in law enforcement has given Bill an inside track on revolver mechanics. "In fact, all four of these 500s for the hunt needed attention."

"Huh?" I'd been one of the first to take the S&W 500 afield (the model name is the cartridge name minus the preceding period). "Problems?" On a Florida pig hunt I had found the 500 accurate and reliable.

"Well, it wasn't really the gun. The cantilevered scope base was actually flexing in recoil, so the forward end contacted the barrel. Warne got to work and provided a base with a reinforcing block. Problem solved." Bill had subsequently installed the Warne base and Bushnell 2-6x scopes on all the guns for this hunt: mine, his, Frank Miniter's and Tom Taylor's. Frank works as an editor at American Hunter magazine; Tom is vice-president for marketing at S&W.

We'd met in Buffalo, Wyoming at Pete Dube's Bear Track Outfitters camp. Wind and light rain had followed us to the range, where Bill and Tom drilled tight groups in the centers of their paper targets. "Good bullets," said Bill of Cor-Bon's sleek 385-grain hollowpoints. Cor-Bon had recently added the load to its three initial offerings. Hornady had weighed in with a 300-grain poly-tipped

Wayne found extended range sessions comfortable. He used Grizzly loads for the 500 WE.

Evolution bullet at 1950 fps, a 350-grain XTP at 1900 and a 500-grain XTP at 1425.

The 500 Smith & Wesson's recoil depends mainly on bullet weight and speed. The 440-grain lead bullets in full-power loads make your hands tingle. However, Cor-Bon's other ammunition was surprisingly manageable in the heavy pistol. The 385 HP has a long ogive for flat flight. It is, to my mind, the best game bullet of the bunch – heavy enough to drive deep, with the legs for easy hits to 200 yards. Not that I shoot that long. My confidence with a handgun reaches about as far as I can hurl a medicine ball.

"One secret to good shooting with this gun is a high grip," said Bill. "You'll absorb recoil better with the web of your hand well up toward the hammer. And you'll find the revolver easier to steady." My first bullet landed at 6 o'clock, the next at 3. Of the next three, only one landed in the middle. I felt like a rookie. Then, as Bill banged a steel chicken at 160 yards with his pistol, I slunk to the far end of the line, and squeezed off 10 more rounds. My last four shots printed a 2-inch group, well centered.

In the morning, guide Mark Kirby took Bill and me into a series of hills creased with coulees and studded with deciduous brush and the occasional

pine. I spied a buck and circled to get the wind. In a classic display of sixth sense, the buck stopped feeding my way and paused, lost in thought. Then he turned and ambled into a draw. Illogical behavior helps deer grow old.

Our binoculars found many other deer that morning, but few mature bucks. Presently I found pieces of mule deer in my 8x32 Pentax. Does. Then Mark whispered, "Buck!" The animal had risen from its bed, but all I could make out were antler tips. Though a crosswind favored us, a doe had zeroed in on my scope lens; we didn't have much time. Mark rolled aside as I squirmed to his spot and pushed my pack under the extended 500. When the reticle quivered to a near standstill on a front rib, I pressed the trigger.

Recoil jerked the revolver up, obscuring my view and then I heard the sharp "thwack" of a hit. Does squirted from the pines. I saw the great buck lunge, recover, then tumble down the steep grade, trailing dust and rubble. He kicked weakly, and then lay still. The Cor-Bon hollowpoint had struck exactly where I had aimed, scrambled the lungs and exited. No rifle bullet would have killed better. Mark's Bushnell rangefinder pegged the shot distance at 94 yards.

Pete Dube drew Bill and me the next morning. We glassed diligently but without effect. Our luck turned, though, when Pete spied an outstanding buck at the hem of a deep draw. We moved slowly up the draw, confident the big deer was still ahead of us. The thump of hooves signaled an end to our game, and Pete saw the buck only as it rocketed away.

Tired and despondent, we shuffled to the truck. "Let's find some pronghorns," said Pete. A couple of hours later, with a red sun at my back, I bellied to a small bush 150 yards from a loose group of antelope. Now, with the 'Smith steadied in a fork of sage, I sighted through a small gap in the bush as the buck angled toward me. I crushed the last ounce from the trigger, heard the explosion and felt the big gun lift through a shower of sage leaves.

The buck crumpled without a twitch, the bullet having smashed its spine ahead of the shoulder. We photographed and field-dressed the pronghorn, then fetched the pickup and loaded it into the back.

Motoring slowly out of the valley between two bluffs, we spotted a fine mule deer buck, statue-still, at the base of a bluff. "He's about 200 yards," said Bill. "I can make that shot if he'll give me a moment." The animal watched us with interest but not alarm as Bill lowered himself to a sit on the prairie, bracing his shoulder against the pickup tire and – at last – fired. The sound of the strike followed close after the blast, and the deer collapsed into the grass. A marvelous shot, it demonstrated not only the 500's reach and power, but Booth's skill with a handgun.

Smith & Wesson now markets a 500 with a 4-inch barrel. You can get other barrel lengths from the company's Performance Center. A caveat: the muzzle porting that keeps long pistols manageable in recoil accentuates noise even more with a short tube, and the front of the pistol lifts faster and farther at the shot. My preference in the 500 is for a 7 1/2-inch barrel. Whatever your barrel preference, accurate shooting with the 500 S&W requires concentration and steady nerves.

A second X-frame gun, chambered

for a new, faster cartridge, appeared in mid-2004. With a case even longer than the 500's, the 460 XVR spits 200-grain Hornady SST bullets at 2211 fps, while 250 Cor-Bons fly at 2291, 325s at 1591 and 395s at 1511. Zeroed 3 inches high at 100 yards, pointed Hornady bullets strike 3.8 inches low at 200, where they deliver 837 fpe – nearly twice the energy of the 45 Colt at the muzzle! Smith & Wesson's 460 revolver has gain-twist rifling, increasing from a throat pitch of 1-in-100 to 1-in-20 at the muzzle. The slow initial spin keeps a lid on pressures and reduces bullet deformation.

Tom Kelly tells me that Performance Center 460s do not have gain twist. "But guns from both shops give us outstanding accuracy." My range time with a PC 460 left me mightily impressed. The revolver showed the fit and finish you'd expect in a best-quality British grouse gun. It shot with the precision of a bolt-action hunting rifle. Its accuracy and downrange energy make it a 200-yard elk gun!

Many shooters accept – some even relish – the length and weight of specialty handguns, and the added bulk of powerful scopes. Indeed, portability and speed don't count for much if you're in deer blind or toting a handgun on a

sling as you would a rifle. But if convenient carry matters, if you must back up a rifle with multiple shots at dangerous game in tight quarters, or if you favor the lines and handling qualities of traditional double-action revolvers, you'll stay with Smith & Wesson's 29 or a Colt Anaconda or a Ruger Redhawk. The 44 Magnum may not match the latest artillery for reach and smash, but it's still a powerful round, with more authority than delivered by many rifle cartridges of the 19th century! If single-actions turn your crank, Ruger's Blackhawk and Vaquero series, along with Colt and Uberti 45s, give you affordable options.

Packaging the smash of a S&W 500 or 460 in a backup revolver is a daunting job for engineers. Such a handgun would deliver fearsome recoil – enough to discourage even infrequent practice and to deny you control for a quick second shot in an emergency. A useful compromise came along 50 years ago, when Dick Casull and Jack Fulmer built their first 50-ounce single-action for a 45 wildcat that would hurl 240-grain bullets 1900 fps. The 454 came within 300 fps and 200 foot-pounds of matching the mighty 460!

The Freedom Arms Model 83 revolver in 454 Casull and 475 Linebaugh

Fully adjustable iron sights take advantage of the Model 83's accuracy. They're of blued steel.

yields explosive power in a portable package renowned for its fine fit and finish. I've stopped several times at the FA shop on the Salt River. Not far from Olympic gold-medal wrestler Rulon Gardner's home, Freedom, Wyoming hardly merits a dot on the map. But it's a celebrated hunting destination. Last autumn, returning from a hunt where permits were more plentiful, I pulled into Freedom Arms again, for an update from company chief Bob Baker.

"I'll give you the tour," he said. "Won't take long."

He did and it didn't. I was impressed by Bob's willingness to host a drop-in shooter – and by the shop's capabilities. Freedom revolvers are made from scratch here. Almost, you might say, by hand. Not only are all the major parts machined to incredibly close tolerances; they're hand-fitted, and then kept together by number and bin during production. Sure, the parts are interchangeable. But to ensure the snug fit and glass-smooth operation and extraordinary accuracy that have earned Freedom its reputation, Bob insists that each pistol come together as a single unit.

There aren't many models. Freedom's flagship is its large-frame, five-shot Model 83, cataloged now for 20 years. Beside 454 Casull and 475 Linebaugh, it also comes in 44, 41 and 357 Magnum, even 22 LR. "Or 500 Wyoming Express," said Bob. "It's new, a straight-walled belted revolver cartridge." He explained that it offers more bullet weight than a 454 and hits about as hard, but doesn't recoil as sharply. He picked a revolver from the finishing station, and a perforated tar-

This pronghorn buck fell to one shot from Wayne's 500 S&W at just over 90 yards.

get from a box nearby. The target's two five-shot groups could each be covered with half a business card. One of them showed four shots cutting one hole, the fifth less than 3/4 inch away. Proofed at 50 yards, this Model 83 did not measure up and was going back through the line! "We don't release pistols that we would not choose for ourselves," Bob said simply. "We demand a lot of our products; that's why they cost more."

He said when prospective buyers balk about the price, he just refers them to customers. "The gist of their message is the same I'd deliver: Hunting is expensive; it just makes sense to take all the accuracy and power you can get. If you're a silhouette shooter, you might as well buy a Freedom revolver, because you'll have to shoot against one." Indeed, over the last decade, Freedom has dominated silhouette matches. Bob chuckled. "I'm not kidding when I say that at some matches you have to look hard to find a revolver that didn't come from this shop. Shooters who demand top performance buy our guns."

I asked about the new 500 Wyoming Express.

"It's actually about a year old," replied Bob. "We designed it as a big-bore alternative to the 454, one that would outperform the rimless 500 Action Express and approach the 500 Linebaugh in a standard revolver cylinder." (The 500 AE, you'll recall, is a rimless round developed in 1991 for the massive Desert Eagle Mk VII autoloading pistol. The 500 Linebaugh predated the 475 Linebaugh and was based on the 348 Winchester case.) "The belt made sense because a rim on a 50-caliber case would have been too small if we sized it to fit our current Model 83 cylinder. Also, a belt strengthens the case head, and since forming the belt is part of the heading operation, it can be made more uniform than a machined rim."

Starting load				Maximum load			
POWDER	BULLET	PRESS/VEL.		POWDER	BULLET	PRESS/VEL.	
29.0 Lil' Gun	350 XTP	34,500	1467	32.0 Lil' Gun	350 XTP	42,700	1617
31.0 H4227	350 XTP	32,400	1378	35.0 H4227	350 XTP	44,200	1584
32.0 H-110	350 XTP	34,600	1486	35.0 H-110	350 XTP	43,100	1629
29.0 Lil' Gun	370 WFNGC	34,200	1460	31.0 Lil' Gun	370 WFNGC	37,100	1528
31.0 H4227	370 WFNGC	33,600	1382	34.0 H4227	370 WFNGC	43,300	1535
34.0 H-110	370 WFNGC	37,500	1527	36.0 H-110	370 WFNGC	41,800	1607
28.0 Lil' Gun	400 WFNGC	38,600	1454	31.0 Lil' Gun	400 WFNGC	45,700	1565
30.0 H4227	400 WFNGC	39,900	1390	33.0 H4227	400 WFNGC	46,700	1509
32.0 H-110	400 WFNGC	39,800	1497	34.5 H-110	400 WFNGC	47,900	1589
26.0 Lil'Gun	440 WFNGC	38,100	1355	28.0 Lil' Gun	440 WFNGC	46,300	1450
26.0 H4227	440 WFNGC	34,400	1220	30.0 H4227	440 WFNGC	48,300	1413
27.0 H-110	440 WFNGC	34,000	1302	29.5 H-110	440 WFNGC	44,200	1415

The 500 WE case is 1.37 inches long, for an overall cartridge length of about 1.76. The head is designed for Large Rifle primers and fits a standard Number 41 RCBS shell-holder. Bob told me Freedom is supplying dies, which should be adjusted to size the case down to within about 0.10-inch of the belt. "Seat and crimp in separate operations," he added. Freedom's own tests show the 500 Wyoming Express cases are long-lived when loads are kept to recommended pressure levels. "We typically get 10 loads per case," said Bob. "Belt expansion of 0.002-inch on the first firing is common, but the belt should never be sized. Subsequent expansion up to 0.003-inch has no effect on chambering."

Designed for bullets scaling between 350 and 450 grains, the 500 WE is well served by Hodgdon Lil' Gun, H4227 and H110 powders. Here are starting and maximum loads for four bullet weights:

Factory-loaded ammunition is available from Grizzly Cartridge Company, POB 1466, Rainier OR 97048. After wresting a Freedom Arms Premier revolver in 500 AE from Bob, I used Grizzly's 370-, 400- and 440-grain loads in range work. All bullets were hardcast flatnose. Loaded to 950 fps, all were pleasant to shoot and accurate. At 1300 and 1250 and 1200 fps, respectively, they were noticeably more frisky but still very accurate. The bullets were beautifully made and would make the short list of missiles I'd choose for hunting. That saucer-size flat would blast a huge hole through vitals; bones of game as big as elk would give way.

While a Ransom Rest or Caldwell HAMMR Machine Pistol Rest would have better tested the 83's inherent accuracy, I chose to shoot this revolver over sandbags. I wanted to feel the 500 WE, and to learn how the grip, trigger, sights – and recoil affect my ability to shoot it accurately. Bob had sent me a Premier model, with impregnated hardwood grips. Standard versions feature Pachmayr Presentation grips. Other dif-

This squirrel fell to a scoped Smith & Wesson 22. Good revolvers aren't all big-bores!

ferences: The Premier has a satin finish, standard models a low-luster matte; the Premier's rear sight is screw-adjustable for windage and elevation, while standard models have a screw for elevation only and must be drifted to change windage. Both grades are of stainless steel (except sights), the parts seamlessly

Wayne killed this Wyoming buck at 95 yards with one of the first S&W 500s, a Cor-Bon bullet.

fitted and the actions so finely tuned that revolvers of other makes seem loose in comparison. Nothing slips or rattles on a Freedom Arms revolver. The cylinder rotates like the hand of a Rolex. Every click is solid, purposeful – and somewhat muted by the weight and snug fit of each part.

A single-action revolver, especially one chambered for potent rounds, should be allowed to rotate in your hand during recoil. I found the 83's grip allowed for that slippage without compromising control. After 25 rounds, my hand was not at all sore, nor was blast

objectionable. The 7 1/2-inch barrel not only gives this revolver good looks and balance but limits muzzle flip with heavy loads and mitigates recoil.

With all three bullets, I was able to print five-shot groups of about 2-1/2 inches at 25 yards – about as tight as I can expect with iron sights. Every group had holes touching. Predictably, the 440-grain bullets struck highest on the target, as they spent more time than the lighter bullets in the barrel during recoil and muzzle lift. The 370- and 400-grain bullets hit lower but right in line. Switching to a more ambitious 400-grain load, I punched holes directly below the 370-grain cluster, confirming that barrel time, not gravity, determines shot placement from pistol barrels up close.

The 83's trigger broke crisply and consistently at 3 pounds 1 ounce. This revolver is easy to shoot!

The 500 Wyoming Express is no threat, ballistically, to the 500 Smith & Wesson. Herb Belin and company can still say that no handgun round is more powerful. Double-action fans can still claim Smith & Wessons as the best such revolvers in the world. But if you prefer the lines and feel of a single-action, in a package that's closer to 50 ounces than 70, there's nothing to compare with a gun from Freedom Arms. The 454 Casull and 475 Linebaugh remain potent options in the Model 83 line. Now, however, you have a 50-caliber alternative. The 500 Wyoming Express offers great flexibility in loading, long case life, and enough power to flatten any North American big game.

An elegant gun with a terrific punch – you might have also said that about S&W's first 357 in 1935, or about the Keith-inspired 44 Magnum revolver two decades following. You could have repeated it 30 years later at the debut of the Freedom Arms Model 83 in 454 Casull. In my view, the current M83 Premier in 500 Wyoming Express merits the accolade now.

The Brownie (1919-1932)

The Little Brownie That Challenged The World: ▮ By Jack A. Myers

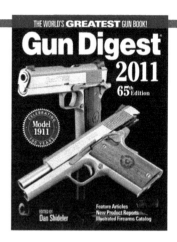

How the Brownie Came To Be

Before the world-wide sales success of its little Brownie pistol launched the O.F. Mossberg & Sons company to its well deserved world-wide recognition, Oscar F. Mossberg had already gained knowledge and experience in the field of gun manufacturing and sales.

Oscar was an industrious young Swede of 22 when he immigrated to America in 1866. And 53 years later, in 1919, he introduced his Brownie pistol, the first and only handgun his small company ever produced. That small company continues today and now holds the distinction of being America's oldest surviving, family-owned, gunmaking company. In my opinion, the little Brownie is as much an example of the American gunmaker's art as Sam Colt's earliest revolver or Oliver Winchester's first lever action rifle.

A truly unique little pocket pistol, Mossberg's Brownie was a four-barrel double-action handgun that weighs in at just 10 ozs. and is 4.5 inches overall, with a cluster of four 2.5-inch barrels. A single pull of the trigger cocks and fires the first barrel and on the same stroke revolves the firing pin to the next barrel's chamber. It is chambered for the .22 Short, Long, or Long Rifle cartridge. Every Brownie left the shop with a small manual extractor rod fitted in a small well behind the left grip. The top of the gun has a very small rectangular opening at top left to accommodate this rod. (Extractor rods are usual missing from the older guns, but new reproduction rods that cannot be distinguished from the originals are readily available on the internet.) Although all of the estimated 33,404 Brownies produced shared the same appearance, with a rich, blued finish and ridged black walnut grips, some were roll stamped with different patent information on the right side of the barrel cluster.

Contemporary writers have reported that due to its diminutive size, ease of concealability, and near superiority to

An original Brownie, as drawn by Canadian illustrator Palmer Cox (1840-1924).

other designs available at the time, the Brownie was an attractive and appealing all-purpose handgun. It was named after a similarly-endowed mythical character which was very popular in that era's literature: the Brownie, a fictitious elfin character created in the late 1800s by Canadian illustrator Palmer Cox (1840-1924). Though perhaps hard to appreciate today, Cox's Brownies were as popular in late-Victorian America as Smurfs would be a century later, and their name inspired a number of popular consumer products. The very popular Kodak "Brownie" camera is a good example; another is the junior division of the American Girl Scouts, founded in 1912, which added a branch for younger girls in grades two and three called "Brownies" with this explanation: "Our Brownie age level gets its name from folk tales of little brownies that would enter homes and help the occupants with housework. This sets the tone for Brownie Scouts who

"Unique" palm pistol made by Mossberg for C. S. Shattuck. Note misspelling of "Shattuck" on roll marking.

Brownie in original factory box.

are learning to help others."

The information we share here will not be a detailed report of the company's early years, but more a synopsis of discoveries about the variations of Brownies that have surfaced over the ensuing years. Both collectors and dealers want to know more how they can recognize an unusual, rare, scarce, or oddball Brownie from the more commonly found specimens, than to study the company history. I feel sure there are more discoveries to come of heretofore unrecognized variations of the Brownie.

Early writers have described Oscar's involvement with the design and production of other small, easily concealed handguns sold by the the C.S.Shattuck Co., stating he was first awarded a patent in 1906 for a four-barrel pistol which came to be known as the Shattuck "Unique" or "Invisible Defender." We know the name "Novelty" has also been used in connection with those early pistols. Those early researchers have also detailed how he toiled alone in his one-man shop in a loft at Hatfield, Massachusetts, to produce those guns for his employers. Mossberg subsequently worked for the Stevens Arms Company and Marlin-Rockell in a variety of production management positions.

In 1919, at the tender age of 75, Oscar –

under the auspices of his newly-formed company, O.F. Mossberg & Sons – started producing his new Brownie pistol, almost a full year before receiving the patent for it. Oscar filed an application for his Brownie with the U.S. Patent Office on Aug. 28, 1919. His pat-

ent (number 1,348,035) was awarded July 27, 1920. It's interesting to note that unlike most such patent applications of that era, the guns he produced actually matched the drawings he had submitted! It is recorded that Oscar moved his gun production facilities to New Haven, Connecticut and still later moved again into larger facilities in New Haven and hired a few mechanically knowledgeable helpers from among his Swedish friends.

Number of Brownies Produced

Since there are no known surviving factory records to verify the actual number of units produced in Oscar's 13 years of fabricating Brownies, guesstimated figures for a total number range from 32,000 to 37,000. Since I've been keeping a database on observed and reported serial numbers on these guns, the highest serial number I would consider reliable is 33,404, found on a gun in Florida. And although I was told of a serial numbered gun lower than any other reported, I never saw it except in a couple of photos, and the person who reported it did not answer my request for additional photographic proof. Therefore, the lowest number I can personally attest to is in my collection and is number 212.

This leads to some interesting speculation. Oscar Mossberg began production of the Brownie in 1919, before receiving the patent he had applied for in August of that year and which was not granted until nearly a year later, on July 27, 1920. Now, do the math. For Oscar to have produced my estimated 33,404 units from 1919 to 1932, as reported, the output of his shop facilities would have to have averaged 2,569 units annually. That averages out at 214 units per week, or 31 units per day. Therefore my Brownie numbered 212 could conceivably have been produced the first or second week of production and was handled by Oscar himself!

However, when one considers the amount of time Oscar probably spent on preparation and experimentation with various production methods, it's doubtful #212 left his shop until sometime in

perhaps the first month. Previous reports are not clear on how many helpers, if any, Oscar hired at the very beginning. Though the name of the company includes "& Sons," his boys were aged 21 and 23 at the time, so is very probably that he hired some more experienced help for his assembly process.

Tough Times Demanded Tough Sales Tactics

Early Brownie ads were primarily aimed at the outdoorsman type of prospective buyer such as hunters, trappers, fishermen and such. As that dark decade of the 1920s inexorably moved toward the Great Crash of 1929 and resulting mass unemployment, many men were resorting to such outdoor vocations in order to feed their families. The initial price of the Brownie was $5. Six years later, probably due to Oscar's improved production methods, Taylor Fur of New York was offering the Brownie for just $3.45 in their 1926 advertisements!

The Brownie ads state they would be shipped "postpaid" anywhere in the U.S..The Brownie was delivered in a small, very plain, boxed unmarked in any manner. The boxes in my collection measure 4.75" X 3.5" X 1" deep, just big enough to accommodate the Brownie, wrapped in brown oiled paper, and accompanied by factory papers. Other writers have reported that these fragile boxes were produced in blue, red or black solid colors with no particular color being more common than any other. The specimens I have are solid black, and the only other two I've been told of were also black. The boxes, being composed of paper, have a much lesser degree of survivabilty than the guns they contained and are therefore more rare to find than the guns themselves. The current price of these guns in Very Good to Excellent condition, with their original box and papers, is quite high. One such specimen advertised nationally in a gun publication in 2007 for $799 was already sold when I inquired about it.

It's interesting to note that the boxes I've handled were of simple cardboard construction, but were then covered with the colored paper that has a somewhat "pebbled" texture to it. It had to have been more expensive to use a plain box with that extra step of production necessary to glue that colored and textured paper over every surface of the box, except most of the interior! I've not yet resolved that puzzling feature.

Variation #1

The information stamped into the right side of the barrel cluster on these earliest guns is shown in the photo at left. In italicized type it reads: PAT. APPL'D.FOR. There are no spaces between the abbreviated words.

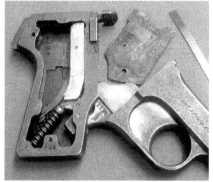

Location of serial numbers on Variation #1.

The location of the serial numbers on this variation may be found in five different locations: 1) under the right grip, on the edge of the gripstrap, down at bottom; 2) with gun open, on right side of the barrel cluster, down near the hinge; 3) with gun open, look up under the little "ears" on the front of the barrel latch lever which lies along the top of the gun; 4) & 5) on back of both metal side plates on receiver section of the gun. Some of the earlier guns also had the serial number written in pencil on the back of the wooden grips. We estimate this model was produced from 1919 until mid-1923 and that there were probably between 10,000 and 11,000 produced.

NOTE 1: So far there have been only 50 of the Variation #1 reported to our database. This is 32.25% of the total production, not quite one third.

NOTE 2: Due to the length of some serial numbers and the limited space available on some parts, only the last three or four digits of the whole number

may be found. These are typically found in locations 2) and 3) shown in the photo, and on back of grips.

NOTE 3: The muzzle of the barrels has not been chamfered (beveled) as on later guns. The face of the muzzle is completely flat.

NOTE 4: Unlike some later Brownies, there is no pin at top center of the metal plate on the right side. Below are photos of the two types of sideplate. Earlier Variations #1 and #2 had no pin.

Warning Regarding Disassembly

The metal side plates on the Brownie have a single screw towards the rear holding them to the frame. When you remove that screw, do not pry up on the plate. This usually results in the sharp edges of both the plate and the frame being marred beyond repair. These metal side plates are beveled into the frame at the front edge. After removing the screw gently loosen the plate by lifting it and/or moving it up and down to loosen it from the frame. Once loose, slide it to the rear for removal. CAUTION: There are some variations with

Location of the pin that identifies later variations. Variation #1 (front) has no pin.

an alignment pin through the metal plate on the right side. On these Brownies, once the screw is removed you must gently lift the rear of the plate until it just clears the top of the pin before sliding it to the rear.

Variation #2

Variation #2 differs from Variation #1 only in that the stamped patent information on the right side of the barrel cluster reads: PAT'D.JAN.27,1920. That is the date which was discovered to be in error. The patent papers are plainly

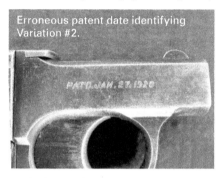

Erroneous patent date identifying Variation #2.

marked as July, not January. I've had only six Variation #2 specimens reported to the database. These represent just under 4% of the total number reported. This would indicate 1,260 units probably were produced from mid-1923 to early in 1924, a guesstimated total of 1,260 units. Personally, I have a hunch it may have been even less.

Variation #2.5

Variation #2.5 differs from Variation #2 in ways which strongly indicate it to be a short-run transitional piece to the later Variation #3, which the company seems to have eventually settled on and

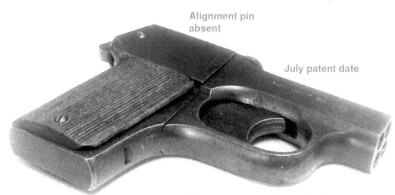

Alignment pin absent

July patent date

No external serial number on butt

Identifying characteristics of Variation 2.5.

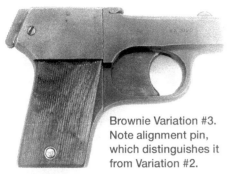

Brownie Variation #3. Note alignment pin, which distinguishes it from Variation #2.

produced in greatest volume. The serial numbers can be found in the same locations as on Variations #1 and #2. The only visible external clue that this is not one of those two earlier variations is that no alignment pin is found in the metal plate on the right side, even though it has the correct patent date stamped on it, which would immediately identify it as a Variation #3. The patent info reads: PAT. JULY 27, 1920. It's interesting to note that the stamped patent information on Variation #2.5 has a space separating each word or group of numerals.

This particular example of Variation 2.5 is a very recent discovery and only three specimens have been observed thus far. They represent only 1.3% of the total production, or less than 400 units produced, probably for only 30 days or so early in 1924. The serial numbers on the reported specimens are just 725 apart, which if Oscar followed the usually consecutive numbering of each piece, would mean there may be at least another 723 units out there. Whichever figures one uses, this means that Variation #2.5 is currently the rarest of the Brownie family and should, especially in the future, demand a premium in its selling price.

Variation #3

Variation #3 had the longest production period and therefore the most units of production, making it the most often encountered Brownie variation found. The stamping found on the right side of the barrel cluster of this variation is the same as the previous Variation #2.5: PAT. JULY 27, 1920. An estimated 20,977 units were produced from 1924 until the end of its production in 1932. Both of the boxed specimens I've managed to obtain are the Variation #3. It

stands to reason that since these were the most recently made guns, the better their chance to have survived in Very Good, or Excellent, and even New condition. (Unfired, pristine guns with their original box and factory papers have come to be commonly known as NIB, or New In Box.) Only four boxes have been reported thus far.

Variation #3 is easily identified by the small alignment pin through top center of the right side metal plate. Its serial numbers are stamped into the bottom of the butt; on right side of the barrel cluster down near the hinge; and under the small "ears" on front of the barrel latch lever along the top of the gun.

NOTE: The full serial number is on butt while the other two stampings may only be the last few digits due to space available, and, these latter two locations can only be seen when the barrel cluster is lowered for loading.

Other Variations?

There is a very good possibility that there are even more variations of this little pistol than the four reported here. Variation #2.5 was discovered only because I had learned to start observing every survivor for the slightest difference from any Brownie heretofore known. I then noticed there was a specimen that had the patent date of one variation but lacked the pinned side plate of that variation. Possibly parts from two different variations joined, I thought? Soon after that a similar survivor became available. The main difference was that the later one was in excellent condition and not likely to be a hodgepodge of parts from different guns.

In the fairly recent past I've observed other, more startling types of Brownies but have passed them off as home-made fabrications involving some original factory parts and a lot of imagination, mainly because none of them had their particular unusual feature ever advertised as available from the factory. There is also a possibility they were experimental display pieces to show and learn if there was a demand for their particular feature. However, nothing has ever been noted in print from that era about

such experimental items. Now I'm not so sure. I may have erred and passed up a great opportunity to unearth and disclose a fifth variation. The moral of the story is: keep your eyes open and keep looking. Maybe you will be announcing the finding of a new Brownie!

A Word of Advice

For those who would like to fire one of these old-timers, be advised they were designed in an era before the advent of our modern steels and higher velocity ammunition. Therefore a real danger exists that the gun may be damaged, and/or the shooter injured, when firing one of these guns using modern hi-vel ammo. I have owned one such Brownie which had a large chunk of metal blown out of the area between the chambers! And as always, with all older guns it's a good idea to have it inspected by a reliable and competent gunsmith before firing it.

An Introduction to the Military Handguns of Imperial Japan

■ By Teri Jane Bryant

I hear it all the time at gun shows: "They're just copies of Lugers, aren't they?" Well, no, they're actually nothing like Lugers, but in a way the question is not surprising. Japanese handguns are very little known, especially in Canada, where I live, and several do have the same general shape as the famous German pistol. Many people have never even seen one Japanese handgun, let alone a collection. However, I have found them to be a fascinating and challenging field of study, and the attention my display gets at gun shows suggests others agree.

Early Tokyo Arsenal Showa 4.2 (February, 1929) Type 14 and late Nagoya Arsenal-Tomimatsu Showa 20.5 (May, 1945) Type 14 show differences in cocking knobs and grips, as well as addition of magazine retention spring on front of grip. Shown with service medals from the Manchurian (left) and Chinese (right) campaigns.

The Type 26

When Japan began to modernize its military in the late 1800s, it first chose a foreign handgun, the Smith & Wesson Model 3 in .44 Russian, for its army and navy. Between the late 1870s and mid-1890s it imported an estimated 16,000 of these revolvers in several variations. Japanese industry progressed rapidly, though, and soon it had an indigenous design, the Type 26 revolver, so named because its design was completed in the twenty-sixth year of the reign of the Meiji Emperor, i.e. in 1893.

The Type 26, a break-top, double-action only revolver, combined features of many of its contemporaries, most noticeably a Smith & Wesson-style latch and a left side plate that swings open like that of the French M1892 revolver. Like its contemporaries, it is chambered for a rather underpowered cartridge, which is similar to the .38 S&W but with a much thinner rim. However, its main flaw is that the cylinder locks up only at the moment of firing. As a result, if the cylinder brushes against something, an empty chamber can easily rotate into the firing position. Modern buyers unfamiliar with this peculiarity often mistake the free rotation of the cylinder as a sign of breakage, but that is just how these guns were made.

More than 59,000 Type 26 revolvers were produced. Although they were obsolete by the 1920s, Japan's chronic shortage of small arms meant they were still in widespread use in 1945, and hence almost all are either very battered or were arsenal refurbished during the 1930s. Specimens with the original finish have much deeper bluing than arsenal reworks and are most easily distinguished by the heat tempered bluing on the hammer, which has a purplish, iridescent appearance.

The Nambus

Shortly after the introduction of the Type 26, Captain (later Lt. General) Kijiro Nambu joined the Tokyo Artillery Arsenal and began work on small arms. Nambu had the same broad influence on small arms development in Japan that John Browning had in the USA. His work touched everything from handguns to rifles and machine guns.

Nambu's first production handgun design was an eight-shot, semi-automatic with a shoulder-stock/holster. Now called the Grandpa Nambu, only about 2,400 were produced between 1902 and 1906, for private purchase by officers. However, this early model included two features that were extremely influential. First, it introduced the 8mm bottle-necked cartridge that became the standard Japanese pistol and sub-machine gun round. The 8mm Nambu is similar in size to the 7.65mm Luger round, but with a lower velocity that makes it ballistically more similar to the .380 ACP. Second, it had a mechanism based on a downward-swinging locking block, variants of which were used in several subsequent models. When the pistol is fired, the barrel and bolt recoil together about 3mm. Then the locking block swings down into an aperture in the rear of the frame, freeing the bolt to continue its rearward movement. Luger afficionados will recognize this as totally different from the upward-breaking toggle action on the much more common Parabellum pistol. In fact, if the mechanism had any German inspiration, it was more likely the Mauser Broomhandle,

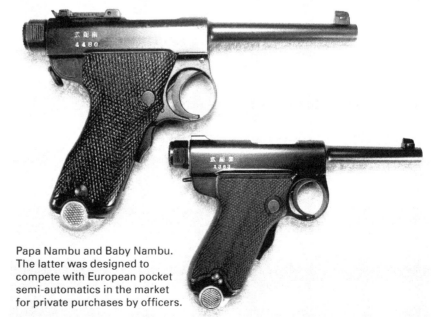

Papa Nambu and Baby Nambu. The latter was designed to compete with European pocket semi-automatics in the market for private purchases by officers.

which also had a downward-swinging locking block, and with which Nambu would have been familiar.

A direct follow-on from the Grandpa was the Papa Nambu, which dropped the shoulder-stock and incorporated some minor improvements such as a slightly larger trigger guard and an aluminum (rather than wooden) magazine base. Tokyo Arsenal and the private firm Tokyo Gas and Electric (TGE) produced more than 10,000 of these pistols between 1906 and the mid-1920s. The Japanese referred to it as the "Rikushiki" (Army-Type), which was ironic, since the Army never adopted it officially, while the Navy did, in 1909. Once again, a chronic shortage of weapons resulted in the Papa continuing in service until 1945, by which time decades of use in the Navy's salt-spray environment had left most of them in very rough

condition. Like the Type 26 revolver, only a handful of mint specimens are known.

Many Japanese officers found the full-size Nambu pistols too bulky and purchased smaller European and American semi-automatics, such as the 1910 and 1914 Mausers, 1903 Colt and 1910 Browning, for their personal use. To provide a domestic alternative for this market, Nambu developed a three-quarter-size version of his pistol. Known as the Baby Nambu, this pocket-sized pistol was mechanically identical to its full-size counterparts but fired a unique bottle-necked 7mm cartridge with muzzle energy similar to that of the .32 ACP. Since they were almost twice the price of a European pistol, they were mostly purchased by senior officers and therefore led pampered lives. Only 6,500 were produced, 90 percent by To-

kyo Arsenal and the rest by Tokyo Gas & Electric. Their rarity and extremely high level of craftsmanship have made them among the most sought-after of Japanese pistols.

The Type 14

The 1920s saw the development of Japan's most common sidearm, the Type 14. Adopted by the Army in 1925 (the fourteenth year of the reign of the Taisho Emperor, Hirohito's father) and by the Navy in 1927, approximately 280,000 were produced between late 1926 and August, 1945. While broadly similar in design to its predecessors, it was much easier to produce and incorporated several improvements, such as dual recoil springs. The first 102,000 or so produced up until September of 1939 had a small, rounded trigger guard. Those produced thereafter had an extended trigger guard to allow the use of a gloved finger in cold weather. The large trigger guard version is sometimes referred to as the "Manchurian Model," "Kiska Model," or "Winter Trigger Guard Model." However, these terms have fallen into disfavour since all pistols produced after September of 1939 had the large guard regardless of where or in what season they were issued.

Type 14 pistols are easily dated since the year and month of production were recorded just below the serial number on the right rear of the frame. They are recorded using the Japanese emperor-based system of dating, with the year of the Emperor's reign first, followed by a period or comma and then the month. For example, a marking of "18.6" indicates the sixth month (June) of the eighteenth year of Emperor Hirohito's reign. To convert these imperial dates to Western style, simply add 1925 (e.g., "Year 18" was 1925+18=1943). The only exception was the first 100-150 or so pistols produced, which were made during the last months of the reign of Hirohito's father, i.e. in 1926. These do not have a reign name character in front of the date, which could range from 15.8 to 15.12, and bear low serial numbers of up to around 100 (note that guns with the dates 1.8 to 15.1, a character

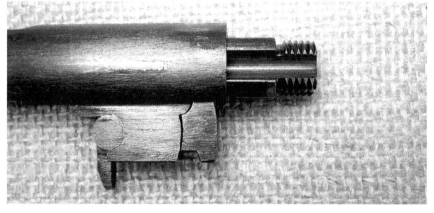

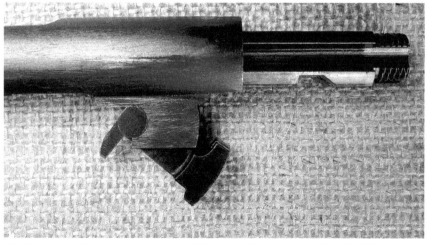

(Top) Here the Type 14 bolt is shown fully forward, with the locking block in the "up" (locked) position. (Bottom) After firing the bolt and barrel move rearward 3mm, then the locking block drops down and allows the bolt to continue rearward. Note the notch in the bottom of the bolt, into which the locking block fits when the bolt is forward and the action is locked.

in front of the date, and serial numbers in the 72000 to 87000 range were made much later, during Hirohito's reign, and are relatively common). If you find one of these ultra-rare pistols, known as "Taisho" Type 14s after the name of Hirohito's father's reign, you have really hit the jackpot!

The Type 14 was Japan's primary sidearm for 20 years. It had several strong points, such as ease of disassembly, great "pointability," a very light trigger that breaks at around 2.5 lbs., good inherent accuracy and mild recoil, all of which made it easy to shoot well. On the other hand, it had three major defects. First, it was prone to misfires due to striker tip breakage and inadequate power of the striker spring. To combat this problem a spare striker was issued with each pistol, and the striker length was reduced from 87mm to 73mm and then 65mm to lighten it.

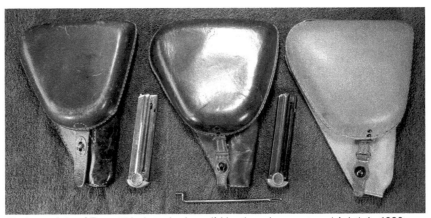

Early models of Type 14 holster had a solid leather closure strap (right). In 1939 a spring –loaded strap was adopted (middle). In late 1942, rubberized canvas was adopted as a leather substitute. It proved much more resistant to rot in tropical climates (right). Also shown are an early magazine (left, with nickel plating), a late magazine (blued, with a notch in the lower front for the magazine retention spring), and a cleaning rod.

Second, the safety required two hands to operate, since it was located too far forward on the left side and had to be rotated 180 degrees. Third, the bolt locked back on the magazine follower after the last shot, making reloading slow and awkward unless one is fortunate enough to have been blessed with three hands. Since the Japanese had a rather limited idea of the military use of handguns, neither of the latter two design shortcomings was considered worthy of corrective action. Indeed, in December of 1939 another highly visible change was introduced that made reloading even slower: a magazine retention spring was added. This spring protrudes through the lower part of the front grip strap and prevents magazine loss by catching a released magazine after about 3mm of downward travel so that it can be manually extracted. Despite these shortcomings, the Type 14 continued in service with the Japanese coast guard until the 1960s!

There were five producers of Type 14s, and numerous variations in cocking knobs, grips, etc. One could make a very interesting collection of just Type 14 variations and their holsters, which themselves come in at least eleven major varieties. Late war Type 14s, particu-

larly those from 1944, the peak year of production, are often available in excellent condition at reasonable prices and therefore make an excellent representative Japanese pistol for the World War II collector, or a starting point for a more ambitious Japanese collection. Their often rough finish should not be confused with actual wear and tear, a common mistake. While early Japanese pistols such as the Baby Nambu had fit and finish equal to the best anywhere, as World War II progressed, less and less attention was paid to cosmetic issues such as polishing and bluing. Eventually poorly trained schoolgirls made up a large part of the labour force in arms factories, resulting in poor quality and an appalling rate of workplace injuries. Oddly, very rough Type 14 pistols made in the last month or two of production (July and August, 1945) are prized by many collectors specifically because of their crudity. These pistols, known as "last ditch," combine poorly made new parts with those scavenged from earlier rejects or damaged pistols sent in for repair. They usually lack final inspection stamps in the area near the date and should definitely not be fired. (Of course, like any antique firearm, even earlier, higher-quality Japanese pistols should be inspected by a competent gunsmith for safety before firing.)

Just before the Type 14 went into production, Lt. General Nambu retired

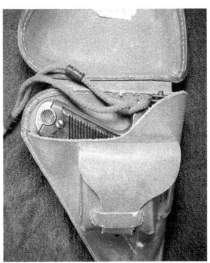

Rubberized canvas holster shows typical Type 14 features: pouch for two, 15-round boxes of cartidges, slot for spare striker to right of ammo pouch, and use of lanyard to draw pistol. Like many Japanese holsters, this one has a tag identifying the soldier to whom it was issued, in this case Superior Private Toru Sayama.

and established the Nambu Rifle Manufacturing Company. Initially it produced only training rifles, but by the late 1930s, after merging with two other companies and assuming the name Chuo Kogyo (Central Industries), it became the largest private producer of military small arms in Japan. Besides pistols, it made the famous "knee mortar" and Type 100 submachine guns, among others. A successor company operated in postwar Japan until the 1970s, when it was

Type 94 with holster, cleaning rod and spare magazine. The Showa 18.7 date translates to July, 1943.

absorbed by Minebea, the Japanese bearing maker. The company's pistol-making heritage was preserved when it was granted a contract to produce SIG pistols under license for today's Japanese Self-Defence Forces.

The Notorious Type 94

The last major design used by the Imperial Japanese military was the Type 94. Its designation results from its adoption by the Army in 1934, which was 2694 by the Japanese calendar (it was never adopted by the Navy). Contrary to reports in some early sources, this pistol was never intended for civilian sale; it was designed at the specific request of the military.

This unusual pistol broke with previous Nambu designs in two important respects. It had a hammer and firing pin rather than a spring-driven striker, and the locking block was a downward-floating wedge. Considered by many to be a good candidate for the title "world's ugliest pistol" or even "world's worst military handgun," the Type 94 perhaps deserves reappraisal. Its small grip and compact overall size actually were ideal for the smaller stature of Japanese soldiers, who averaged only 5'3" and 123 lbs. Its compactness was especially appreciated by those working in confined spaces, such as pilots and tankers. The holster magnified the advantage, as its tailored design contrasted sharply with the bulky clamshell designs issued with most prior Japanese sidearms. The safety was also better positioned and can be operated with one hand.

On the down side, the design of the Type 94's locking mechanism was weak and prone to premature wear, the sights are poor and the trigger is long and creepy. However, by far its most notorious feature was undoubtedly its exposed sear bar on the left side. Pressing on its forward tip when the safety is disengaged allows the pistol to be fired without depressing the trigger. Although inherently an undesirable, unsafe feature, in practice such discharges require sufficiently focused pressure on a small area that they were never a serious operational issue. About 71,000 Type 94s were made by Chuo Kogyo, the only producer. Frequent changes in machining and the placement of markings and the late-war use of slab wooden grips instead of the earlier checkered bakelite mean there are also numerous variations for the serious collector to pursue. "Last ditch" Type 94 pistols often show even worse quality than the late Type 14s and, although of great historical interest, they should certainly not be fired.

Tips for the Beginning Collector

If you've been keeping score, you have probably figured out by now that total production of handguns by Imperial Japan during the entire period 1893-1945 was less than 450,000, even including a small number of rare weapons produced late in the war, such as the Hamada. (By comparison, Germany made several million Lugers during the same period, not to mention the many other sidearms it adopted.) Most Japanese handguns were destroyed at the end of WWII; most of those that survived were brought home as war trophies by US troops. Many of these pistols are still being dug out of attics,

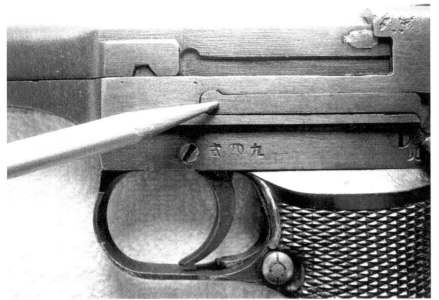

The Type 94 had an exposed sear bar. When the safety is off, pressing on the forward portion (indicated by the pencil tip) will fire the pistol.

ask me why I chose such an obscure field to collect. My long-term interest in Japan was one factor, but I also thought it would be interesting to do something no one else in my area was doing. In addition, although they can be hard to find, especially in Canada, when they do turn up, prices are still quite reasonable compared to some of the more popular collectible handguns like Colts and Lugers. You probably won't find one at your local gun shop even in the USA, but if your curiosity has been piqued, you can often find them on the major gun auction websites, Banzai's newsletter or one of the bulletin boards devoted to Japanese weapons and militaria (see my website for a list of them). Be careful, though: once you get started you may end up a "Nambu nut" like me!

NOTE: Teri Jane Bryant's interest in guns and militaria was sparked by visiting gun shows with her father as a child.

Japan began to fascinate her when she visited the country on an exchange during her university years. Her two interests came together when she saw a battered Type 14 for sale cheap at a gun show. She has since developed an extensive Japanese collection and published numerous articles on Japanese weapons and militaria. She can be reached at tallteri@shaw.ca.

garages and closets and put on the market by the heirs of the servicemen who brought them back. A good start to a collection would be a Type 26 revolver, two Type 14s (small and large trigger guard versions) and a Type 94. These examples would represent over 90% of all the Japanese handguns made. From there one can easily branch out into collecting the many variations of either the Type 14 or Type 94, or (if one's budget allows) attempt to complete the "Nambu Family" with the rarer types such as the Papa, Grandpa and Baby. There are now excellent sources of reference information available to guide the beginning collector or help the established one reach new depths of understanding. Two outstanding reference books have been published recently. The most comprehensive is Japanese Military Cartridge Handguns 1893-1945 by Harry Derby and James Brown. Mr. Brown's Collector's Guide to Imperial Japanese Handguns 1893-1945 is also available at a very modest price for those on a strict budget (it even has some new information that has turned up since the larger volume came out, as well as advice on valuation). Online resources are also available, such as my website, www. nambuworld.com. I strongly recommend doing some research before you

plunge into a purchase, as few sellers know what they really have due to the specialized nature of Japanese weapon collecting. Joining a group like Banzai, the Japanese militaria collectors' association, is also a good idea: I have found the advanced collectors very forthcoming with help and advice as they warmly welcome newcomers to the field.

Very few Japanese handguns made their way to Canada, so many people

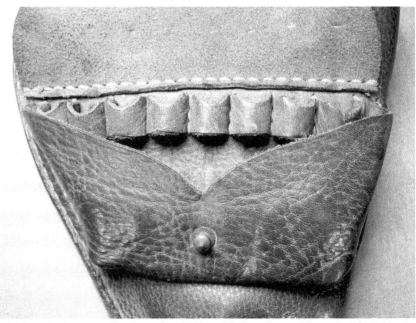

Baby Nambu holsters, like those for the Type 26, Grandpa and Papa, had individual loops for spare cartridges in their ammo pouches.

Oddballs–
Why we love'em

They're not as common today as they once were, but unusual vintage handguns can still be a lot of fun. The author shares four of his favorites with us. ▌By Andy Ewert

Generally speaking, the reasons for owning a handgun fall under two categories: need and desire. Protection, law enforcement, and recreation are functions of need. But when one owns numerous handguns, possession may be more a function of desire than need.

A good number of veteran handgunners who have all they need, myself included, find themselves in this predicament. Today's new-product-driven marketplace is awash in brand name revolvers, semi-autos, and other action types for every conceivable purpose. Specialization has replaced utility as marketers cajole us at every opportunity to discard the old in favor of the new and improved.

There is a subset of handguns on the market today that time has passed

One of few succesful 9mm Parabellum blowback designs, the Astra 600 is impressively accurate and reliable.

by. They're usually old and long out of production; made of steel; of obscure, sometimes foreign origin; and usually a bit "dated" looking, compared with their modern counterparts. They go by the names Astra, Webley, Ballaster Molina, and Makarov, to name a few. I refer to this subset affectionately as "oddballs" and I love 'em. So do other like-minded independents who snap them up for no other reason than pure desire to own, shoot, and admire. Not that they're incapable of meeting the needs they were designed for. They do, usually very well, but not with the pizzazz of high-capacity firepower, exotic materials, or blockbusting ballistics.

Oddballs are usually encountered unexpectedly and off the beaten path: in small town gun shops, at rummage and garage sales, in the shadowy corners of gun shows, or on the back pages of pulpy firearms-peddler publications. You can even find them on the Internet if you are willing to drill. At first glance, they appear to be second-rate, second-class clunkers. Ah, but as we know, appearances can be deceiving.

Oddballs are an eclectic bunch. Some date to before the turn of the twentiethth century, but most originate from the 1900s to the 1960s. Many are of military origin and from Old World countries. They're often referred to by the unenlightened as obsolete, surplus, or, most cruelly, as old iron.

The Webley No.1 Mark VI

My favorite oddball is the Webley No.1 Mark VI, the last in a distinguished line of break-top, self-extracting, double-action revolvers. Manufactured in England from 1915 to 1928, the Mark VI served with distinction across the British Empire, from the trenches of France during World War I and the African deserts in World War II to across former possessions for decades after production ceased. Webleys still appear in active duty from time to time, usually in the hands of irregular mountain warriors prowling the border regions of middle-eastern civilization.

Chambered for the .455 Webley Revolver, Mk 2 cartridge, the Mark VI's

A small sampling of "oddballs" includes (top to bottom) England's Webley No.1 Mark VI, converted to .45 ACP; Argentina's Ballester-Molina in .45 ACP; Spain's Astra 600 in 9mm Parabellum; and the 9X18mm Makarov, this example manufactured in the former East Germany. Exotic history, old-world, quality manufacture, and uniqueness set them apart from today's handguns. Despite their age and foreign pedigree, all are more than capable in defense or informal target shooting. They're still available at reasonable prices, though not as reasonable as in times past, if one takes the time to search.

265-grain round-nose lead slug, traveling at a leisurely 600 fps, delivers a lethal blow up close. The sixgun itself exudes a rich heritage of exotic places, hard combat with determined foes, and empiring. Its 6" barrel and 2 lb. 6.5-oz. heft balances well and steadies without muscle fatigue. The Mark VI is rugged, fast to reload, and is capable of delivering its payload fast and true. It earned the reputation as arguably the best combat revolver ever produced.

The Webley No.1 Mark VI was available in the U.S. at least since the 1960s at move-'em-out prices. To heighten their appeal, importers converted many to the more available and affordable .45 ACP cartridge. And a good thing they did. Today, as back then, .455 ammo costs more than twice its ACP peer. You can still find Mark VIs about, but not at rock bottom prices. I acquired mine without dickering at a Milwaukee, Wisconsin, gun show after a protracted search.

Its markings indicate that my Mark VI dates to 1916 and is of Royal Navy issue. Like many of its brothers, this Brit was converted to .45 ACP, which is fine by my wallet and .45 reloading dies. In excellent condition, it accommodates

ACP cartridges in half- or full-moon clips for speedy loading, or .45 Auto Rims for slightly improved accuracy.

Fired offhand at 25 yards, it will place six 250-gr. lead flatpoint slugs, powered by 3.5 grains of Bullseye, at approximately 700 fps, into a group you can cover with your hand. Not bad for an octogenarian! Recoil is mild. To be on the safe side, I keep reloads near factory .455 levels and forego stouter ACP ballistics.

The Webley's V-notch rear and squared front sights are conducive to good shot placement. Its single action trigger pull is accommodating, less so double action. The issue hard rubber grips are non-slip and the right size. My Webley's boxy, high-center-of-gravity look draws stares on the firing line, but so what?

The Astra 600

My second favorite oddball is the curious Astra 600. This single-action, enclosed hammer, blowback 9mm Parabellum originates from an extended family of military- and civilian-issue semi-automatic handguns produced by Unceta y Compania in Spain's historic firearms manufacturing region. It should be noted that the 600 is one of very few successful (read durable) blowback 9mm Parabellum designs. The Astra's long, narrow, tubular look sets it decisively apart from other handguns.

Introduced in 1943, the 600 carries a history as interesting as the Webley's. During World War II, the German military required more sidearms than its indigenous manufacturers could supply. Impressed with the Astra 400 9mm Largo semi-auto used by both sides during the Spanish Civil War and by the Wehrmacht in limited quantities during early World War II, Germany ordered 38,000 Astra 600 pistols, specifying they chamber the German military-issue 9mm Parabellum cartridge and feature a 5-1/4" barrel, compared with the 400's 6" tube. The magazine release was also modified to a button located on the lower side of the left grip frame. The Germans designated their supplemental sidearm the Pistole Astra 600/43.

Some 10,000-plus 600s made it to Germany before the shifting tides of war ended deliveries. A number of the 28,000 undelivered pistols were sold for issue to the Portuguese Navy, and later exported as surplus. Others ironically were delivered to West Germany after the war, this time for police use. Astra 600 production terminated in 1946 with a total run of approximately 60,000 pistols.

I came across my 600 through a classified ad several years ago. The pistol is marked "MRP" (Marina Republica Portugal) on the frame, indicating naval issuance. It appears never to have been used and, other than a few storage dings, is as it was when it arrived in Portugal 60-plus years ago. Fit and finish are as fine as any semi-auto I've encountered. Evidently, the Spanish aimed to please their German customers.

By today's double-action, high-capacity, locked-breech 9mm semi-auto standard, the 600's design is past its prime. Single-action, nine-shot 9mms with a grip safety and fixed sights are passe. However, at the range it's another matter.

The Astra's rigidly secured barrel is promotes unusually good accuracy. Despite a stiff trigger and rudimentary (though user-friendly) sights, on a good day I can place a magazine full of economical, Russian steel-cased 115-gr. 9mm ball into a bit over 2 inches at 25 yards. I challenge any wondernine to do noticeably better. Perhaps with tailored handloads one might cut this to under 2 inches, but why bother? I have no use for costly hollowpoints and other high-performance rounds for punching holes in paper.

Recoil from blowbacks tends to be more pronounced than that of comparable locked-breeched pistols. The 600's heavy slide and impressive recoil spring mitigate the sensation satisfactorily.

The Ballester-Molina

Oddball number three is Argentina's home-grown Ballester-Molina .45 semi-auto. This Colt 1911 variant represents a successful attempt to upgrade the proven John Browning design – a quarter of

a century or more before doing so became popular.

Produced by Hispano Argentina de Automovites, S.A. around 1935, the Ballaster's developers did away with the 1911's grip safety, switched to a pivoting-type trigger from Colt's bar-type design, and added a larger grip tang than the Colt. In my experience, all three changes are for the better. The 1911's laterally mounted safety makes its grip counterpart redundant. The Ballaster's pivoting trigger is noticeably smoother its Colt counterpart, and its extended tang provides needed protection to the web of the shooting hand. Others may take a different view, but I know what works for me.

The Ballester-Molina had its moment in history, albeit brief and murky. A number of the pistols were supplied to the British Special Operations Executives for use on convert missions during World War ll. Why it was chosen is unclear. Perhaps its origin provided a degree of deception in identifying users. History is mum on its performance in battle.

Judging from the variety of slide markings encountered, Ballester-Molinas were distributed profusely among various branches of the Argentine military and law enforcement communities during its five-year, 100,000-pistol production run. Mine, acquired through a print advertisement, is marked "Armada Nacional," indicating naval issue. (Judging from the condition of surplus naval pistols I've come across, sailors didn't spend much time with sidearms.)

Like its oddball peers, the Ballester-Molina reflects quality manufacturing. All parts fit tightly and function as they should. The pistol's smooth, evenly applied parkerized finish is as attractive as it is practical, particularly in a marine environment. Available on the U.S. surplus firearms market periodically for almost four decades, this sidearm never was popular, but it always seems to sell. It remains an economical alternative to the Colt 1911.

Though certainly nowhere near as prestigious as its legendary American stepfather, the Ballester-Molina more

The Author believes this Cold War-era EastGerman 9X18-mm Makarov strikes a reasonable balance between power and size. Surplus holster and economical Russian ball ammunition suit range needs, while translated operating manual provides a wealth of useful and interesting data, including shooting from horseback! Like its fellow oddballs, this Mak is reliable and suitably accurate for a combat pistol.

than holds its own at the range with stock military 1911s. With a smooth pull, courtesy of the aforementioned pivoted trigger, and adequately proportioned fixed sights, my Ballaster groups 230-gr. ball comparably with other unaltered military 1911s and is totally reliable. Lead SWC handloads improve accuracy and function good enough for perforating paper, but not for lifesaving. I'm perfectly content to stick with factory ball or equivalent handloads and avoid the cost and uncertainty of modification.

The Makarov

My last oddball dates back to the Cold War. The Russian Markarov semiautomatic is an interesting product of German and later Russian desire to produce a compact, lightweight, 9mm blowback for their armed forces. Interestingly, firearms producers in Italy, France, Germany, England, Israel, and the U.S. have attempted to do this on and off since before the First World War through the 1980s. Perhaps someone somewhere is at it today.

German efforts, led by small arms manufacturer Carl Walther and ammunition maker Gustave Genschow, at the request of the Luftwaffe, culminated in a shortened, lower-operating-pressure, 9mm cartridge and some prototype pistols – but no production sidearm – by the war's end. Russia, suitably impressed by the German weapons technology that bloodied it so, discovered documentation detailing Germany's 9mm blowback project. The Russians adopted the cartridge and pistol concepts, added their own touches, and introduced the

Pistolet Makarova in 1951. This double-action sidearm, chambered for a special 9X18mm cartridge referred to as the 9mm Markarov, was adopted by some East Bloc countries and later China, along with parts of Soviet-influenced Africa, Asia, and South America. To meet these geographically dispersed needs, Markarovs were produced in Russia and, with Soviet assistance, in Bulgaria, China, and the former East Germany.

After the fall of the Iron Curtain, all sorts of East Bloc hardware ranging from firearms to greatcoats and jet aircraft became available in the U.S. When Markarovs made it to our shores, favorable reviews begin popping up and the pistols began to disappear. Those that didn't suddenly were more expensive. New batches arrived, including Markarovs manufactured with adjustable sights for the U.S. civilian market.

Some firearms authorities refer to the Markarov as obsolete. True, it's a product of the 1950s and has been supplanted in parts of the former Soviet Union by a high-capacity, double-action, full-power Wondernine. But when grasping this compact eight shooter, you realize there is an ideal size for a belt pistol and this is it. For someone lugging a sidearm around in battle, the Makarov strikes a workable balance between full-size and pocket pistol in power, bulk, and weight. I carry mine in a briefcase during the day and park it on the bedroom nightstand when the sun goes down. I don't feel undergunned.

My Makarov is of German 1960s vintage, apparently unissued, and without a scratch. It came to my door in a box along with a spartan shoulder holster and extra magazine. Fit and finish are the traditional German standard – excellent, not surprising since it came from the captured Walther plant in Zella-Mehlis, in what was then Russian-occupied East Germany.

With Russian 9X18mm ball, featuring a 94-gr. FMJ bullet at around 1,050 fps, I can place my shots offhand within the span of my fingers at 25 yards. This is quite good for an almost-but-not-quite pocket pistol with a 5" sighting radius.

The basic square-rear-notch and square-front sights suit my 50-year-old+ bifocaled eyes well. The single action trigger pull is adequate for defense or informal paper punching. Its double action pull, however, is atrocious. Recoil is surprisingly sharp and a bit painful in extended shooting sessions, but not unbearable.

Oddballs:
Where To Find 'Em

As you can see, oddballs are all about history, high quality manufacture, and innate uniqueness. I've only scratched the surface of this fascinating group. All four of the handguns profiled here are capable of protecting one's hide and hearth, besides piercing X-rings, potting small game, or making tin cans dance.

Taking the oddball plunge requires forethought. I favored the pulp route in locating most of mine, perusing Shotgun News and Gun Digest Magazine until my fingers are black with ink. I also keep an eye on importers' websites. (Editor's note: We've also found a fair number of oddballs at AuctionArms.com, Gunbroker.com and GunsAmerica.com.–DMS)

If you don't have a Federal Firearms License, you'll have to find someone who does and, for a modest fee, will conduct your transaction in accordance with federal, state, and any local laws. Surplus arms dealers periodically receive new shipments, some large, some small. Once an oddball catches on, they're gone in a hurry, so it pays to move fast. I'm completely satisfied with my three sight-unseen purchases. Most surplus arms dealers have reasonable return policies.

Another route is to canvas gun shows. Some dealers specialize in ordering quantities of surplus firearms, marking them up for profit, and selling them one by one at shows. Although more costly than placing orders with an accommodating FFL owner, this approach permits buyers to examine the merchandise, sometimes still coated in cosmoline and wrapped in waxed paper, along with mysteriously marked crates of imported ammunition, holsters, magazines, and all sorts of miscellaneous

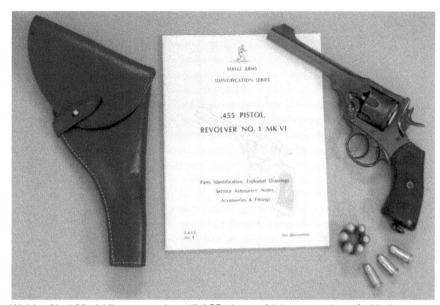

Webley No.1 Mark VI converted to .45 ACP along with homemade period holster, full- and half-moon clips, and detailed literature that add luster to this historic, battle-tested old timer. Despite its reputation for ruggedness, author keeps reloads to .455 levels, though surplus .45 ACP ball has been fired through converted Webleys for decades without reports of mishaps.

paraphernalia. Getting to know these dealers and maintaining dialog gives you an edge in getting in on the ground floor of new offerings.

The final option is akin to panning for gold. Visiting small town gun shops, hardware stores, garage and yard sales, and pawn shops is an adventure in search and discovery. It's truly amazing what a diversity of firearms and miscellaneous second-hand Americana awaits you.

During one foray to a southern Ohio sporting goods store, for example, I came across a Waffenamt acceptance-marked Astra 600, complete with original holster bearing its German owner's name – and priced to sell. I let that one get away and I've regretted it ever since. This way of procuring oddballs is admittedly time- and fuel-consuming, but it's fun. As a city slicker, I find exploring small towns a pleasurable exploit in itself.

A bit of advice for beginners: When buying an oddball, always spend the extra money required for prime specimens. Worn out, battered, malfunctioning wrecks are frustrating at best, a danger to human health at worst. There is no guarantee that you'll be able to find

replacement parts or gunsmiths capable of performing proper repairs. Be forewarned: Buying long-out-of-production oddballs is not without risks.

You've Found an Oddball – Now What?

So you've found your prize, lightening your bankroll in the process, and are admiring it in your easy chair. If you have any doubts about your handgun's caliber, operation, condition, or disassembly, you have more work to do.

Operating manuals or literature detailing your prize's specifications, disassembly, functioning, and idiosyncrasies are usually available. I unexpectedly came across a translated Soviet Markarov operating manual and a wonderful booklet detailing the Webley at local gunshows. Using the Internet can speed up literature location. Gun magazines, books, specialty firearms publications, and Gun Digests from the past are treasure troves of information on oddballs.

With oddballs, there are a few "best practices" to observe.

#1: Examine your newly acquired handgun thoroughly for signs of wear or damage. Do this by field stripping it (or further disassembling it if you're capable) using The Gun Digest Book of Firearms Assembly/Disassembly (separate volumes for semi-automatic pistols and revolvers) by J.B. Wood and the NRA Guide to Firearms Assembly (separate volumes for handguns and rifles and shotguns). Many valuable out-of-print books dealing at least in part with oddball handguns can be found at Amazon.com.

Some oddballs are tricky to take apart and/or reassemble. The Astra 600 leads my menagerie in this characteristic. With its powerful recoil spring, you have to be careful: a slip of the fingers sends a piece of steel flying at eye-threatening velocity.

If you have any doubts about your handgun's operating condition or safety, take it to a reputable gunsmith before your first trip to the range.

#2: Do not use ammunition exceeding the operating pressures your sidearm was designed for. Cartridges of the World by Frank Barnes and reloading manuals list factory load specs. Exceeding these jeopardizes your hide and your prize. Remember, most oddballs were built before the advent of high-pressure +P loads and their ilk. To be safe, stick to standard factory ball or equivalent handloads.

#3: Select your ammunition with care. If you're lucky, your oddball is chambered for a common caliber. If not, be prepared to dig deeper into your wallet. Be sure to keep track your empties at the range. The reliability of most semi-automatic oddballs begins to suffer with hollow point and lead bullets. Military surplus ammunition is a cost-effective option, but proceed with care. Some of it is great while others are less so. Thanks to entrepreneurial importers, ammunition is today a global commodity. You can purchase ammunition from Asia to Eastern Europe and Australia and many locales in between. Try to stay away from corrosive or "semi-corrosive" ammunition if possible, unless you enjoy mandatory, extended strip-down cleaning sessions.

If you have a real oddball that you can't find ammo for, or don't know the proper caliber, consult The Old Western Scrounger at (304) 262-9870. If Dangerous Dave Cumberland can't help you out, you're in trouble. After firing your oddball for the first time, examine the fired cases for any signs of cracks or blown primers. Either indicates something amiss with either with the gun or ammunition. It may be time to contact a gunsmith.

Reloading for Oddballs

Reloading saves money and solves problems. Varying tolerances in firearms and ammunition are normal. You want to keep variances within a range where safety, performance, and case life are maximized. The first way is by measuring your bore diameter. Do this by driving an oversize, soft lead slug through the bore and measuring it with calipers. When buying or casting bullets, keep them close to bore diameter or a little over for optimum accuracy.

The second way to maintain tolerances is to periodically measure your fired cases. When they exceed your manual's recommended maximum length, trim with a case trimmer and chamfer the rough edges with a chamfering tool.

Slight case bottom bulges in blowback empties are not unusual, as are blackened case mouths. If you notice signs of excess pressure, such as unusually heavy recoil or flattened or pierced primers, consult your reloading manual and back off the powder charge.

If oversize chamber variance is a problem (split cases are the warning sign), you may want to purchase a custom resizing die manufactured to your handgun chamber's dimensions. I followed this route with a World War ll vintage Japanese Ariskéa rifle and saved mucho dinero in prolonging the life of pricey Norma brass.

Now you see the big picture of owning and using oddballs. They're not for everyone, but for those eccentric, nostalgic pistoleros who treasure quality manufacturing and are willing to forgo the trendy for the uncommon, the desire for oddballs burns hot and bright. For us, desire is what it's all about.

Bibliography

Barnes, Frank C. Cartridges of the World. Iola, Wisconsin: Krause Publications, 2006.

Ezell, Edward C. Handguns of the World. New York: Barnes and Noble Books, 1993.

Gangarosa, Gene Jr. "Germany's ULTRA Pistols," Gun Digest, 53rd Annual Edition, Iola, Wisconsin: Krause Publications, 1998.

Gebhardt, James F. (translator). The Official Makarov Pistol Manual. El Dorado, Arizona: Desert Publications, 1995.

Hogg, Ian V. The New Illustrated Encyclopedia of Firearms. Secaucus, New Jersey: Wellfleet Press, 1993.

James, Garry. Guns & Ammo The Big Book of Surplus Firearms: The Best of Volumes l, ll, and lll. Los Angeles: Petersen Publishing Company, 1998. (Webley Mk VI.)

Malloy, John. "Blowback Nines." Gun Digest 1993, 47th Annual Edition. Northbrook, Illinois: DBI Books, 1992.

Metcalf, Dick. "East Meets West – The 9 mm Makarov Arrives!" Shooting Times Nov. 1993.

Shimek, Robert T. Guns & Ammo The Big Book of Surplus Firearms, The Best of Voumes l, ll, and lll. Los Angeles: Petersen Publishing,1998. (Astra Models 400, 600, and 300.)

Shimek, Robert T. Guns & Ammo The Big Book of Surplus Firearms, The Best of Voumes l, ll, and lll. Los Angeles: Petersen Publishing,1998. (Makaro.v)

Skennerton, Ian. Small Arms Identification Series: .455 Pistol, Revolver No. I MK Vl. Labrador, Australia: Ian D. Skennerton, 1997.

Thompson, Jim "Surplus Handguns For Home Defense." Guns & Ammo Surplus Firearms, Vol. Vl. Los Angeles: Petersen Publishing,1998.

Six Decades of Automatic Pistols

■ By John Malloy

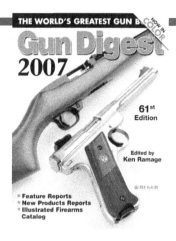

In the final years of the Great Depression, just before the start of World War II, only two U. S. manufacturers produced what were then known as "automatic" pistols. Foreign autoloaders were made, but relatively few were used in America. The revolver, designed and brought into common use in America, remained the most popular type of handgun.

During the World War II, the American public understood the value of proficiency and knowledge related to firearms. After that devastating war was over, there was a great interest in firearms of all types, but in particular in semi-automatic pistols. Servicemen during the war had been exposed not only to the U.S. service semi-automatic pistol, but to those of other countries. After the war, new developments took place in America, and foreign makers were eager to sell to U. S. markets.

The first edition of GUN DIGEST

Inset: The 2005 GUN DIGEST cover showed Ruger's new Mark III 22 and the company's trim new 45, the model 345. After only appearing four times in almost four decades of the early covers, autoloading pistols were featured on eight of the last 23 covers.

came out in 1944, during the course of World War II. The first edition was well-received, and the second edition of GUN DIGEST was published in 1946, immediately after the war. It soon became an annual reference. It provided historical information, tips and advice on how to shoot various types of firearms, and let post-war America know what guns were available. As time went by, students of firearms realized the publication was a valuable reference to the history and evolution of the types of guns available to the American shooter.

Now, that first thin book has grown to the present 61st edition. With sixty-one editions of GUN DIGEST, we can look back and see the gradual changes in what has been available in various types of rifles, shotguns and handguns. We can also see the pattern of background events that led to the offerings of certain types of guns.

However, nowhere has this evolution been more striking, or the changes more numerous or more dramatic, than the field of what were originally called "automatic" pistols. Starting with just a handful of possibilities in the first edition, this category grew and grew. Today, autoloading pistols form a dominant portion of the volume, far outnumbering revolvers or any specific action type of rifle or shotgun.

So, GUN DIGEST is a useful reference to chronicle the history and development of semi-automatic handguns in the six decades since the first slim volume appeared.

Of course, the "automatic" pistol had been introduced to America long before 1944. In 1900, Colt had introduced the 38-caliber autoloader designed by firearms genius John M. Browning. The cartridge, the 38 Automatic Colt Pistol cartridge (38 ACP) is still produced--more than a century later--as the 38 Super. One of Browning's great achievements came in 1911, when the Browning-designed Colt automatic in 45 ACP was adopted by the United States military. If there was any valid criticism of the Colt 1911, it is that the pistol was so good that it discouraged competition by other makers. Savage and Remington

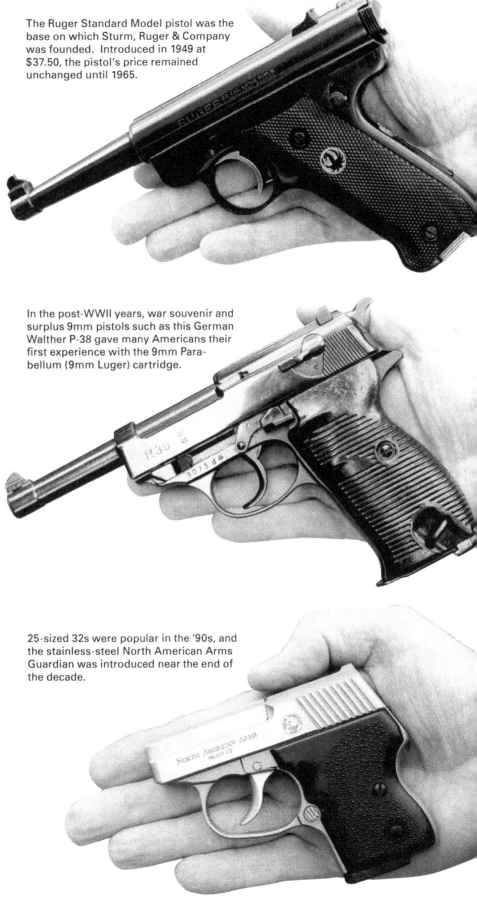

The Ruger Standard Model pistol was the base on which Sturm, Ruger & Company was founded. Introduced in 1949 at $37.50, the pistol's price remained unchanged until 1965.

In the post-WWII years, war souvenir and surplus 9mm pistols such as this German Walther P-38 gave many Americans their first experience with the 9mm Parabellum (9mm Luger) cartridge.

25-sized 32s were popular in the '90s, and the stainless-steel North American Arms Guardian was introduced near the end of the decade.

shelved their designs for 45-caliber service pistols.

Those two makers, and others such as Smith & Wesson, Harrington & Richardson and Warner, did challenge Colt in the field of American pocket pistols, but by the late1930s, only the Colt pocket pistols were left.

The 22-caliber automatic pistol arrived in 1915, actually prior to our entry into the First World War, and was another Colt/Browning design. Today, with a wide variety of dependable 22 pistols from which to choose, it is easy to lose sight of the difficulties Browning faced. The rimfire 22 Long Rifle (22 LR) cartridge had been developed only 28 years before, in 1887. 1915 ammunition was loaded with varieties of black, semi-smokeless, and smokeless powders, all with corrosive priming. The greased lead bullets were only lightly held in very thin copper or brass cases. It amazed experts of the time that the new Colt 22, later to be called the Woodsman, worked so well.

Several variants of the Woodsman were made, and became very popular. Non-corrosive priming arrived in 1926 and high-velocity 22 LR cartridges arrived in 1930. By 1932, competition for the Woodsman had also arrived, in the form of the Hi-Standard 22 automatic. High Standard Manufacturing Co. had acquired a Hartford Arms design for

The Colt Government Model 45 was the only pistol listed in the first edition of GUN DIGEST that continued virtually unchanged into the post-WWII years.

a 22 pistol, and produced it as the Hi-Standard Model B. Similar in shape to the Colt, it was of different construction. Several variations were made in succeeding years.

Colt had brought out several variants of its basic Government Model. In 1929, the 38 Super was introduced. Soon, target versions—the National Match 45 and the Super Match 38—were added. The big frame was adapted to the 22 LR cartridge in the Ace and Service Ace variants.

That was it.

In the period leading up to our involvement in World War II, we had variants of two big-bore automatic pistols, two models of pocket pistols, and a smattering of 22 automatics—all from two manufacturers, Colt and High Standard.

This was the autoloading pistol situation prior to the publication of the first GUN DIGEST in 1944. In addition to the paucity of pre-war self-loading models, wartime production needs meant that few automatic pistols were actually available to civilians.

During the war, the country switched over to wartime production. Firearms that could be used for some military function were kept in production. Others were dropped "for the duration," some to be resumed after the end of hostilities, others to never again be made. The automotive industry also switched to war production, and no cars were made between 1942 and 1945. Ford switched one of its properties to aircraft production, building a mile-long factory that ran 24 hours a day. Parts and materials entered one end, and every hour a four-engine B-24 heavy bomber rolled out the other.

People at home were deeply impressed with the need for guns and shooting. Training programs grew throughout the country to train young men in marksmanship. America was still largely rural then, and hunting was a way to supplement a family's food supply during a period of rationing and "Meatless Tuesdays." Hunting and target shooting continued in the face of a dwindling supply of factory ammunition for civilian use.

The first GUN DIGEST came out in 1944, during this period. There was a tremendous interest in guns and shooting, but except for the *American Rifleman* magazine of the National Rifle Association (NRA), little published in-

The Colt Commander of 1950 was the smallest, lightest 45 that had been produced to that time. It was also made for the 9mm Parabellum cartridge, the first 9mm pistol made in America.

Top Left: In 1957, Smith & Wesson introduced a 22-caliber target pistol, later named the Model 41. The company thus joined Colt, High Standard and Ruger in producing 22 semi-automatic target pistols.

Middle Left: In the mid-1960s, High Standard began using a "military" grip on its line of 22 target pistols, a grip of the same angle as the service Colt 45 pistol.

Bottom Left: After the Gun Control Act of 1968 went into effect, importation of small pistols such as the Walther PPK was no longer allowed.

Below: In 1970, Colt revised its standby Government Model with a collet-type barrel bushing, and it became the Mk. IV / Series '70.

formation was available. The 1944 GUN DIGEST introduced the basic format that was to continue through the years—feature articles, and a catalog section of handguns, rifles and shotguns. The catalog section, of course, could not be accurate, as availability changed markedly during the war. Essentially, the catalog section of the first edition listed the guns made prior to the war. The automatic pistol listings consisted only of the pistols by Colt and High Standard. Colt handguns were the Government Model 45, Super 38, and 22-caliber Ace, and their target models, and the 22-caliber Woodsman series. High Standard listings were all 22s, in the early "letter" series A, B, D and E, offered both as hammerless and visible-hammer models.

After the end of fighting in 1945,

servicemen began returning home. A joke of the time was that returning servicemen were only interested in two things—and the second one was hunting. The first interest created the baby boom. The second created a demand for inexpensive firearms that could be used for hunting and recreational shooting.

The Second Annual Edition came out in 1946, again published by Klein's Sporting Goods. The addition of "Annual" to the name indicated the intention to revise and publish a new edition each year. A note mentioned that the publication had been "revised since the end of World War II." However, the automatic pistol listings were exactly the same as they had been in the first edition. Considering the turbulent state of firearms manufacturing at that time, this was

certainly understandable.

The U.S. firearms industry had problems switching from expanded wartime production to more restricted peacetime production. A number of companies never put some of their prewar offerings back into production, and a new section was added to the second GUN DIGEST. "Discontinued Metallic Cartridge Arms" gave shooters an idea as to what was no longer available.

The Third Edition came out in 1947. Colt listings had been changed to include only the Government Model 45, the Super 38, and the Woodsman Target, Sport and Match Target 22s. The

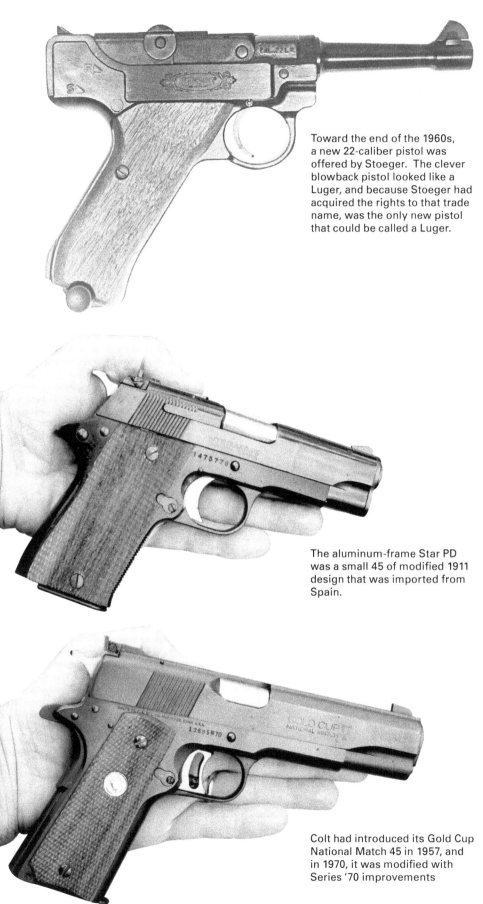

Toward the end of the 1960s, a new 22-caliber pistol was offered by Stoeger. The clever blowback pistol looked like a Luger, and because Stoeger had acquired the rights to that trade name, was the only new pistol that could be called a Luger.

The aluminum-frame Star PD was a small 45 of modified 1911 design that was imported from Spain.

Colt had introduced its Gold Cup National Match 45 in 1957, and in 1970, it was modified with Series '70 improvements

Pocket Model 25 was also included, but it was not actually available.

High Standard pistol listings were reduced to only one model. Only the Model H-D Military (which had been made for the military during the war) was then in production, with 4 1/2- or 6 3/4-inch barrels. A note was included that the Model B hammerless "may be produced in 1947."

"Discontinued Models" was continued as a section, and a new section, "Foreign Sporting Arms," was added. Consisting mostly of rifles and shotguns, there were passing references to automatic pistols, primarily as war souvenirs.

The fourth GUN DIGEST began a tradition that was to serve the publication well in some ways. Brought out in 1948, it was listed as the "4th Annual (1949) Edition." This got it into the hands of hunters before the beginning of the 1948-1949 hunting season, and was the most current listing of available firearms. This tradition has been followed ever since, and explains why the book for each year has been copyrighted the year before.

Automatic pistol listings had changed, but only a little. Colt's big news was the redesign of the Woodsman models. The Woodsman now had a longer grip frame, a slide hold-open, a pushbutton magazine latch, and Coltwood plastic grips. The Government Model 45 and 38 Super were still the flagships of the automatic line.

High Standard still offered the H-D Military, and added a new Model G, a 380 pistol with a barrel lock on the frame to permit easy field-stripping. This was to be the beginning of the interchangeable-barrel system that is still in use in the present day.

More people were interested in handguns, and a new section, "Handgun Facts," was written by Charles Askins, Jr. This section was the predecessor of the "Handguns, Today" sections in the current GUN DIGEST. Askins was the earliest writer of the handguns section, joined in later years by such knowledgeable writers as Julian S. Hatcher, Kent Bellah, Pete

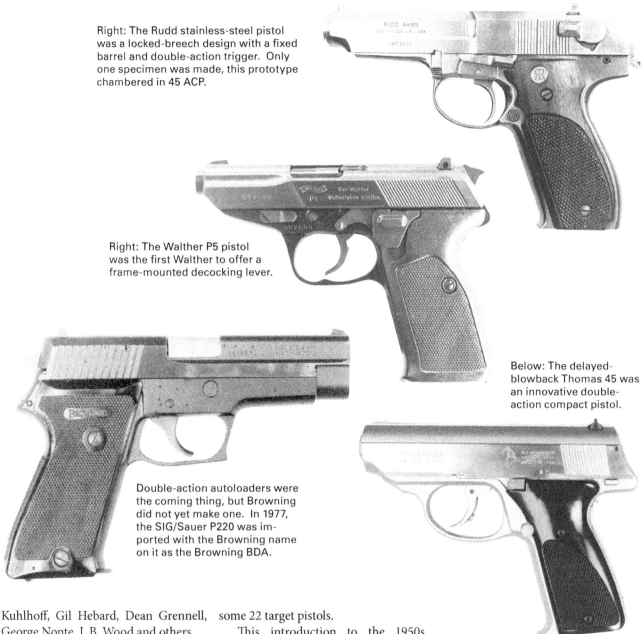

Right: The Rudd stainless-steel pistol was a locked-breech design with a fixed barrel and double-action trigger. Only one specimen was made, this prototype chambered in 45 ACP.

Right: The Walther P5 pistol was the first Walther to offer a frame-mounted decocking lever.

Below: The delayed-blowback Thomas 45 was an innovative double-action compact pistol.

Double-action autoloaders were the coming thing, but Browning did not yet make one. In 1977, the SIG/Sauer P220 was imported with the Browning name on it as the Browning BDA.

Kuhlhoff, Gil Hebard, Dean Grennell, George Nonte, J. B. Wood and others.

Some notable changes were made in the 5th Edition, 1951. Copyrighted and published in 1950, it was still copyrighted by Klein's Sporting Goods, but published by a new entity, The Gun Digest Company. The editor was now John T. Amber, who was to remain in that position for twenty-eight years, through the 33rd Edition, 1979. Charles Askins' report was in the new section, "Handguns Today." A "Foreign Firearms" section made an appearance, with illustrated coverage. In the automatic pistol section were offerings of Astra, Beretta, Bernardelli, Star and Unique, mostly pocket pistols in 25, 32 and 380 calibers, with some 22 target pistols.

This introduction to the 1950s tied in to the changes going on in America.

The 1950s were generally a time of optimism and enthusiasm for America. New cars had once more become available in 1946, but most new designs arrived only in 1949. Styling was to grow more flamboyant and engines more powerful as the '50s went on.

Not even the Korean Conflict of 1950-1953, important as it was, dampened America's enthusiasm. The fighting, however, reinforced the ideas of many that all young men needed firearms training. Shooting clubs, veterans' organizations, police departments and other groups operated youth shooting programs.

Dwight D. Eisenhower was elected President in 1952. The Korean War ended in 1953. "Ike" was reelected in 1956.

Serious motion-picture Westerns—*High Noon*, *Shane* and *Hondo*—were screened in the early '50s. Also, a new medium—television—began a number of popular Western series. Such entertainment increased interest in single-action revolvers and lever-action revolvers, but did little to spur interest in semi-automatic pistols. However, some

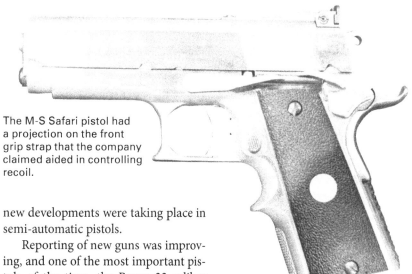

The M-S Safari pistol had a projection on the front grip strap that the company claimed aided in controlling recoil.

new developments were taking place in semi-automatic pistols.

Reporting of new guns was improving, and one of the most important pistols of the time, the Ruger 22-caliber Standard pistol, introduced in 1949, was reported by GUN DIGEST in 1950. This pistol was the one on which Sturm, Ruger & Company was built. 1950 was the year of introduction for the lightweight Colt Commander. With a 4 1/4-inch barrel and weight of 26-1/2 ounces, it was the smallest, lightest 45 automatic made, and was also offered in 38 Super and 9mm Parabellum (9mm Luger). It was the first U. S.-made 9mm pistol. Colt also introduced the Challenger, a low-price version of the Woodsman. High Standard improved new models for competitive target shooting and introduced its Supermatic in 22 LR and the Olympic in 22 Short.

By 1951, Ruger had brought out its Mark I target pistol. That year, High Standard dropped the "letter" designations completely, and had new names for all pistol models.

By 1954, High Standard introduced the simplified Dura-Matic pistol, priced at $37.50 to directly compete with the Ruger Standard. In that year, Smith & Wesson brought out a double-action 9mm pistol. Not numbered for several years, it became the S&W Model 39. In 1954, Belgian-made Browning pistols— the 9mm High Power (HP), the 380 and the little 25—were imported into the postwar American market for the first

The elegant Sokolovsky stainless-steel 45 target pistol had no visible screws or pins...or controls. Everything was operated by subtriggers on either side of the trigger.

time.

1956 saw some modifications of previous designs. The Colt Huntsman was another modified Woodsman, and Sears, Roebuck's J. C. Higgins Model 80 was a High Standard Dura-Matic with some cosmetic changes. (Yes, Sears sold pistols without government paperwork in those carefree days.)

Two new designs also appeared. The Whitney Wolverine was a completely new 22 pistol by firearms designer Robert L. Hillberg. With an aluminum frame and futuristic styling, the light new 22 was unlike anything made before. Praised for its natural pointing features, the Whitney fell victim to company financial problems and disappeared by the early 1960s.

One of the most ambitious new projects of 1956 was the Kimball pistol. It was chambered for the 30 Carbine cartridges that were available as surplus. The Kimball was a delayed blowback design that proved to be not satisfactory for the pressure of the cartridge. The few made are collector items, but the Kimball foreshadowed later attempts to produce handguns for this cartridge.

In 1957, S&W introduced their 22-caliber target pistol. Introduced without a model number, it soon became the S&W Model 41. Target shooters now had a choice of Colt, High Standard, Ruger or S&W pistols for 22-caliber competition. Colt also introduced its new 45-caliber National Match pistol, the Gold Cup. The new match pistol was considerably more refined than the pre-war National Match, which had not been produced again following the war. Bullseye target shooting was a popular sport in the '50s, and a number of custom gunsmiths were building "accurized" 45s. The appearance of the Gold Cup National Match provided a readily-available pistol that was satisfactory for competition. It soon became the standard target pistol for 45-caliber shooting.

1958 saw more refined target models from High Standard. The Colt 25 had not been produced after WWII, but there was a market for a small 25. In 1958, Colt introduced the Colt "Junior"

25, made in Spain by Astra.

Entry-level shooters in the bullseye target sport were price-conscious, and in 1959, S&W offered its 22-caliber Model 46. Mechanically the same as the Model 41, the new Model 46 had plastic grips and a dull finish, and sold at a substantially lower price.

By the latter part of the 1950s, military modernization was taking place. Governments all over the world were clearing their armories of obsolete military equipment, including firearms and ammunition. Most of these items were sold to private citizens in the country with the greatest degree of personal freedom—the United States. Many previously little-known automatic pistols were among the items imported during the late '50s and into the '60s. American shooters had their first chance to try out Lugers, Walthers, Mausers, Astras, Radoms and other foreign pistols. The pistols were fed with inexpensive surplus ammunition, predominantly 9mm. It was the first time the average shooter had a chance to gain experience with the 9mm round, and set the stage for its later acceptance.

As the guns changed in the 1950s, so did the GUN DIGEST. The "Handgun Review" section, which still combined automatics and revolvers, was a standard feature in every issue. The catalog section relating to American-made autoloaders had grown from a few models made by two companies to a full four pages which featured the pistols of five different companies. In the order of the listings, handguns still came in third behind rifles and shotguns, but this would change with time. Foreign guns were still considered separately, but more and more were being imported, and the foreign handguns were mostly automatics. By the end of the decade, foreign-made autoloaders filled five pages.

With the 1955 edition, a semi-automatic pistol appeared for the first time on the cover of GUN DIGEST. A 9mm Smith & Wesson pistol appeared on both the front and back covers. A single-action version of the S&W Model 39, the pictured Model 44 was never produced.

Most shooters of the '50s were not aware that there was a growing anti-gun sentiment among some public officials. To make people aware, GUN DIGEST dedicated its 1953 edition to the National Rifle Association and encouraged NRA membership. Annual membership was $4, and Junior membership was 50 cents.

The 1960s began as an extension of the 1950s, but changed drastically before the end of the decade.

In 1960, John F. Kennedy was elected President of the United States. When he took office, he was a Life Member of the NRA, as had been Eisenhower and previous presidents. Kennedy was no stranger to firearms, and while a Senator, had acquired an M1 Garand from the Director of Civilian Marksmanship (DCM). Kennedy did not serve his full term. On November 22, 1963, he was assassinated under circumstances that arouse speculation to this day. Officially, a lone killer with unknown motives had committed the murder with a surplus military rifle.

As a result, gun-control advocates stepped up their demands for further restrictions on firearms. Senator Thomas Dodd added surplus military rifles to a restrictive bill he was preparing.

The Civil War Centennial period, 1961-1965, created some new interest in firearms, but primarily the percussion re-

Above: In 1986, Smith & Wesson offered its first 45-caliber semi-automatic pistol, the Model 645.

Left: ODI introduced the 45-caliber Viking, a 1911 design with the Seecamp double-action mechanism.

volvers and rifles used during the Civil War.

By the mid-1960s, the United States was involved in Viet Nam. Protests began against American involvement. Somehow, in the minds of some, firearms became involved with the Asian war. A political viewpoint was formed that was both anti-war and anti-gun.

The 1966 killings at the University of Texas, and the 1968 assassinations of Robert F. Kennedy and Martin Luther King added momentum to the anti-gun bandwagon. In 1968, the year of the Tet Offensive in Vietnam, the Gun Control Act of 1968 (GCA 68) was passed by Congress and signed into law by President Lyndon B. Johnson. The GCA 68, among other things, stopped importation of many firearms, including surplus firearms, placed restrictions on all firearms made after 1898, and initiated federal restrictions for purchasers of firearms.

It was the passing of an era. In that same year, traditional family TV enter-

The 9mm MAB PA-15 was a 15-shot pistol imported from France.

tainment such as "The Andy Griffith Show" went off the air.

In other forms of entertainment, a change was also obvious. The Beatles, who had achieved popularity in the United States in 1964 with their harmonic versions of rock-and-roll songs, gradually evolved during the '60s into a group performing songs that involved protest and drug use.

The '60s were to involve some changes in the handguns America preferred. In 1960, America was still a revolver country. The 1961 15th Edition GUN DIGEST, which came out in late 1960, showed this in its catalog section. Under "U. S. Handguns," nine pages were devoted to revolvers, and only four to pistols (which included single-shots as well as autoloaders). The foreign handguns, however, were represented by 27 automatics and only three revolvers. During the decade, American interest in autoloading handguns would increase.

In 1961, Colt celebrated its 125th anniversary, and in that year introduced the new 38 Special Gold Cup National Match. High Standard was the largest maker of 22-caliber handguns in the world, but other companies were making 22s. Browning introduced a new 22 LR automatic that year. Walther was importing its Model PP Sport in 22 LR.

By 1962, the Browning 22 line had grown to the Nomad, the Challenger and the Medalist, with increasing fea-

tures and prices. Smith & Wesson, not to be outdone by Colt's 38 Special auto, brought out the S&W Model 52 target pistol in 38 Special.

Bullseye target shooting remained very popular and High Standard, S&W and Ruger all introduced bull-barrel 22-caliber target pistols in the mid-60s. By that time, Browning was considered an American, rather than a foreign, company. Also in the mid-60s, an unusual pistol, the Universal Enforcer, was introduced. The Enforcer was a 30-caliber 30-shot pistol with a 12-inch barrel, based on the M1 Carbine. It was the first of a type that would later be demonized as "assault pistols."

In 1965, High Standard introduced its "military-grip" autoloaders, with a grip angle the same as that of the military 19llA1 pistol. The Ruger Standard, which had been introduced in 1949 at a price of $37.50, had its first price increase, to $41.50. Sixteen years of production before a price hike is a record that still stands. The Heckler & Koch HK4 was imported, a novel pistol with interchangeable barrels for 22 LR, 25, 32 and 380.

At the end of the decade, after the passage of GCA 68, little new came from the major manufacturers. Colt put out a series of four World War I commemorative 45 autos. Browning dropped the 25- and 380-caliber pistols due to the new import restrictions.

However, in 1969, two companies introduced new 22-caliber autoloaders. The Sterling pistols were full-size pistols with external hammers and fixed barrels. They looked quite a bit like the early Hi-Standard autos. The other offering was the Stoeger 22-caliber Luger pistol. Stoeger held the trademark on the "Luger" name, and used it for the new pistol, a clever blowback design that had a striking resemblance to the original German pistol.

There were changes in GUN DIGEST

during the 1960s. There were a number of editorials relating to the assassinations, proposed legislation and the passage of the Gun Control Act. GUN DIGEST's tradition of putting out each year's edition during the previous year fell afoul of the timing of these events. The Kennedy murder took place in November 1963, after the 1964 edition had been published. Thus, the 1965 edition was the first that had an editorial touching on the tragedy and its effect on the right to bear arms. In similar fashion, the 1970 edition contained the first editorial response to the Gun Control Act of 1968. During the decade, more feature articles dealing with semi-automatic pistols were included, by writers such as Gil Hebard, Larry Sterrett, Kent Bellah, James B. Stewart and Raymond Caranta.

In the 1965/19th Edition, the Townsend Whelen Award was announced, to honor Whelen, who had died in 1961. It offered a $500 prize "for significant contributions to the literature of guns and shooting." The third Townsend Whelen Award presented (23rd-1969 Edition) was won by Raymond Caranta for his feature, "History of French Handguns."

The country moved into the 1970s. In the aftermath of the GCA 68, the restrictions contained in that law kept many ordinary people from acquiring firearms. Because the restrictions applied to those who obeyed laws, criminals ignored them. In the framework of rebellion against authority and drug use by increasing numbers of the younger population, the crime rate skyrocketed.

In the face of increasing crime, many people thought more seriously about guns for protection. Many of the small foreign pistols previously favored were prohibited by GCA 68. Soon, American manufacturers began providing pistols to fill the niche.

Politically and economically, the '70s were a turbulent time. Richard Nixon was reelected President in 1972, but the Watergate scandal forced his resignation, and Gerald Ford assumed the office. A messy retreat from Vietnam did not sit well with America. In 1976, the year of the nation's Bicentennial, Jimmy Carter was elected President.

One of Carter's campaign points had been the increasing rate of inflation, caused initially by the Organization of Petroleum Exporting Countries (OPEC)'s severe cutback on oil production in 1973. Before Carter's term was over, the Arabs turned off the tap again in 1979, and inflation soared to record levels. The uncertainty caused many businesses to founder or fail.

These conditions also affected the firearms industry. However, interest in autoloading pistols was still strong, and the Gun Control Act actually stimulated the development of new models in the United States. Redesigned foreign pistols began coming back in. George Nonte called this "rebellion by compliance," a situation in which prohibited guns were revised and dressed up to qualify for importation.

An indication of the rapid development of the autoloading handgun during the 1970s is the situation involving the 45 automatic. Surplus 45s were popular, and both custom and home gunsmiths were building target pistols from them. However, in 1970, only one American company—Colt—was making new 45 automatics. In that year, Colt had introduced its Mark IV Series '70 variation, which used a finger-type collet barrel bushing.

Toward the end of the decade, other new designs of 45 ACP pistols, both American and foreign, had begun to arrive on the scene. The Thomas 45 of 1977 was a compact American-made 45 with a unique retarded blowback system. The Spanish Star PD was a compact aluminum-frame locked-breech pistol. Sterling, a company that had started making pistols after GCA 68, developed and displayed (but never commercially produced) their model 450, a double-action 45. Hawes, an American company, by 1977, imported under its name the SIG/Sauer P220 in 45 ACP chambering. Soon, Browning imported the same P220 pistol as the Browning BDA 45.

The Detonics 45, an innovative scaled-down 45 based on a highly-modified 1911 design, appeared on the market. Crown City, a company that had made parts, decided to make complete pistols, essentially slightly-modified 1911s. The Essex company made 1911-type frames and slides, and surplus parts were available to build complete pistols. Later in the decade, AMT brought out its line of all-stainless-steel 1911-type 45s. These included the Combat Government, the Hardballer (adjustable-sight target version) and the Long Slide Hardballer (with a 7-inch barrel). Llama 45s, modified from the 1911 design, were imported from Spain.

The Heckler & Koch P9S arrived in 1977, first in 9mm and then in 45. The Rudd pistol, an innovative double-action 45, was displayed in prototype but never produced. The Vega, another 1911 lookalike, did go into production. Mossberg advertised, but did not produce, its AIG "Combat Model" pistol, based on a Clerke design.

Other new pistols, primarily small ones, but some large, were designed and manufactured by both old and new companies during the 1970s. The Walther PPK was made in a slightly larger version, the PPK/S, to meet the absurd point system of GCA 68. American-made small pocket pistols also appeared from old companies. S&W brought out its 22 LR Model 61 Escort, and Colt introduced an American-made Colt Junior 25, a new copy of the Astra Cub pistol.

A new company, American Firearms Manufacturing Company, brought out a new stainless-steel 25 auto. The company would later become American Derringer, and would continue the little 25 in with its line of double derringers. From across the seas came the Astra Constable and the Beretta Model 90, modern double-action pocket pistols. The Heckler & Koch HK4 four-caliber pistol qualified for importation by Harrington & Richardson.

With all the interest in pocket pistols, there was a new niche developing. Interest in long-range pistol silhouette shooting and handgun hunting had opened opportunities for more powerful pistols. The '70s saw the introduction of the AutoMag (44 AutoMag) and

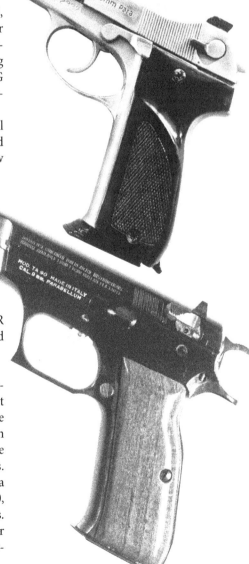

Below: This rare LES P-18 Rojak pistol was the stainless-steel American counterpart of the Austrian Steyr GB pistol.

Bottom: Another CZ 75 clone was the TA-90, made by Tanfoglio of Italy.

the Wildey (45 Winchester Magnum), semi-automatic pistols of much greater power than had previously been produced in a practical autoloader.

As the 1970s wound down, the trends had already begun to develop that would reach a peak in the next decade. These trends were double-action (DA) trigger mechanisms, large-capacity magazines, and stainless-steel construction. Not every new design had all of them, but the trends seemed clear. The DA Smith & Wesson 59, with its 14-round magazine, was introduced about 1973. A few years later, the 18-shot Steyr P-18, and its American counterpart, the stainless-steel LES Rojak P-18, were offered. The HK VP70Z, an 18-shot DAO pistol originally designed as a combination pistol/submachine-gun, was approved for importation as a pistol.

Gun Digest itself changed during the decade of the '70s. Foreign guns became such a part of the American handgun scene that U. S. and foreign pistols were grouped together for the first time, and were just listed alphabetically in the catalog section. More feature articles had autoloading handguns as their subjects. Articles about autoloading pistols by Jeff Cooper, Raymond Caranta, George C. Nonte, Mason Williams, Larry Sterrett, James B. Stewart, J. B. Wood, Kenneth L. Waters and others appeared.

The Townsend Whelen awards, which in the early years seemed to favor rifle topics, were presented in 1978 to Donald M. Simmons for "The Remington Model 51," and in 1979 to Dennis

Riordan for "The Model of 1911 Colt."

Toward the end of the decade, runaway inflation made it difficult to keep prices current, and some guns were listed in the catalog section without prices.

The company identification had changed from "Gun Digest Publishing Co." in the 25th-1971 Edition to "Digest Books, Inc." the following year. By the 30th-1976 Edition, it was DBI Books. In the last edition published during the 1970s, John T. Amber had stepped down after 28 years as editor. A new editor, Ken Warner, was at the helm.

The decade of the '80s began with the election of Ronald Reagan as President in November 1980. In March 1981, only a few weeks after taking office, President Reagan was shot, and three others were also injured. Anti-gun forces prepared to use the incident to further their program of further restrictions. However, Reagan stated publicly that he saw no need for additional gun controls.

Economic problems still remained, but whereas President Carter had blamed Americans for a "malaise," President Reagan voiced his optimism and enthusiasm for America. Conditions slowly improved, and he was reelected in 1984.

In 1986, the Firearms Owners Protection Act was passed which modified a number of the provisions of Gun Control Act of 1968. One of the most visible was the resumption, after almost two decades, of importation of surplus firearms.

In 1988, George H. W. Bush was elected President. Bush was not particularly supportive of firearms rights. After the killing of five schoolchildren in Stockton, California in 1989, the useless "Gun Free School Zone" legislation was passed in 1990.

The Berlin Wall came down in 1989.

The small Beretta 22 Short pistol of the 1950s evolved into the double-action Model 21 in 22 Long Rifle.

Then, from the standpoint of automatic pistols, the breakup of the Soviet Union opened the door to the importation of new and surplus handguns from the area behind the Iron Curtain.

The first Shooting, Hunting, Outdoor Trade Show (SHOT Show) had been held in January 1979, as a trade show specifically aimed at the shooting and hunting aspects of outdoor sports. Organized by the National Sport Shooting Foundation (NSSF), the new annual show grew steadily through the next decade. The show was to be a factor in providing accurate information on the types of autoloading handguns available each year.

Automatic pistols at the beginning of the 1980s continued the trends of the late 1970s. However, there was a veritable explosion of creativity, and autoloaders gained prominence. There were more double actions, more stainless-steel pistols. The 9mm seemed to be the most popular round, but the 45 got plenty of attention. American police, wedded to the revolver in the previous decades, were adopting automatics in the 1980s.

The category some called the "wondernine" pistols had expanded. With large-capacity magazines and DA triggers, often stainless, the new 9mms were offered by many makers. Development was encouraged by the fact that the U. S. military was conducting testing for a new 9mm pistol to replace the 45. The tests rejuvenated the 9mm/45 controversy, but on January 14, 1985,

A 45-caliber BackUp pistol was introduced by AMT in the middle 1990s. Double-action-only, it was made of stainless steel.

the United States adopted the Beretta 9mm pistol as the M9. Commercially, it was sold as the Model 92 SB.

Many companies got into the "wondernine" business during the 1980s. At least four copies of the CZ 75 were offered before the original pistol became available. The Swiss-made AT-84 was handled by Action Arms. FIE offered the Italian TZ 9, and Excam the Italian TA-90. Springfield introduced their P9.

Other foreign designs, such as the South African Mamba pistol, the Spanish pistols Llama Omni and Astra A-80 and Star Models 28 and 30, the French MAB P-15, and the Italian Bernardelli PO 18 were offered. The Browning HP was made in a DA version. The Ruger P85 took a long time getting into production, but eventually joined the group. The 15-shot Walther P88 was a German entry.

One of the most influential new 9mms was the Austrian Glock 17. With a frame of polymer plastic, the 17-shot Glock was immediately denounced by anti-gun politicians as able to pass undetected through airport security devices. It would not, of course, but even long after DC police adopted the Glock, Capital Hill anti-gunners continued to rail against "plastic pistols" that were useful only to criminals and terrorists. The Glock's unique action caused the re-evaluation of other mechanisms.

Even amidst a flood of new larger-capacity nines, the 45 auto received plenty of attention. Most, but not all, of the new 45s were copies or modifications of the basic 1911 design. Colt offered its Series '80 pistols, which had a new firing-pin block. A stainless version was offered, and (since the Detonics had already demonstrated the feasibility of a very small 45) the scaled-down Colt Officers ACP was introduced. ODI brought out a commercial 1911-type pistol with a Seecamp double-action trigger system.

During the decade, new copies of the basic 1911 design were offered by Springfield Armory and Auto-Ordnance (Thompson). The Randall company made stainless-steel versions, and then brought out a dramatic true left-hand variant, in which every part was reversed. Randall went out of business during the decade, but a new left-hand pistol, the Falcon Portsider, appeared. Unfortunately for southpaws, Falcon also disappeared.

M-S Safari offered 1911-style pistols, distinguished by a projection on the front strap of the frame that provided a hollow place for the shooter's middle finger. Many felt the configuration helped control recoil. The company closed down, but the Safari-style pistols were acquired and continued in production by Olympic Arms.

Large-frame Spanish Llama 45s were built on the 1911 design, but not all parts would interchange with the Colt. The original Detonics company had gone out of business, but a new company, called New Detonics, took over. The Arminex Tri-Fire pistol was generally based on the 1911, with a number of modifications. The "Tri-Fire" name came from its ability to switch barrels and parts and use 45 ACP, 38 Super or 9mm ammunition.

Not all the new 45s of the '80s were based on the 1911 design. The Sokolovsky was a gorgeous (and expensive) stainless-steel pistol with no external screws, pins or controls. All operations were controlled by two "subtriggers" on either side of the actual trigger. The German Korth and Korriphila pistols were also of unique design and were also in the expensive category. The British Victory pistol was introduced in 45 ACP and other chamberings. Magnum Research planned to market it in the United States, but the pistol never reached full production status. The SIG/Sauer P220 was imported into America, this time under its own name.

Smith & Wesson, a company that had made large numbers of 45 ACP revolvers, finally introduced a 45 automatic. The double-action Model 645, introduced in 1985, was followed in 1986 by the limited-production single-action Model 745.

Small pistols were in demand. The Budischowsky TP-70 design was made in small quantities by a succession of companies. Other small 22- and 25-caliber pistols were offered by companies such as Wilkinson, Iver Johnson, Raven, RG, Jennings, Seecamp (the Seecamp 25 was modified later into a 32), Sterling and Bauer. CB Arms introduced the 22-caliber Double Deuce. The company changed to Steel City Arms, then Desert Arms, with few pistols produced.

New 32- and 380-caliber pistols were offered by Davis, Sterling and TDE (later AMT). A new polymer-frame 380, the Grendel P-10, was introduced in 1987. Small 9mm pistols were represented by the Detonics Pocket Nine and the Sirkis (later Sardius) DAO 9mm. Both of these early attempts at a very small 9mm were blowbacks, and shooters complained of heavy felt recoil.

More powerful pistols also found a market. The Coonan 357 was a modified 1911 design that handled the 357 Mag-

By 1991, 9mm Stallard-design pistols were offered with aluminum frames and in larger calibers. During the '90s, the variations were all marketed under the name "Hi-Point."

num revolver cartridge. The Eagle pistol, an Israeli design handled by Magnum Research, was also offered as a 357 Magnum. Before the decade ended, the pistol was called the Desert Eagle, and was also available as a 44 Magnum. The LAR Grizzly, looking like a 1911 on steroids, was offered in 45 Winchester Magnum. The AMT AutoMag III was offered in 30 Carbine in 1989, filling a

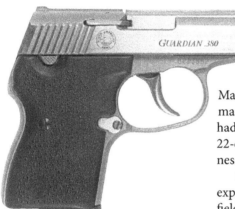

Top: The Taurus PT 145, introduced after the turn of the century, is a compact polymer 45.

Above: Following the success of their 32-caliber Guardian, North American brought out an enlarged version in 380.

niche the old Kimball of the '50s could not. Dornaus & Dixon introduced the Bren Ten, chambered for a new 10mm cartridge that got a nod from pistol guru Jeff Cooper.

During the 1980s, a new class of semi-automatic pistol became popular. The new pistols were large and vaguely resembled submachine guns. In the early years of the decade, writer J. B. Wood called them an "as yet unnamed category." It did not take long for the anti-gunners to hate them, and "assault pistol" was the name applied. Used frequently by the major media, the term, unfortunately, has stuck.

The Universal Enforcer in 30 Car-

bine was still made. However, the category was now also represented by the Bushmaster 223, the Ingram M-10 (45) and M-11 (9mm), the 9mm Inter-dynamic KG-9 (later KG-99), the UZI pistol, the Holmes MP83, the Goncz and Claridge high-tech pistols, the Intratec TEC-9, the 45-caliber Encom, and the Calico 9mm, with its 100-round helical magazine.

Not all developments were so spectacular. 22-caliber pistols quietly remained popular for hunting, plinking and target shooting. The Ruger Standard pistol had passed the One Million mark by 1988, and had been modified into the Ruger Mark II. However, the High Standard Manufacturing Company, which had made 22 automatics since 1932, and had been the largest manufacturer of 22-caliber handguns, went out of business in late 1984.

GUN DIGEST noted the tremendous expansion of the autoloading handgun field. Autoloading handguns now came first in the catalog section. More and more articles about semiauto pistols appeared. In the 36th-1982 Edition, the cover showed a Heckler & Koch P9S Target pistol. That same issue instituted the John T. Amber Literary Award, to honor Amber, the editor emeritus. The new award, which doubled the previous monetary prize, replaced the original Townsend Whelen Award. Amber himself died later in the decade, in 1986. By the end of the decade, in 1989, the John T. Amber Award was awarded to John Malloy for "Early Rivals of the Model 1911 45 Automatic," a history of early autoloaders that had challenged the Colt design.

Much happened during the 1990s, and some events influenced the world of autoloading pistols.

The Gulf War of early 1991 was over quickly, and Americans were impressed with the power of the military. However, the Los Angeles riots of April 1992, in which over 50 people were killed, and

the August 1992 tragedy at Ruby Ridge, where government agents killed people at their home, made many uncomfortable with the idea that the government could provide protection for them.

Bill Clinton was elected in November 1992, and the Clinton Justice Department was involved in the killing of at least 74 people near Waco, Texas on April 19, 1993.

Politicians wanted more gun control, and in 1994, the "Brady Bill" and the "Assault Weapons Ban" took effect. In 1996, Clinton was reelected, but Congress reflected gains in pro-gun members. At the state level, "Shall Issue" concealed-carry laws were passed in a number of states.

The tragic murders at Columbine High School, near Littleton, Colorado, occurred on April 19, 1999. The tragedy was played up by the major media, and more calls for restrictive gun control were prompted.

Not content with the way the legislative process was working, a number of municipal politicians began to sue the firearms industry. The excuse was that crimes committed by people with guns cost the cities money. The real intent seemed to be to force companies out of business through legal costs.

All this had an effect on the firearms industry, but did not stop the creativity and the development that had characterized the previous decade. More use of injection-moulded polymers (we no longer said "plastic") created new opportunities for makers of autoloading pistols.

The 1990 introduction of the 40 Smith & Wesson cartridge took some of the fun out of discussions as to whether the 9mm or the 45 ACP was the better cartridge. AMT actually beat Smith & Wesson into production with a 40 S&W, but soon the S&W 4006 appeared. The FBI had adopted the 10mm, but few agents could handle the full-power load well, and a reduced load (some called it "10mm Lite") was used. S&W shrewdly realized that a smaller cartridge could duplicate the reduced load, and the smaller round could be used in smaller pistols. The 40 S&W caught on rapidly, and within a short time, SIG, Taurus, Glock, Browning, Star, Heckler & Koch, Auto-Ordnance, Springfield and others were offering pistols for it.

The Assault Weapons Ban (AWB) of September 1994 had a greater impact on automatic pistols than on the rifles it purported to restrict. With magazine capacity restricted to 10 rounds, interest waned in the large-capacity full-size wondernine. A large-capacity pistol without a large-capacity magazine lost some of its appeal. 9mm pistols became smaller, with magazines that would just hold the "legal limit" of 10 rounds. So, smaller guns, with shorter grips, became popular. Polymer plastic as a frame material allowed lighter pistols, faster production and lower-priced offerings. This situation fit well with the nationwide interest in "license-to-carry" legislation that was growing from state to state.

The 45 ACP was seen with even greater favor. Seven or eight rounds of 45 didn't look so bad when compared with ten rounds of 9mm.

Still, large-capacity pistols did not fade away. Many companies had, before the AWB went into effect, cranked out as many big magazines as they could, and offered these as an incentive with their larger pistols.

New cartridges arrived during the '90s. Colt introduced the 9x23, sort of a rimless 38 Super with a reinforced case to take high pressure. In 1993, S&W brought out the 356 TSW (Team Smith & Wesson), a somewhat similar round. AMT brought out the 400 Cor-Bon (a 45 ACP necked to 40) and the 440 Cor-Bon (a 50 AE necked to 44). The 41, 44 and 45 Wildey Magnums were the company's 475 Magnum case necked down appropriately.

Companies came and went. FIE and Excam went, but two companies, Quality Firearms, Inc. (QFI) and European American Armory (EAA) picked up most of the lines of imported pistols.

The Bren Ten had disappeared, but a slightly-modified version was marketed in 1991 as the Peregrine Falcon. It too disappeared after a short while.

Mossberg got back into the pistol business in 1996, planning to market Israeli IMI pistols under the name UZI Eagle.

The arrangement ended three years later, with few pistols actually sold.

The LAR Grizzly, a giant 1911-style pistol, started out as a 45 Winchester Magnum and added new chamberings throughout the '90s, including 50 AE. By the end of the decade, however, the Grizzly was no longer made.

The major companies were active. Colt brought out the Double Eagle 45 in 1990. In 1991, the company introduced its lower-price line of 45s, the 1991A1 series. Colt's 9mm All-American 2000, the polymer DAO pistol, didn't work out, and was dropped in 1994. Colt had not made a 22 since the Woodsman, but in 1994 brought out the Colt Cadet, with a Woodsman slant to the grip, and the Colt Target 22 the next year.

Smith & Wesson expanded its line of 9mm, 40 and 45-caliber autos, with conventional double-action and DAO versions. In 1994, the polymer-frame Sigma series made its debut. In 1995, the 45-caliber Model 645 was replaced by the 4506. By 1997, a new line of redesigned 22 pistols appeared.

Ruger also expanded its pistol line, bringing out the 22-caliber Model 22/45 in 1992. The polymer frame had the same grip angle as a 1911. The centerfire line grew, with polymer frames included.

Beretta introduced the Cougar, a compact pistol with a rotating barrel lock, in 1994. Soon, a Mini-Cougar appeared.

Springfield, in early 1994, introduced a wide-frame 45 with a 13-round magazine. The AWB of later that year refocused the emphasis on the company's line of standard 1911 pistols and 10-shot compacts.

Heckler & Koch introduced the new USP (Universal Self-Loading Pistol) line in 1993, in 9mm and 40 S&W. By 1996, the USP and a new Mark 23 were available in 45 ACP.

Glock had introduced subcompact versions of its original pistols by 1996. A year later, subcompacts in 10mm and 45 were added.

AMT introduced its On Duty, an aluminum-frame departure from its stainless-steel tradition, about 1994. The AutoMag line expanded to 45 Winchester Magnum

and 10mm, and later to 50 AE. In 1992, the DAO BackUp 380 arrived. A larger DAO BackUp was offered a few years later. By the end of the decade, in 1998, the rights to manufacture most AMT pistols had been acquired by Galena Industries.

SIGarms brought out a P220 "American" version with side magazine release button, and in 1996, the P239, the first SIG made in the USA, was offered.

Some companies came into prominence during the '90s. Kahr introduced its stainless-steel K9 pistol in 1994. The company expanded, and by the end of the decade, had acquired Auto-Ordnance.

Para-Ordnance, having got its start by making large-capacity replacement frames for 1911 pistols, began marketing complete guns in 1990.

Kel-Tec, with the experience of the polymer-frame Grendel pistols on which to draw, introduced its 14-ounce 11-shot DAO 9mm, the P-11, in 1995. The P-11 introduced a whole new category of popular pistols for concealed carry. It was light, simple to use, shot a relatively powerful cartridge, and didn't cost a whole lot. It was soon made in 40-caliber in 1997. By then, Heritage had introduced its Stealth polymer-frame pistol in 9mm, soon also in 40. In 1997, Republic Arms entered the category with a polymer-frame DAO 45.

Some pistols came with a story. The Raven was a reliable, inexpensive 25 auto, but the factory had burned down in 1984. The design was acquired by another

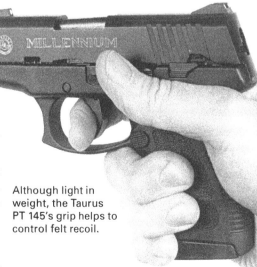

Although light in weight, the Taurus PT 145's grip helps to control felt recoil.

The FN Five-seveN, a 20-shot polymer pistol designed originally for military and law enforcement uses, was announced in 2002. It uses a high-velocity bottleneck cartridge, the 5.7x28.

company, and figuratively "rising from the ashes," the new company became Phoenix Arms. By 1993, Phoenix had added a nice little 22-caliber pistol to its line. Other small companies were active. Lorcin introduced 32 and 380 pistols in 1992. The Wyoming Arms Parker pistol was modified into the Laseraim pistol in 1993.

The 9mm blowback Maverick pistol became the Stallard in 1990. Then, 40- and 45-caliber versions were added in 1991, as the Iberia and Haskell pistols. To avoid confusion, they were all marketed under the name Hi-Point a few years later. Hi-Point grew, and became a leading producer of low-priced but dependable handguns.

Kimber, a rifle company, got into the making of 1911-style pistols in the mid-1990s. The company went into it in a big way, and became one of the leading makers of 1911-type pistols.

Several custom pistol makers realized that many of their customers wanted pistols that were basically similar. They offered such variations as production items. Thus, the appearance of "production custom" pistols, mostly 1911s, took place in the '90s.

GUN DIGEST covered all this, of course. Autoloading handguns were becoming a greater part of the shooting world. They were always listed first now in the catalog section, and filled 38 pages by the end of the decade. Numerous articles, by writers such as Gene Gangarosa, Lee Arten, C. Rodney James, J. B. Wood, C. E. Harris, Holt Bodinson and Raymond Caranta discussed semi-automatic pistols. One automatic pistol piece, "Blowback Nines" by John Malloy, won the John T. Amber Award for 1993.

The covers featured autoloaders three times. On the 1991-45th Edition, two SIG/Sauer pistols were featured. Two years later, the new Ruger 22/45 appeared. Then, the next edition featured the Heckler & Koch USP pistol.

Following the publication of the 1996-50th Edition, J. B. Wood stepped down, after having written the "Handguns Today, Autoloaders" section for 15 years. John Malloy filled in at that position, and Wood continued to have articles about semi-automatic pistols included.

After the 1990s ended, January 1, 2000 arrived on schedule without much trouble. There had been substantial concern about "Y2K," the possibility of widespread computer failure, as the new year clicked into place. Prudent people had made preparations just in case, and part of the preparations of many involved the protection afforded by firearms.

George W. Bush was elected President of the United States—not in November 2000, but over a month after Election Day—after lengthy court proceedings over vote counts.

On September 11, 2001, America was attacked. Terrorists in highjacked jetliners killed thousands of people. The U. S. economy, already in a slump, went into a nosedive. For a while, the only things selling well were American flags, gas masks, Bibles and… firearms. A lot of people wanted a dependable handgun. The U. S. military responded to the threat of further terrorist action with strikes in Afghanistan, and in March 2003 went into Iraq.

2004 was a significant year for gunowners. On September 13, 2004, the "Assault Weapons Ban" did actually sunset. It was the only time in the memory of many that an onerous gun law had gone away. On November 4 of that year, George W. Bush was reelected.

The period following the 1990s has thus been a time of change for the firearms world. By 2000, lawsuits had driven Lorcin out of business, and other companies were hard-pressed. Colt discontinued almost all its handgun line, including guns introduced only the year before. Only a few 1911 models, in 45 ACP only, and single-action revolvers were retained. Colt recovered, and the product line gradually increased again. Galena took the AMT operation from hostile California to Sturgis, SD, but things did not work out. By late 2001, AMT was gone. The Davis, Talon and Republic companies were out of business by 2002.

However, useful designs are sometimes just not allowed to fade away. In 2002, Cobra Enterprises had been formed, and was offering improved Davis, Talon and Republic pistol designs again. In 2003, Lorcin-style guns had been added to the Cobra line. In 2004, the newly-formed Crusader Group, which included High Standard, had acquired AMT designs. AMT BackUp and AutoMag pistols were put back into production by 2005.

The 1911 design, with its 100th birthday just down the road, has never been more popular. Besides the traditional Colt offerings, companies such as Springfield, Olympic, Kimber and others had already gone heavily into 1911 production before 2000. Dan Wesson, a name related to revolvers since 1968, introduced its own 1911 line in the year 2000. That same year, High Standard also added a line of 1911 45s. In 2001, Century International Arms brought out an offering of 1911 pistols.

Smith & Wesson introduced their SW1911 in 1903, and Sigarms followed the next year with their 1911-type GSR pistol. In 2005, new 1911 pistols from Taurus, U. S. Fire Arms and Iver Johnson also entered the market. Colt has "reissued" older models such as the original World War I-type 1911, the military-style 1911A1 pistol of World War II, the Series '70 and the pre-'70 Government Model.

Polymer frames have become more widespread. Browning brought out its PRO-9 and PRO-40 pistols in 2003. Beretta, between 2000 and 2005, introduced its 9000S polymer compact pistol, its 22-caliber U22 NEOS and the new modular Storm Px4 pistol. Glock, a leader in polymer usage, added its Model 36, a compact single-column 45 ACP, and its later offerings for the new 45 G.A.P. (45 Glock Automatic Pistol) cartridge—the models 37, 38 and 39.

Hi-Point had used polymer for some time, with smaller-caliber 380 and 9mm models. In 2002, the company began phasing in polymer-frame 40- and 45-caliber pistols. HS America had introduced its HS2000 pistol, a polymer-frame design from Croatia with a "Glock-type" trigger, in 2000. By 2002, the design was modified and offered by Springfield Armory as their new XD (Extreme Duty) pistol.

Kel-Tec, whose head was an early pioneer in the use of polymers, had its popular P-32 in use by 2000. The company added a 380 version, slyly called the P-3AT, in 2003. Kahr, beginning with stainless-steel pistols in the '90s, introduced polymer-frame variants in 2000. Kahr's first 45-caliber pistol, the P45, was a polymer-frame design introduced in 2005. Ruger added a new polymer 45 auto, the P345, in 2004. The company's new Mark III 22/45 pistols also have polymer frames.

Full-size pistols are still here, as are compacts and also very small pistols. Today's small pistols may be of greater power than those of years past. The new little Rohrbaugh 9mm pistol, in production during 2004, weighs less than 13 ounces. North American Arms has introduced powerful new bottleneck cartridges for its little Guardian pocket pistols. The 32 NAA was in production by 2003, the 25 NAA a year later. From their short barrels, the bullets exit at about 1200 feet per second.

GUN DIGEST recorded these developments, and there were some changes to GUN DIGEST itself after the end of the 1990s. In 2000, Ken Warner stepped down as editor-in-chief, after serving in that capacity for twenty years. Ken Ramage, the present editor, took over at that time. He had held the position of senior staff editor prior to then. DBI had already been bought by Krause Publications before 2000, and in 2003, F&W Publications took

over Krause. Autoloading pistols remained the largest individual portion of the catalog section, and a number of excellent feature articles added to the store of knowledge about semi-automatics. Writers such as Jerry Burke, Jim Foral, Raymond Caranta and Lee Arten wrote on different aspects of autoloading handguns. In the 2004-58th Edition, the John T. Amber Award was reported won by John L. Marshall for his coverage of "Service 45s of the Twentieth Century." In the following 2005-59th Edition, the front and back covers were graced by new Ruger semi-automatic pistols.

Anti-gun forces seem to hate all autoloading pistols, but they love to hate some more than others. Some, such as this 45-caliber MAC-10, were labeled "assault pistols" and banned by the Assault Weapons Ban of 1994, which finally sunset in 2004.

The "Handguns Today, Autoloaders" section in that edition covered 15 pages, the largest single section in the volume. Thirty pages of the catalog section were devoted to current autoloading pistols.

So, after six decades, creativity continues in the field of automatic pistols. Yet, a few things are not much different than they were. In 1944, there were only two American manufacturers of automatic pistols. Both Colt and High Standard, the original two, have had problems, but both are still here. Of the models listed in the first GUN DIGEST, only the Colt 1911 design still survives, only little changed. Many companies have made their own modifications, but the popularity of the original 1911 design lives on.

Foreign automatics were given little coverage in the early years of GUN DIGEST. As the years went by, the foreign autoloaders were given greater coverage, then combined with the American pistols. Because foreign designs are now manufactured in the United States, there would no longer be any way to separate the guns by countries, as was done in the past. Some of the European pistol designs of the pre-WWII era are also still with us, such as the Walther PP and PPK pistols, and the 1935 Brown-ing Hi-Power.

Most of today's companies that make autoloading pistols did not exist in 1944, yet some, such as Ruger, and later Glock, have grown to great importance. Some designs have stayed with us, such as the CZ 75 and the Beretta 92, and their importance has gone beyond their production by the original maker.

The world of autoloading handguns has grown with the years. It is an exciting world. There are always new materials and new manufacturing processes to be tried. New cartridges are introduced that might fill a new niche. There are always new ways to accomplish the functions of feeding cartridges from a magazine into a chamber, firing the cartridge, controlling the pressure, ejecting the empty cartridge case, and then doing it all over again. Some designs arrive, and then fade away. Some designs arrive and thrive. Through it all, for just over six decades, GUN DIGEST has recorded these efforts.

.44 Special begins its second century

■ By John Taffin

The Road To The .44 Special

In 1857, two entrepreneurs, Horace Smith and Daniel Wesson, produced the first successful cartridge-firing revolver, the Smith & Wesson #1. This little seven-shot, tip-up revolver was chambered for what would become the most popular cartridge of all time, the .22 rimfire. They would go on to build both .22 and .32 rimfires in the Models 1, 1-1/2, and 2, and they had plans to bring out a big-bore version, but those plans were pushed to the back burner with the coming of the Civil War in 1861.

Meanwhile, over at the Colt factory, Sam Colt had decided cartridge cases would never catch on and shooters would always want to load their own using powder, ball, and cap. When Colt received a very lucrative contract to build 1860 Army Model .44s for the Northern Army not, only was the company's immediate future assured but there

Taffin shooting the USFA .44 Special Single Action.

definitely was no further thought of building cartridge-firing revolvers. Smith & Wesson kept producing their little pocket guns, which were quite popular as hideout weapons during the 1860s, but they did not forget their plans to build a .44-caliber version.

Sam Colt died in 1862, but his ideas persisted and percussion revolvers remained as the number one focus of the Colt Company. Then it happened! I can let my imagination run loose and see the executives of Colt sitting around the boardroom in late 1869 when the messenger arrives. He talks to the president, Richard Jarvis, who immediately scowls. He shares the information with the rest of the group. That other gun company, that Smith & Wesson group, had just announced a large-frame, break-top, six-shot, cartridge-firing .44 sixgun!

The new Smith & Wesson was known as the American and was chambered in both .44 Centerfire and .44 Henry Rimfire. Then when the U.S. Army ordered 1,000 .44 S&W Americans, Colt really knew they had some catching up to do.

Meanwhile, someone else was taking a serious look at the first .44 from Smith & Wesson: the Russians. They eventually negotiated a large contract for 150,000 guns with the Springfield firm to supply single-action sixguns for the Czar's army. However, they insisted on a change in the ammunition that would affect all future cartridge-cased ammunition. The original .44 S&W American was made just like the .22 Rimfire and used an outside lubricated heel bullet; that is, the diameter of the main body of the bullet was the same as the diameter of the outside of the brass case, but the lower part of the bullet was slightly smaller in diameter to fit inside the cartridge case. The Russians made a great improvement in ammunition when they asked for a bullet of uniform diameter with lube grooves inside the case itself. The result was the .44 Russian and the beginning of modern ammunition.

Those first Russian contract guns were nothing more than American models chambered in .44 Russian. Eventually the rounded back strap was changed with a hump at the top to prevent the

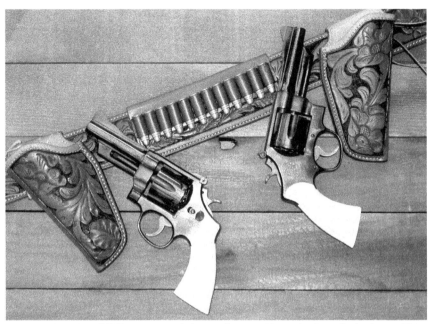

In the early 1980s S&W resurrected the .44 Special Model 24 for a limited run. This matched pair of 4" sixguns wear carved ivory stocks by Bob Leskovec and are carried in floral carved Tom Threepersons holsters from El Paso Saddlery.

Smith & Wesson 4" .44 Specials: 1950 Target with shortened barrel, Model 624, Model 24-3, and original 4" 1950 Target.

grip's shifting in the hand when the gun was fired, and a spur was placed on the bottom of the trigger guard. (The argument still remains as to just what that spur was for: to parry a sword thrust? To keep the sixgun from falling when carried in a sash? To serve as a steadying rest for the middle finger when firing the revolver? All these theories have been advanced.) This sixgun became known as the Model #3 Russian. With the removal of the spur and a slightly rede-

signed grip frame, the Model #3 Russian evolved into the New Model #3 in 1878 chambered in, of course, .44 Russian. The New Model #3 is without a doubt the epitome of Smith & Wesson single action production, and could easily be argued as the finest single-action sixgun to come from the nineteenth century. It was beautifully built with tight tolerances that actually worked against it in a black powder age with the fouling resulting from shooting.

In 1881, Smith & Wesson looked at that beautiful New Model #3 and redesigned it with a double-action mechanism, and so the first Double Action Model arrived in .44 Russian. These are not the finest-looking double-action sixguns ever made, far from it, but they were dependable and would represent the best big-bore double-action sixguns from Smith & Wesson for more than 25 years. In fact, the Double Action .44 would stay in production right up to the eve of World War I.

By the late 1890s, Colt was producing swing-out cylindered double-action revolvers, and Smith & Wesson soon followed suit. In 1899, Smith & Wesson produced their first K-frame, the Military & Police, which would go on to be one of the most popular revolvers of the twentieth century. It was chambered in .38 Special, but the engineers at Smith & Wesson were looking at something a bit bigger. In 1907, the Military & Police was enlarged to what we now know as the N-frame, fitted with an enclosed ejector rod housing, and had a third locking mechanism added. By this time, the M&P locked at the back of the cylinder and the front of the ejector rod; this new sixgun received a third lock with the crane locking into the back of the ejector rod housing.

The new sixgun had many names, including the .44 Hand Ejector 1st Model, New Century, Model of 1908, .44 Military, but it is best known among collectors and shooters alike as the Triple Lock. Such a beautifully built sixgun deserved a new cartridge, and that cartridge was the .44 Special. To arrive at the .44 Special, the .44 Russian was simply lengthened from .97" to 1.16". But having gone to the edge of perfection, Smith & Wesson then drew back. The longer cartridge in a stronger sixgun was loaded to duplicate the .44 Russian! The Russian carried a bullet of approximately 250 grains at a muzzle velocity of about 750 fps. They should have at least duplicated the .45 Colt round and bumped the .44 Special up to 850-900 fps – and 1,000 fps would have been even better. It would remain the task of experimenters in the 1920s through the

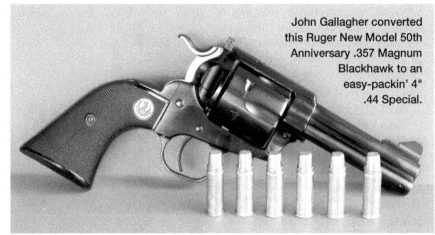

John Gallagher converted this Ruger New Model 50th Anniversary .357 Magnum Blackhawk to an easy-packin' 4" .44 Special.

The excellent, and very rare, Texas Longhorn Arms 4-3/4" South Texas Army .44 Special.

1940s to discover the real potential of the .44 Special.

Smith & Wesson .44 Specials

The Triple Lock, perhaps the finest double-action revolver ever produced, had a very short life span, lasting only until 1915 with just over 15,000 being manufactured. They sold for $21 at a time when one dollar was a lot of money, but because of an attempt to save $2 on its price, the Triple Lock died. True! It was replaced by the .44 Hand Ejector 2nd Model, which lacked the third lock, a shortcut that allowed it to retail for $2 less than the Triple Lock. To add insult to injury, the Triple Lock's shrouded ejector rod housing was also dropped. The result was simply a larger Military & Police.

More 2nd Models were built than 1st Models, about 2,000 more, but it would take 35 years to accomplish. Both the

Triple Lock and the 2nd Model are rarely, very rarely, found in other chamberings such as .45 Colt, .44-40, and .38-40; however they were first and foremost .44 Specials. As soon as the Triple Lock was replaced by the 2nd Model, sixgun connoisseurs began calling for a return to the Triple Lock. As so often happens with gun companies, the pleas for the return to what a double-action sixgun should be fell on deaf ears, at least until 1926.

What individual shooters could not do, Wolf and Klar, a gun dealer in Fort Worth, Texas, could do. An order was placed with Smith & Wesson for several thousand revolvers chambered in .44 Special with the enclosed ejector rod housing. Except for the missing third lock, these revolvers were every bit as good as the 1st Models and were eagerly accepted by shooters and especially by Southwestern lawmen. The 4",

1st, 2nd, and 3rd Generation 7-1/2" .44 Special Colt SAAs with leather by Circle Bar T.

fixed sighted, double-action .44 Special Smith & Wesson was just about the perfect defensive sixgun in the 1920s, and there is some doubt that it has ever been pushed to second place. This 3rd Model, also known as the Model 1926, would be produced until the start of World War II, when all production of civilian arms ceased, and then resurrected in 1946 for only a short time until the next model appeared. As great as the Model 1926 was, it did not replace the 2nd Model as both were produced simultaneously until the eve of World War II.

The Model 1926 is even more rare than the Triple Lock, with only about 6,500 being produced in the two runs from 1926 to 1941 and 1946 to 1949. Just as with the 1st and 2nd Models, this 3rd Model was offered in both fixed-

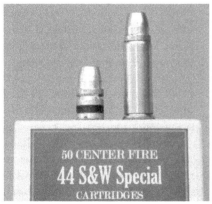

The most popular bullet for the .44 Special is the Keith design; this version is from RCBS.

sight and target-sight versions. By 1949, the Model 1926 was about to be changed to become the 4th Model Hand Ejector of 1950. The Model 1950 was offered in two versions: the rare fixed-sight Military Model with only about 1,200 being produced, and the magnificent 1950 Target Model. Both were offered in barrel lengths of 4", 5", and 6-1/2" with the 4" 1950 Target being rare and the 5" Target extremely so. Just under 5,100 4th Model Target .44 Specials were made from 1950 to 1966. In 1957, when all Smith & Wessons lost their personality and became mere model numbers, the 4th Model Military became the Model 21 and the Target version was dubbed the Model 24.

The Model 21 demands prices in four figures today. In the early 1970s I purchased a 5" Model 21 for $65 and since it was not considered rare or a collector's item at that time, I converted it to a Target Model with a 1950 Target barrel cut back to 5" and a S&W adjustable rear sight installed. One of the top gunsmiths in the country did the work and it is a beautiful sixgun, but imagine what it would be worth today if I had left in its original condition! Eight years later I actually came upon a 6-1/2" Model 1950 Target. I had placed a Winchester 1886 on layaway at the Gunhaus and when George called me to tell me about the Smith & Wesson, I backed off the Winchester and took the 1950 Tar-

get instead.

Then I did it again! I wanted the 6-1/2" 1950 Target, but I also wanted a 4" version even more and had the barrel shortened to four inches. Strike Two! Fortunately, thanks to regular readers of *Guns* and *American Handgunner*, I have been contacted about .44 Special Smith & Wesson sixguns for sale and in recent years have purchased three 4" .44 Specials, a 1926 Model made the same year I was, a 1950 Military, and a 1950 Target, as well as a 6-1/2" Model 1950 Target. There will be no Strike Three and the sixguns will be enjoyed exactly as the beautiful works of art they really are.

Not only was the 1950 Target a magnificent sixgun in its own right, it became the basic platform for the .44 Magnum. In 1954 Smith & Wesson began experimenting with a new Magnum in a 4" 1950 Target with special heat-treating and the cylinder re-chambered to the longer .44. When the .44 Magnum became reality, it was a 1950 Target with

An excellent choice for a hunting bullet in the .44 Special is the Speer original jacketed bullet with a lead core in a full copper cup.

a longer cylinder, bull barrel, high polish Bright Blue finish, and adjustable sights consisting of a white outline rear sight and a front ramp sight with a red insert. The 1950 Target with its special heat-treating could handle the .44 Magnum, but shooters could not, and an extra half-pound was added to the weight by going to the longer cylinder and bull barrel.

The coming of the .44 Magnum pushed the .44 Special aside very quick-

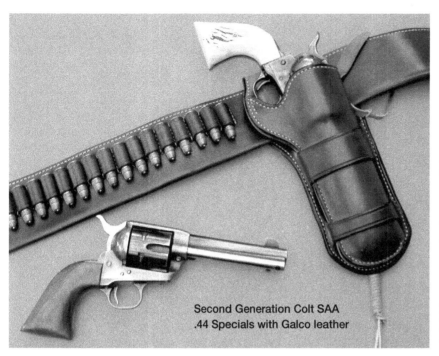

Second Generation Colt SAA
.44 Specials with Galco leather

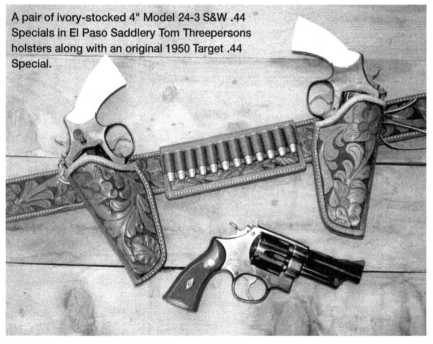

A pair of ivory-stocked 4" Model 24-3 S&W .44 Specials in El Paso Saddlery Tom Threepersons holsters along with an original 1950 Target .44 Special.

ly. Some shooters, such as sheriff of Deaf Smith County Texas, Skeeter Skelton, sold his 4" 1950 Target .44 Special and replaced it with a 4" .44 Magnum, only to find it was a lot harder to pack all day and the ammunition was much too powerful for law enforcement use. Of course, a handloader could tailor-make .44 Magnum ammunition at the .44 Special level, but if one is going to shoot .44 Special ammunition, why carry the heavier sixgun? Skeeter admitted he was

sorry he ever sold his .44 Special.

In 1966 Smith & Wesson dropped the 1950 Target/Model 24 from production. Of course, as always happens, when something disappears a demand appears. It would be Skeeter Skelton who would help keep the fire burning for .44 Specials by publishing an article in the early 1970s about converting the Smith & Wesson .357 Magnum Highway Patrolman to .44 Special. In those days Smith & Wesson .44 Special barrels were

still available so it was simply a matter of re-chambering the .357 cylinder to .44 Special and fitting a new barrel.

It would take a while, but finally in 1983 Smith & Wesson brought back the .44 Special as the Model 24-3. To ensure selling all of these guns they promised to make only so many. They were offered in both 4" and 6-1/2" versions with a production run of one year and 7,500 being produced. They sold quickly; in fact the demand for these resurrected .44 Specials was greater than the number produced. Now what? Smith & Wesson had backed themselves into a corner by promising only to produce a certain number, and yet the market was out there for more .44 Specials. This dilemma was solved by offering the stainless-steel version, the Model 624, with the same barrel lengths from 1985 to 1987. Both the blued 24-3 and stainless-steel 624 .44 Specials were also specially ordered and offered as 3" round-butted versions by Smith and Wesson distributors.

The Smith & Wesson .44 Special died in 1966, was resurrected in 1983, and died again in 1987. However, the .44 Special is too good to stay buried for very long. In 1996, the Smith & Wesson .44 Special returned as the Model 696, a stainless steel, five-shot L-frame with a 3" barrel and round butt grip frame. It was followed by the Model 396Ti, the same basic revolver with an alloy frame and titanium cylinder. And then after nearly 20 years we got back to basics with a full-sized, six-shot, N-frame .44 Special: the Model 21-3, a 4" round–butted, fixed-sight, blue steel revolver with an enclosed ejector rod. It first appeared as the Thunder Ranch Special and now is a standard catalog item.

Smith & Wesson also produces two 4" .44 Magnums, the Model 29 Mountain Gun with the tapered barrel of the 1950 Model and the 26-oz. scandium/titanium 329PD. If the truth be known, both of these Magnums are better suited to .44 Special use. Just this past year S&W introduced, or I should say re-introduced, the Model 1950 Target as the Model 24-6 Classic with the same 6-1/2" barrel length as the original. The

.44 Special is definitely alive and well at Smith & Wesson.

Colt .44 Specials

In 1913 Colt began chambering the Single Action Army in .44 Special. From then until 1941, only 506 Single Action Army Models would be so chambered, and only one Flat-Top Target, which belonged to Elmer Keith. In the beginning these sixguns were marked on the left side, "RUSSIAN AND S&W SPECIAL 44". One of the most beautiful examples of an engraved .44 Special so inscribed was the 7-1/2" personal sixgun of Ed McGivern shipped to him by Colt in 1919; it is pictured in *A Study Of The Colt Single Action Army Revolver* by Graham, Kopec, and Moore. In 1929, barrel markings were changed to "COLT SINGLE ACTION ARMY .44 SPECIAL".

I had one of these 7-1/2" .44 Special Colts marked the same as the McGivern Colt as related in my book *Big Bore Sixguns* (Krause Publications 1997).

As I relate in that book:

My new wife solidly entrenched herself in my heart forever our first Christmas together as she presented me with a brand new 6-1/2" .44 Special Smith & Wesson Model 1950 Target. I had begun a lifelong love affair with the .44 Special. Not only did my wife present me with my first .44 Special, she also combined with a very special .44 Special to make it possible for me to meet another vocal proponent of the .44 Special. It has always been my regular habit to read section 640 GUNS every day in the morning paper's want ads expecting to find maybe one special sixgun per year. In the early 1970's the ad read Colt Single Action .44 and old belt and holster.

The address was a trailer park just outside of town and I hustled over to find a 1st Generation 7-1/2" Colt Single Action with cartridge belt and holster. The owner explained the .44 had belonged to his uncle and he wore it regularly as a sheriff in Colorado, and the pitting on the top strap were from his blood when he was shot and was more concerned about having himself patched up than

cleaning the Colt. As I handled the Colt I could scarcely contain myself. Except for the minor pitting on the top strap, the old Colt .44 Single Action was in excellent

shape mechanically and the case coloring had turned a beautifully aged gray. The left side of the barrel was marked "RUSSIAN AND S&W SPECIAL 44". A very

(Top) This pair of .44 Specials built on S&W and Ruger .357 Magnums were finished in matte blue by Hamilton Bowen for heavy-duty field use. (Middle) In the mid-1980s Smith & Wesson offered a limited number of stainless steel .44 Special Model 624s. (Above) The Freedom Arms Model 97 is the finest production .44 Special single-action ever produced.

rare single action!

How much? I asked as I contemplated my budget. $450. I was sorely tempted but with paying for three kids to attend private school, I felt it was out of the question. I reluctantly thanked the man for his time and left. My excitement stayed high all the way home and it was impossible to contain my disappointment as I told my wife all about the Colt .44 Special. She was more than a little surprised I was able to resist buying that beautiful sixgun.

Later that day she headed out to do some shopping and I asked her to stop at the local boot repair shop. I had been so stirred up by the .44 Colt I had forgotten to pick up my finished boots. When she returned home she handed me the boots with a slight smile on her face. As I took the boots I realized they felt a few pounds heavier than normal. In the left boot was the Colt! She had gone out on her own and purchased the .44 Special! You hold on tightly to a wife such as this one!

After doing a little research on the Colt and finding out how really rare it was, we decided it belonged to a collector not a shooter as I was. So we traded it for the $450 we paid for it plus two shooting Colt sixguns, a 2nd Generation Colt Single Action Army 5-1/2".44 Special and a 7-1/2" New Frontier chambered in .45 Colt. But that isn't the end of the story as this Colt .44 Special and Russian was my ticket to meeting someone very special.

Later that year I attended the NRA Show in Salt Lake City and carried pictures of the old Colt, especially a close-up of the barrel inscription, all for a purpose. I was looking for one particular individual. When I found him dressed in a dark suit, wearing colored shooting glasses and a white Stetson, I simply handed him the picture of the barrel close up. He grabbed me by the arm and said: "Son, let's go find a place to talk." The man was Skeeter Skelton and I had found the way to his heart. Skeeter was second only to Elmer Keith in praising the virtues of the .44 Special during his writing career. Keith retired his .44 Specials after the .44 Magnum arrived; Skelton tried the .44 Magnum, found the Special better for most purposes, and went back to his first love.

This first-year production .44 Special Triple Lock is carried in a George Lawrence #34 Elmer Keith holster.

The 1st Generation Colt Single Action Army was dropped from production in 1941, never to be seen again. After the war, Colt made it very clear they had no intention of ever resuming production. Television changed all that! A whole new generation of shooters and would be shooters discovered the Colt Single Action Army through all the B Western movies that filled the screens in the early days of television and then were followed by the made-for-TV westerns. Shooters wanted Colt Single Actions and in 1956 the 2nd Generation Single Actions appeared.

The .44 Special arrived in the Single Action Army one year later in 1957 with both 5-1/2" and 7-1/2" barrel lengths. For some unknown reason the 2nd Generation .44 Specials were never offered with 4-3/4" barrels. While not as rare as the 1st Generation .44 Specials, just over 2,300 were offered before they were removed from production in 1966. A companion sixgun to the Single Action Army was the New Frontier, a modernized version of the old Flat-Top Target Model of the 1890s. These are very rare with only 255 total being made with 5-1/2" and 7-1/2" barrels from 1963 to 1967. They are also some the finest single actions ever produced by Colt.

By 1974, the Colt machinery was wearing out and the decision was made to drop the Colt Single Action Army once again. This time instead of 15 years it only took two years to resurrect the Single Action, as the 3rd

Generation began production in 1976. This time around the .44 Special would be produced from 1978 to 1984 in all three barrel lengths: 4-3/4", 5-1/2", and 7-1/2" and a total production of about 15,000 with about 375 Buntline Specials with 12" barrels. Colt just recently announced the return of the .44 Special Single Action Army to their catalog. The .44 Special was also offered as the New Frontier from 1980 through 1984 when all New Frontier production ceased. Something over 3,500 3rd Generation .44 Special New Frontiers were produced and only with 5-1/2" and 7-1/2" barrels. Most shooters hold 2nd Generation .44 Specials in much higher esteem than their counterparts among 3rd Generation examples and the prices demanded reflect this.

Two S&W .44 Specials that command high collector prices now are the five-shot 696 and the Mountain Lite.

Colt not only produced the first big-bore double-action revolvers a few years before Smith & Wesson – the Model 1878 in .45 Colt – but they would also be the first to produce what we consider a modern double-action revolver., i.e., one with a swing-out cylinder. These Army and Navy Models on the .41 frame would evolve into the larger New Service in 1898. Immensely popular, the New Service overtook the Single Action Army in total production numbers due to the fact that more than 150,000 New Services chambered in .45ACP with 5-1/2" barrels and known as the Model 1917 were ordered for the use of the troops in World War I.

The .44 Special, as with the Single Action Army, first appeared in the Colt New Service in 1913. Before it was

Two very easy-carrying .44 Specials by Andy Horvath and Bob Baer.

dropped, the .44 Special New Service was offered as a standard model with barrel lengths of 4-1/2", 5 1/2", and 7-1/2" with either blue or nickel finish, or the beautifully shooting New Service Target Revolver with a choice of either a 6" or 7-1/2" barrel. Stocks were checkered walnut and the trigger was checkered, as were the front and back straps; the finish was a deep blue; sights were adjustable, with a choice of a Patridge or bead front sight.

Colt's ultimate .44 Special New Service was the deluxe target revolver, the Shooting Master. This 6"-barreled revolver featured a hand-finished action, sights and a top strap that were finished to eliminate glare. It represented the highest-quality revolver that Colt could build until the Python arrived in 1955. Along with the Colt Single Action Army, the New Service was dropped in 1941.

New Services chambered in .44 Special are very hard to find, at least at my price level. A few years ago a reader came to the rescue with a late-model New Service in .44 Special, which he offered to send to me for inspection. It had several problems: it was out of time, its lanyard ring was missing, and someone had installed a Smith & Wesson adjustable rear sight while leaving the front sight intact. This, of course, resulted in a sixgun that shot way high. But it had possibilities and it came for very reasonable price. The 4-1/2" New Service .44 Special was sent off to Milt Morrison of QPR (Qualite Pistol & Revolver), one of the few gunsmiths qualified to work on the old New Service. He totally tuned and tightened it, fitted a ramp front sight and re-blued it. A lanyard ring was found and installed, and stag grips were located and fitted to the frame. The final result is one of the finest New Service .44 Specials around.

In the time between the two World Wars, John Henry FitzGerald ("Fitz") was Colt's representative, traveling to all the shooting matches, working on shooters' Colts and generally sharing shooting information. He is best known for his Fitz Special built on the Colt New Service: "Perhaps some would like to ask why I cut up a good revolver and here is the answer: The trigger guard is cut away to allow more finger room and for use when gloves are worn…. The hammer spur is cut away to allow drawing from the pocket or from under the coat without catching or snagging in the cloth and eliminates the use of thumb over hammer when drawing….The butt is rounded to allow the revolver to easily slide into firing position in the hand…. The top of the cut-away hammer may be lightly checked to assist in cocking for a long-range shot." It was common knowledge among his contemporaries that Fitz always carried a pair of .45 Colt

RUGER'S FIRST FACTORY .44 SPECIAL!

The .44 Special sixgun many of us have been waiting for since 1955 is finally here!

It was in that wonderful year that Ruger introduced their first centerfire revolver, the .357 Magnum Blackhawk (known to sixgunners today as the Flat-Top). It was the same size as the Colt Single Action Army but in addition to its virtually unbreakable coil spring action, it also had a flat-topped frame fitted with a Micro adjustable rear sight. Elmer Keith reported the next step would be a .44 Special. However, before that happened the .44 Magnum arrived. Ruger tried to chamber the .357 Blackhawk in .44 Magnum, but with further proof-testing the cylinder and frame proved to be too small and one of their prototypes blew. The frame and cylinder of the Blackhawk were subsequently enlarged to properly house the .44 Magnum and the .44 Special became a dead issue.

Thanks to Lipsey's ordering 2,000 .44 Specials built on the original sized frame, Ruger is now doing what they intended to do more than 50 years ago. The .44 Special Flat-Top New Model Blackhawk is available in an all-blued steel sixgun with the choice of 4-5/8" or 5-1/2" barrel length. I have been shooting one of each and they have proven to be superb sixguns. Suggested retail price is $579 from your local dealer. Don't miss this one!

USFA offers the barrel marking as found on the original Colt Single Action .44 Special.

Fitz Specials in his two front pockets. He definitely knew how to use them.

I've wanted to have a Fitz Special ever since I was the kid learning to shoot big-bore sixguns in the 1950s, and just recently decided to have one made up on a Colt New Service. I found what I thought would be the perfect candidate

Andy Horvath built this .44 Special "Fitz Special" on a Colt New Service.

for a Fitz Special, a 5-1/2" Late Model New Service in .45 Colt. Although having considerable pitting on the right side of the barrel and part of the cylinder, it was mechanically perfect and the interiors of both barrel and cylinder were like new. Instead of sending it off to be converted, I shot it first and found it shot much too well to touch as it placed five shots, fired double-action standing at 50 feet, in less than 1-1/2". By now I have learned not to fix what ain't broke, so it remains untouched.

Thanks to a reader I came up with a Late Model New Service chambered in .44 Special. It needed some help and made a perfect candidate for a Fitz Special, so off it went to one of the premier gunsmiths in the country, Andy Horvath. Horvath said of this New Service: "It's got a few miles on it and somebody got a little carried away with the buffing wheel. I bushed the cylinder to get

out most of the endplay, and installed a ball lock on the crane to help with the lock-up. Instead of cutting the old barrel I just made a new one using up a piece of Douglas barrel blank too short for anything else. The grip frame has been shortened and rounded and fitted with fancy walnut grip panels, and the top of the hammer serrated for shooting single action by starting the hammer back with the trigger and then grabbing the hammer with your thumb." The end result is a .44 Special Fitz Special that is one of the finest in existence. built by one of the finest gunsmiths ever. My everyday working load for .44 Special sixguns, the 250-gr. Keith bullet over 7.5 gr of Unique in the short barrel of the "Fitz" registers 830 fps, or just about the perfect equivalent of Fitz's .45 Colt loads.

Other .44 Special Single Actions

The .44 Special has never been the everyman's cartridge but rather the favorite of true connoisseurs of big-bore single-action and double-action sixguns. As a result, production numbers are usually very low for any company producing single-action sixguns exclusively. In 1954, Great Western began producing a single action, the Frontier Six-Shooter, in Los Angeles. Bill Wilson, president and one of three founders, had contacted Colt in 1953 and was assured they had no plans to resurrect the Colt Single Action Army. The Great Western looked so much like a Colt Single Action Army they actually used real Colts in the early advertising. In fact, some of the Great Western parts came from Colt. When Colt resumed production of the Single Action Army in 1956, Great Western's demise was only a matter of time. They lasted until 1964.

No one really knows how many Great Westerns were produced in eight years, or if they do they aren't telling. The standard caliber was .45 Colt, but the GW was also offered in .22, .38 Special, .357 Magnum, .357 Atomic, .44 Magnum, and .44 Special. The last two are especially rare and, until recently, I had only seen one of each in my lifetime and purchased both of them. In the

From top left counterclockwise: First came the .44 Special Triple Lock of 1908, then the Model 1926, which was used as the platform for the .38-44 Heavy Duty of 1930 which in turn became the building block for the .357 Magnum of 1935.

past few years, again thanks to readers, I have come up with two 5-1/2" Great Western .44 Specials, one unfired and nickel-plated with factory pearls, and the other standard blue and case colored with plastic stag grips. The nickel plated version required considerable 'smithing to put it into shooting condition but all have now proven to be excellent sixguns.

Bill Grover started Texas Longhorn Arms in 1981 building a single-action sixgun different than anything ever previously offered. It was his belief Sam Colt was left-handed and his designs show this. I am right-handed and I load and unload a Single Action Army by switching the sixgun to my left hand, working the ejector rod with my right hand and also using my right hand to reload and then switching the sixgun back to my right hand for either holstering or shooting. Grover's idea was to reverse everything. That is, both the ejector rod housing and the loading gate are on the left side of the sixgun and the cylinder rotates counterclockwise. This allows the right-handed shooter to hold the gun in his right-hand while both loading and unloading operations are performed with the left hand. The sixgun never leaves the shooting hand.

Grover's first right-handed single actions included the West Texas Flat-Top Target with a 7-1/2" barrel, the South Texas Army with fixed sights and a 4-3/4" barrel, and the Improved Number Five with a 5-1/2" barrel. Texas Longhorn Arms' version of Keith's Famous #5SAA managed to maintain the flavor

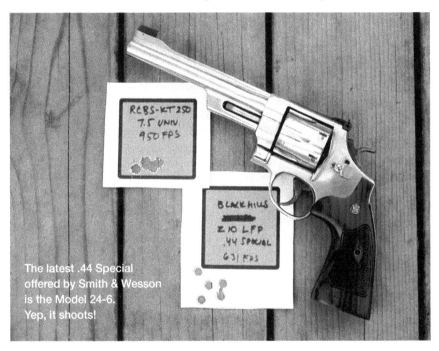

The latest .44 Special offered by Smith & Wesson is the Model 24-6. Yep, it shoots!

of the original while being stronger and replacing Keith's favorite cartridge of the 1920s-1950s with his choice from 1955 on, the .44 Magnum. Even with its larger frame and cylinder, the TLA Improved Number Five still maintains Colt-style balance rather than seeming overly large. Both the West Texas Flat-Top Target and the South Texas Army were offered in .44 Special, and like the Great Westerns, are very rarely seen. Texas Longhorn Arms, unfortunately,

closed their doors in the mid-1990s and their beautiful .44 Special sixguns are no more.

I first ran into USFA (United States Firearms Co.) at a SHOT Show in the early 1990s. Arrangements were made to do a test and evaluation of their single actions, and one of those sixguns ordered was a blued and case colored 7-1/2" version with the barrel marked "RUSSIAN AND S&W SPECIAL 44". At the time USFA was importing Uberti

Southwest lawmen who were true pistoleros often chose the 4" 3rd or 4th Model Hand Ejectors from Smith & Western chambered in .44 Special.

parts and assembling and finishing them in this country. That .44 was beautifully finished and fitted up tightly with very little cylinder movement either fore, aft, or side-to-side. The goal of USFA was to eventually provide an All-American made sixgun and they have now arrived at that point. Their Single Action Army is a beautifully made, totally American .44 Special.

USFA offers the Single Action Army and the Flat-Top Target both made the old way as Single Actions were before World War II. Since my original Colt Single Action Army with its 7-1/2" barrel marked with both .44 Special and .44 Russian was sold, I decided to replace it with the USFA version. In fact, at the 2004 SHOT Show I ordered two USFA .44 Specials, one to replace the old Colt, with identical markings, and a full blue Flat-Top Target also with a 7-1/2" barrel. These are beautiful (I know I'm overusing the word but they really are!) .44 Special sixguns and are made as well or better as any the old revolvers we now call classic. They are finely finished, tight with no cylinder play either front to back or side to side, and they shoot as good as they look.

The Freedom Arms Model 97

One exception to the rule of a full-sized, six-shot .44 Special is the Freedom Arms Model 97. This little sixgun, smaller than the Colt SAA, has a cylinder that is 1.575" in diameter; however it is an extremely strong five-shot little sixgun built to very tight tolerances and with the bolt cut on the cylinder in between chambers so there is no weak point there. My most-used standard load for the .44 Special for more than 40 years has been the 250 gr. Keith hard cast bullet over 7.5 grains of Unique. With this load, a 250-grain Keith bullet clocks out at just over 1,000 fps from the 5-1/2" barrel of the Model 97 .44 Special; and the same RCBS Keith bullet over 17.0 grains of H4227 gives 1,002 fps. These are easy shootin' and very accurate loads from this .44 Special.

For heavy-duty use in the Freedom Arms .44 Special, Speer's 225-gr. jacketed hollow point over 16.0 grains of #2400 gives 1,240 fps and the exceptional accuracy of four shots into 5/8". This bullet is not the normally-encountered jacketed hollowpoint but rather the copper cup with a lead core. The standard Keith load using RCBS's version clocks out at

1,270 fps from the short-barreled Model 97. Switching over to Ray Thompson's design, Lyman's #431244GC, 17.5 grains of #2400 also travels well over 1,200 fps and shoots equally well. The Model 97 has a relatively short cylinder; however, all these loads with the Keith bullet chamber with room to spare. *[Editor's note: These loads have proven safe in the author's Freedom Arms Model 97. Other, older .44 Specials may not tolerate them; thus we do not recommend their use.]*

Most double action connoisseurs hold the original .44 Special in the highest esteem even to the point of labeling the old Triple Lock as the finest revolver ever built. It has had no equal let alone been surpassed by any other factory produced .44 Special; until now. The .44 Special Model 97 from Freedom Arms is the number one challenger to the title.

Ruger .44 Special Blackhawks

In 1953 Bill Ruger modernized the single action and introduced the Single-Six .22 with the first major change (coil springs instead of flat springs) since the Paterson arrived in 1836. Two years later the Single-Six was increased to the same size as the Colt Single Action Army; its frame was flat-topped, adjustable sights were added, and we had the .357 Magnum Blackhawk. Ruger had the full intention of bringing this same sixgun out in .44 Special, and if we lived in a perfect world that is exactly what would have happened; however we don't, and it didn't. The coming of the .44 Magnum in 1956 changed all that and instead the Blackhawk frame and cylinder were enlarged to become the .44 Magnum Blackhawk. Ruger never did produce a .44 Special Blackhawk.

What Ruger did not do, custom sixgunsmiths can do. Earlier mention was made of Skeeter Skelton's article converting the .357 Magnum Highway Patrolman from Smith & Wesson into a .44 Special. In that same article he also covered the conversion of the Three Screw .357 Magnum Ruger Blackhawk to .44 Special. The Three Screw .357 Blackhawks are divided into two categories: the Flat-Top, which was produced from 1955 to 1962, and the Old

Model, from 1963 to 1972. Both of these .357 Blackhawks were built on the same size of frame as the Colt Single Action Army. When the New Model arrived in 1973, the .357 Magnum-size frame was dropped and instead the .357 Magnum Blackhawk was built on the same size frame as the .44 Super Blackhawk. Converting a New Model to .44 Special results in a .44 Magnum-size sixgun.

To convert a .357 Magnum Blackhawk to .44 Special, it is only necessary to re-chamber the cylinder and fit a different barrel. That's the basic idea, but different sixgunsmiths take over from here and exercise their artistic side. Gunsmiths I know of who can convert the Three Screw .357s to very special

Blackhawk frames.

Grip frames can be polished bright or re-anodized; Flat-Top grip frames can be installed on Old Model frames to give more of a Colt feel, or stainless steel Old Army grip frames can be fitted to either Three Screw Model. Even Colt two-piece grip frames can be attached to allow the use of one-piece grips, or 'smiths can use the new Colt-style, two-piece grip frame offered by Power Custom and sold through Brownells. Some Ruger .357s came with an extra 9mm cylinder which allows two .44 cylinders to be used, one Special and the other in .44-40. No matter what route is chosen, nor which of these gentlemen does the work, the result is an easy-handlin', easy-

S&W – is the .44 Special still viable for hunting? I had taken deer-sized game in the 125- to 250-lb. pound class, but what about bigger game? The most popular big game animal, second only to deer, is the poor man's grizzly: wild hogs, feral pigs, Russian boars. For a feral hog hunt I chose the .44 Special loaded with a hollowpoint cast bullet (Lyman's #429421 Keith) at 1,200 fps muzzle velocity from the 7-1/2" .44 Special Texas Longhorn Arms West Texas Flat-Top Target.

On the first pig, the bullet went in right behind the upper part of the front leg and, as we found out later, came out on the other side right through the center of the upper part of the leg on the off-side. The bullet gave total penetration in a 500-lb. animal! That was to be the end of it, as far as I was concerned.

I intended to take one pig and be on my way. But there were two pigs there, and the dead pig's big buddy would have none of that. By now he was up on his feet and using his snout to move that 500-pounder. He was not about to leave. So! At the shot he turned around, started to run, and I put a second shot in him and down he went. The smaller, 500-lb. pig had 4" tusks, while this 650-pounder had tusks curling around for a full 6". We would later find out the .44 Special hollowpoint had gone through the heart of the second boar, the second shot was only two inches away from the first shot, and the bullet was perfectly mushroomed and lodged under the hide on the far side. In both cases the .44 Special bullets did everything a sixgun, load, and bullet combination are supposed to do.

In 1966, the .44 Special was pronounced old, antiquated, out of date, ready for the bonepile. Skeeter Skelton started the resurrection of sixguns firing this first big-bore cartridge of the twentieth century and I have tried to carry the torch since his passing in 1988. I'm sure Skeeter is smiling as he sees all the .357 Three Screw Blackhawks being turned into .44 Specials, as well as the new .44 Special sixguns from USFA and Freedom Arms and the revival of S&W's N-frame .44 Special. The .44 Special is ready for its second century of service.

Great .44 Special sixguns from the middle part of the twentieth century: Great Western SA, 2nd Generation Colt SAA, and a pair of 3rd Generation Colts.

.44 Specials include Bob Baer, Hamilton Bowen, David Clements, Ben Forkin, John Gallagher, Alan Harton, Andy Horvath, Gary Reeder, and Jim Stroh, and I have considerable hands-on experience with examples built by these different gunsmiths/metal artists. Some of these men re-bored the existing barrel to .44 Special; others fitted custom barrels; and others used .44 Magnum barrels from other Ruger Blackhawks. Barrel lengths offered include but are not limited to the standard 4-5/8", 5-1/2", and 7-1/2", as well as 3-1/2" and 4" Sheriffs Model styles. Colt 3rd Generation .44 Special or .44-40 New Frontier barrels can even be fitted to Three Screw

packin', easy-shootin' .44 Special.

With the coming of the Ruger 50th Anniversary .357 Magnum Flat-Top in 2005, we suddenly had a new platform for building Colt SAA-size .44 Specials on a Ruger. Both Ben Forkin and John Gallagher have converted 50th Anniversary .357 New Model Blackhawks to .44 Special for me with the former using a 7-1/2" New Frontier barrel and the latter opting for a custom 4" barrel. I have to say it again: they are beautiful sixguns!

Hunting with the .44 Special

In these days of heavy-loaded .44 Magnums and .45 Colts – let alone the .454 Casull, .475 Linebaugh, and .500

The Colt 1911: The First Century

∎ John Malloy

Students of firearms are aware of the significance of the year 1911. In that year, a century ago, the Browning-designed Colt Model 1911 was adopted as the sidearm of the United States military forces. Perhaps no single semiautomatic handgun is better known, or has had more influence on pistol design, than the 1911. Now, 100 years later, the Colt/Browning 1911 design lives on, little changed, and it remains amazingly popular.

Since its introduction, the 1911 has proven itself as the United States military pistol in two World Wars and a number of other conflicts. Other countries produced the Colt/Browning design, made under license. Still other countries made unauthorized close copies of the pistol.

Civilian use of the big Colt pistol reinforced its value. By the midpoint of the 1900s, the 1911 was on its way to becoming one of the winningest target pistols in use. In the latter part of the century, law enforcement agencies were won over to the semiautomatic pistol, and many went with the time-tested 1911.

For almost half its history, the 1911 reigned supreme as the premier semiautomatic pistol in America. During that time, no other big-bore pistol was even produced in quantity in this country. In the latter part of the 20th century, other companies made competing semiautomatic pistols of more modern design, but the 1911 retained its popularity. With patent protection long gone, other firms began to make nearly exact copies—part-for-part-interchangeable 1911-type pistols—under their own names. New names, some

New names keep coming up for companies offering new 1911s. Legacy Sports now offers their Citadel 45 in full-size and compact versions.

now almost forgotten, entered the firearms lexicon. By the closing decade of the 1900s, other producers such as Springfield, Para-Ordnance and Kimber achieved major positions as 1911 manufacturers.

By the beginning of the 21st century, even companies that were making pistols with more modern features decided to get on the gravy train and began making their own 1911 pistols. Companies such as Smith &Wesson, SIG-Sauer and Taurus introduced 1911s.

The 1911 design, now a century old, seems to be at a peak of popularity.

Historical Background

In the 1890s, the semiautomatic pistol was successfully introduced to the firearms world in Europe. In 1893, the Borchardt became the first commercially-successful autoloader, followed by designs of Mauser, Bergmann, Mannlicher and Luger. To these European developments was added one with an American name — Browning. John M. Browning's 32-caliber pocket pistol was introduced in 1899 by Fabrique Nationale (FN) in Belgium. Early developments were relatively small in bore size, ranging from less than 30-caliber to an upper limit of 9mm. Around the turn of the 20th century, the concept of a larger-caliber semiautomatic pistol had been experimented with in several countries, including Great Britain. However, it took a design of American inventor John M. Browning to bring a truly successful big-bore pistol into being.

Browning, along with his handgun work for FN, had provided designs to Colt. Colt saw promise in military sales and introduced a Browning-designed 38-caliber automatic in 1900. This caliber appeared to be a favorable one, as the US military was by then using 38-caliber revolvers.

However, the need for a larger-caliber handgun became evident during the Spanish-American war of 1898 and the subsequent Philippine Insurrection. When the United States acquired the Philippine Islands from Spain as a result of the war, it was an unpleasant surprise to find that many Filipinos did not like American control any more than they had enjoyed Spanish rule.

The resulting insurrection was officially over in 1901, but deadly conflict, especially in the southern islands, continued well into the next decade. These southern islands were inhabited by fierce Moro tribes that had been converted to a form of Islam. The service sidearm of the time, the double-action .38 Long Colt revolver (marginal even in "civilized" warfare), proved to be inadequate to stop a charging Moro. Old Single Action Army 45-caliber revolvers were withdrawn from storage, had the barrels shortened to 5-1/2 inches, and were sent back into service. A quantity of 1878 double-action Colts, modified with a strange long trigger and enlarged guard, were also issued.

The stopping power of the old big-bore .45s proved to be far superior. However, they were stopgap measures. An effective standard modern handgun was needed.

What was needed? The famous Thompson-LaGarde tests, which involved shooting live stockyard cattle and human cadavers, provided one part of the answer: the new handgun would be a 45-caliber. Thus, the search for a new sidearm began in the early 1900s. Although semiautomatic pistols were coming into use, the cavalry still firmly favored the dependable revolver. The stage was set that any "automatic" considered must have reliability equal to that of the revolver and be a .45. A series of tests, to begin in 1906, was contemplated by the Army.

Prior To The Test Trials

Two 45-caliber cartridges would be used: a rimmed one for revolver use, and a rimless one for the automatic pistols.

The rimless version was essentially similar to a commercial round produced by Winchester for Colt since the spring of 1905. The Winchester ammunition was made for Colt's new 45-caliber autoloading pistol, which had been introduced in the fall of 1905.

The 1905 Colt .45, developed by John M. Browning, was a logical development of the locked-breech 38-caliber Colt/ Browning pistol. The new .45 had a five-inch barrel, which gave it an overall length of about eight inches. It weighed about 33 ounces. Capacity of the magazine was seven rounds. The cartridge, in its original loading, pushed a 200-grain bullet at about 900 feet per second. It was a potent load for a semiautomatic pistol of the time.

To today's shooters, the 1905 pistol might seem strange. It had no grip safety and no thumb safety. The shooter just cocked the hammer when he was ready to shoot. The hammer itself was of a rounded burr shape. The recessed magazine release was at the bottom of the grip frame. The only visible control was the slide stop on the left. It worked well, and a contemporary writer called it "a good fighting pistol." It was the only .45 automatic in commercial production, a fact that gave it a decided advantage when the tests began.

It is worth commenting on the slide of the early Colt automatics. We are so used to semiautomatic pistols hav-

In the early post-WWII decades, the only 45-caliber semi-automatic pistols available to give the Colt Government Model any competition were the Spanish Llama (upper) and Star (lower) pistols. Neither design was a part-for-part copy of the 1911, but the guns were look-alikes of comparable size and weight.

The 1905 Colt was the first successful 45-caliber semiautomatic pistol. Having a gun already in production gave the Colt com-pany a head start when the U. S. military tests began in 1907.

In 1971, Colt brought out the Combat Commander, the same size as the original lightweight Commander, but with a steel frame.

ing slides that it is difficult to realize now what an innovation Browning had introduced. The earliest high-power auto pistols — the Borchardt, the Bergmann, the Mauser, the Mannlicher and the Luger — had exposed barrels with the locking mechanism completely behind the barrel. Browning designed the slide as a totally new concept, a moving breechblock that extended forward over the barrel. Not only did this make a much more compact pistol for any barrel length, but the slide and barrel could have mating lugs to form the short-recoil locking mechanism.

The Colt .38 automatics had been linked to the frame at both the front and rear of the barrel. Lugs on the barrel mated with recesses in the slide. Thus, the barrel and slide were locked together during firing. Then, as the barrel moved down after firing, the slide was free to move rearward, ejecting the empty case and feeding in a new cartridge on its return cycle. This same system was used with the 45-caliber Model 1905.

The 1907-1911 Test Trials

The initial tests were scheduled for 1906, then rescheduled for early 1907.

When the board convened on January 15, 1907, eight applicants had submitted nine designs. Three were revolvers, and six were automatic pistols. The revolvers, Colt, Smith & Wesson and Webley-Fosbery, were soon dropped from consideration.

The autoloaders, at that early stage of history, represented a variety of concepts in competition for the first time. Having the 1905 already in production made Colt the front-runner. However, besides the Colt, the Army also tested pistols from Bergmann, Knoble, White-Merrill, Luger, and Savage. Three of the entries — the Bergmann, Knoble and White-Merrill pistols — were rejected early in the tests as being unsuitable. The Colt was considered the best and the Savage worthy of additional testing. The Board authorized the purchase of 200 each of the Colt and Savage pistols for field tests. Colt, of course, readily accepted, but the fledgling Savage company, then just 12 years old, was unwilling

Revolvers had been made of stainless steel for some years, but in 1977, AMT brought out the first 1911-style 45 automatic made of stainless steel. The AMT Hardballer was essentially a stainless copy of the Colt Gold Cup National Match.

to tool up for such a relatively small production run, so the contract was offered to the third-place Luger. The German DWM company (*Deutsche Waffen- und Munitionsfabriken*), the maker of the Luger/Parabellum pistols, accepted the contract but then backed out. Apparently, the larger Luger .45 could not have been made on existing production machinery, and the German firm may have also been reluctant to redesign production tooling for a small contract. Also, DWM may have wanted to put more resources into the final development of its 9mm pistol. This pistol was indeed shortly thereafter adopted by the German Army as the Pistole '08 (P08).

The failure of DWM to supply 45-caliber Lugers for the field tests gave Savage a chance to reconsider. A semiautomatic pistol would give the company a chance to expand its product line, which then consisted only of the hammerless lever-action rifle designed by Arthur Savage. Savage accepted the contract.

The competition of the Savage was a good thing. During the field tests, which ran from 1907 into 1911, the Savage was good enough to show that the original 1905 Colt design could use substantial improvement. Browning, 52 years old at the beginning of the tests, worked with Colt, making changes to the design as the continuing testing indicated they

were needed. The result of the changes was an increasingly superior Colt pistol.

The final test was a 6000-round endurance test, held during March 1911. Pistols would cool after every 100 shots, and would be inspected, cleaned and oiled every 1000 shots. Both pistols fired over 1000 rounds without problems, but as the shooting continued, the Savage developed problems with malfunctions, and parts defects appeared. The refined Colt fired shot after shot, 100 after 100, 1000 after 1000, until the full 6000 rounds were completed without a stoppage or parts problem.

The tests were a milestone in the development of the semiautomatic pistol. The end result of four years of extensive testing was the most reliable large-caliber pistol in the world. The final report on the Colt stressed "its marked superiority...to any other known pistol."

Adoption of The 1911

The Colt design was adopted, on March 29, 1911, by the US Army as the Model 1911 pistol. Colt would be the supplier. The Navy and Marine Corps also adopted the 1911 within a short time.

As adopted, the 1911 pistol had a 5-inch barrel and weighed about 38 ounces. The unlocking was still accomplished by downward movement of the barrel, but the barrel had only one link at the rear, with the muzzle supported by a barrel bushing. It had both thumb and grip safeties. A pushbutton magazine release had been added. For better pointing characteristics, the grip-to-bore angle had been changed from a straight 84 degrees to a slantier 74 degrees.

Colt immediately discontinued the 1905, and as its replacement, put the Model 1911 into commercial production also. With what was then probably the most thoroughly tested pistol in the world, Colt not only offered the 1911 as a commercial model, but additionally looked for other markets beyond the United States.

Foreign Variations

Norway was the second country to adopt the 45-caliber Colt 1911. Because guns based on Browning's patents could not be handled in Europe by Colt FN in Belgium made the arrangements. In 1912, the Norwegians standardized the Colt design to their liking and adopted it. The modifications apparently consisted primarily of changing the checkering pattern on the hammer and applying Norwegian markings. Only about 500 Model 1912 pistols were made. Minor changes were suggested in 1914, and in 1919, after World War I had ended (Norway was neutral during World

War I), these were incorporated into the Model 1914 Norwegian pistol. The most noticeable change involved a redesigned slide stop, with the thumbpiece lower and slightly rearward. Having a small army, Norway produced about 22,000 1914 pistols, felt this to be adequate, and stopped production.

While Norway sat out World War I as a neutral nation, Great Britain had been one of the principal participants. The British were poorly prepared for war, and had shortages of most small arms. In 1912, the British had adopted a large-bore autoloading pistol, the Mark I Webley self-loader. The pistol was chambered for the .455 Webley Self Loading cartridge (also called .455 Eley). Independently designed, the round was similar in dimensions and power to the .45 ACP cartridge.

The precisely-fitted Webley autoloader proved unreliable in conditions of sand or grit. The 1912 Webleys were restricted to sea duty, and the British looked for another type of .455 pistol. The one they acquired was the 1911 Colt. The first of the 455-caliber Colts was reportedly shipped in mid-1915. It is believed that about 13,500 were shipped to Great Britain for military use.

The next country to adopt the Colt 1911 was Argentina, in 1916. The Colt

was adopted as the Pistola Automatica Sistema Colt, Calibre 11,25mm Modelo 1916. Essentially, the Argentine 1916 was identical to the commercially-made US Colt except for markings.

United States Use
Through WWI

As they became available to the American military, 1911 pistols were sent to the Philippines, where fighting with native tribes continued. The new .45s were also used in the1916 Punitive Expedition, led by General John J. Pershing, that went into Mexico after Pancho Villa.

Colt made all the early 1911 pistols. However, the U. S. Government, previously content to manufacture only long guns (and to purchase handguns from commercial manufacturers), reconsidered. The Ordnance Department wanted an arrangement by which it could manufacture the 1911 at Springfield Armory if it so desired. After some negotiation, Colt conferred the right to manufacture the pistol to the government for a royalty of $2.00 each. After a contract for 50,000 Colt-made pistols, the government could manufacture pistols at the rate of one pistol for every two ordered from Colt.

The Springfield pistols were essentially identical to the Colt-made pistols except for markings. Visually, they could be recognized by the sharper (less-gradual) termination of the scallop at the front of the slide.

World War I had broken out in Europe in 1914. In hindsight, it was only a matter of time until the United States was drawn into the war. America entered on the side of the Allies on April 6, 1917. At that time, apparently without any actual analysis, Ordnance believed that Colt "…would be able to take care of the entire pistol program…." However, the new conditions of trench warfare caused military planners to increase the distribution of sidearms. At first, 10% were to be armed with the 1911, then, up to 60%. Eventually, up to 72% of front-line troops were authorized to carry pistols as well as rifles.

The United States was not prepared

Taurus, a 1911 manufacturer since 2005, makes a variety of 1911 pistols, including this rail-equipped variant.

Kimber, one of the major forces in the 1911 world, recently introduced the SIS variant, in several different sizes.

129

to achieve this kind of pistol production. Because of the need for more rifles, Springfield Armory stopped pistol production during 1916 and 1917. (It did resume Model 1911 production in 1918, after the use of the 1917 Enfield had eased the need for 1903 Springfield rifles.)

In 1917, Colt delivered pistols at a monthly rate of about 9000 guns. In 1918, production increased from about 11,000 to a monthly peak of over 45,000 by the end of the war. This was not enough.

Even by the winter of 1917, it had become obvious that Colt production alone could not supply enough pistols. A new source was found in Remington-UMC. Remington had been manufacturing 3-line Mosin-Nagant rifles for Russia, but the contract ended when Russia withdrew from the war in 1917. By mid-1918, with full cooperation from Colt, Remington-UMC began production of the 1911. By September, completed pistols were being shipped. By the end of 1918, Remington-UMC was up to 4500 pistols a month. The total made was 21,676. Except for markings, they were the same as the Colt pistols.

Even with the Remington pistols (and with .45 ACP-caliber 1917 Colt and S&W revolvers), there were still just not enough handguns. Orders were placed with a number of other firms. However, the end of the war came in November 1918 before any additional production was established. One instance of actual pistols being made took place in Canada. The North American Arms Co. (in the Ross rifle plant) made some finished 1911 pistols, although probably fewer than 100 were made.

The 1911 pistol proved itself in combat during World War I. Many instances of excellent performance of the 45 were reported. The exploits of Corporal Alvin York are probably the most memorable use of both rifle and pistol. York almost single-handedly captured 132 German soldiers. His actions stopped a German counterattack in France's Argonne Forest. (And, yes, I know — the Gary Cooper movie depicted York as using a captured German Luger. However, that was

only because the moviemakers could not get the 1911 to work with blanks! York used a 1911.)

Between the Wars

After any war, military development generally slows down. Pistol development during the decades of the Roaring Twenties and the Great Depression was relatively minor.

Use in the World War had pointed out a few minor complaints concern-

World War II Model 1911A1 pistols, like this Ithaca-made specimen, were standardized with parkerized finish, plastic grips and flat hammers. (This pistol, bought through the DCM, was the author's first 45 automatic.) Ithaca, now located in Upper Sandusky, Ohio, is once again making 1911s.

ing the 1911. Soldiers with small hands had experienced some trouble gripping the pistol and controlling the trigger properly. The hammer spur sometimes pinched the fleshy web of a shooter's hand against the tang of the grip safety. The fine sights were difficult to see under conditions of low light. It tended to point low during instinct shooting.

Accordingly, subtle changes were made to the pistol to answer these situations. The trigger was shortened, and the frame was recessed on the sides near the trigger to provide better access. The tang of the grip safety was lengthened. The sights, although still small by today's standards, were made with a larger square notch at the rear and a wider square front sight. The flat mainspring housing was replaced by an arched housing. Subtle changes were also made to the rifling.

These changes were approved in 1923, and by 1925, Colt had put them into production. In June 1926, the nomenclature was changed to Model 1911A1.

With the adoption of the 1911A1, much of the 1911 tooling at Springfield became obsolete. No more 45-caliber pistols were made at Springfield. Only that tooling able to produce spare parts common to 1911 and 1911A1 pistols was retained.

Colt, of course, changed its commercial offering as soon as the military specifications were implemented. The military pistols were marked Model 1911A1, but the commercial pistols were, for the first time, marked "Government Model."

Mexico had adopted the 1911 after WWI and had purchased pistols directly from Colt. After about 1926, pistols with the 1911A1 modifications were supplied.

Argentina, as noted previously, had adopted the 1911 as their Modelo 1916. After 1927, Colt supplied 1911A1 pistols. Markings on the Argentine Colts remained the same, except that the modified pistol became known as the Modelo 1927. In the early 1930s, Colt agreed to license manufacture by the Argentine government. The Argentine-made Colts were made at Fabrica Militar de Armas

Portatiles (FMAP) in Rosario, Argentina. Unlicensed modified pistols, the Ballester-Rigaud and Ballester-Molina, were also made in Argentina.

During the 1920s, the automobile had become common, and had become widely used by criminals. Law Enforcement found that bullets from the traditional .38 Special revolver, and even the big .45 automatic, would not reliably penetrate car bodies. In 1929, Colt introduced its Super 38 pistol. The Super 38 was a Government Model modified to use a high-powered version of the old .38 ACP cartridge introduced in 1900. With a velocity of almost 1300 feet per second (fps), the new Super 38's 130-grain jacketed bullet earned a good reputation for penetration.

A 22-caliber pistol based on the 1911 design would be a good training and target pistol. In 1931, Colt introduced a .22 Long Rifle blowback pistol, the Ace. Later, about 1937, Colt incorporated the floating chamber designed by David Marshall Williams ("Carbine Williams"), and the new pistol became the Service Model Ace. The Ace was discontinued in 1941, but the Service Model Ace was used for training during World War II.

Target shooting with handguns, previously a sport for single-shot pistols and revolvers, saw the use of semiautomatic pistols becoming more common. At the 1930 National Matches, Colt introduced its National Match 45-caliber pistol. Based on the Government Model, it had a match-grade barrel, honed action, and could be supplied with fixed sights or with Stevens adjustable sights. Barrels and slides were fitted and numbered to each other. The National Match pistol was well-received, and Colt put it into their catalog as a regular production item in 1932. About 3000 were made before production stopped in 1941. A similar pistol was subsequently available in .38 Super, as the Super Match.

World War II

World War II began officially on September 1, 1939, with the German invasion of Poland. The success of the German blitzkrieg surprised even the Nazis. The Germans needed additional arms to supply their occupation troops, and began a program of producing and utilizing the suitable firearms of captured countries

Norway had been neutral during WWI, and reaffirmed neutrality during WWII. However, Nazi Germany viewed Norway as a base of operations against the Allied blockade, and as a possible staging area for an attack on Great Britain. German forces attacked Norway on April 9, 1940, and the country fell within two months. When production of the 1914 Norwegian Colt resumed, it was under German, not Norwegian, control. Apparently issued only in Norway to occupation troops or subservient Norwegian troops, about 10,000 additional

tols were made during the war. Colt, involved with other war production, was not the largest producer of the WWII .45. That honor went to Remington-Rand, the typewriter and business-machine manufacturer.

About 1,032,000 pistols were made by Remington-Rand. This amounted to almost 55% of production. In the year of 1944 alone, the company produced over one-half million pistols. Historian Donald Bady called this "the largest annual production by a single manufacturer in the history of firearms."

Colt produced about 480,000 pistols, over 22% of the total production. Ithaca Gun Company, a shotgun maker, manufactured about 369,000, amounting to almost 20%. Union Switch & Signal Co.

Military National Match pistols used at Camp Perry had the trigger weighed and a tape placed on the trigger guard to show it met specifications. This gun was fired at Camp Perry in 1967 by the author, and still has the 1967 tape on the trigger guard.

Norwegian 45s were produced before the German surrender in May of 1945.

When the United States was forced into World War II by the Japanese attack on Pearl Harbor on December 7, 1941, we were again poorly prepared for war. However, many of the production problems experienced during WWI were avoided. It had been realized that manufacturers other than those making firearms could be utilized for pistol production. About two million 1911A1 pis-

made 55,000 guns. The Singer (sewing machine) Manufacturing Co. was given an "educational order" of 500 pistols.

Production was aided by the early determination of a "standard" pistol to be made by all companies. Essentially all WWII 1911A1 pistols were "Parkerized" (a rust-resistant phosphate finish), had brown plastic grip panels, and had flat-sided hammers. The trigger/stirrup unit was made from stamped components, and grooving replaced checkering on some parts. Colt worked with the other manufacturers, and this cooperation assisted production.

In addition to production of new 45s, a number of old Model 1911 pistols that had been placed in storage were refurbished for WWII use. They were parkerized, and if parts were needed, 1911A1 parts were installed. Work was done at Augusta Arsenal, and such pistols were stamped with the letters "AA."

Again, the Colt/Browning 45 pistol proved itself as a reliable, powerful sidearm. It stood apart from other handguns used during the Second World War.

Post-War, Through   the 1950s

The basic 1911 handgun had gone through its second world war with an exemplary record. Essentially every American serviceman held the pistol in high regard. This feeling was well-represented in the 1959 novel, *The Pistol*, by James Jones. The novel follows the movement of a 45-caliber pistol among U. S. servicemen after Pearl Harbor, in which every man who has any contact with the pistol wants it for his own personal protection.

Still, after 1946, for the first time in almost four decades, U. S. military planners considered the possibility of a lighter pistol, and also began to consider a change to the 9mm Parabellum (9mm Luger) ammunition used by both wartime adversaries and allies.

Colt investigated the possibilities of a lighter Government Model, and developed an association with ALCOA Aluminum. A number of frames were made of aluminum alloy, and test pistols were made. To further reduce weight, the barrel length was shortened to 4-1/4 inches, and the slide shortened accordingly. A rounded "burr" hammer was used, which also allowed use of a shorter-tang grip safety. The test pistols were made in the by-then traditional .45 ACP and .38 Super, and — with an eye to possible military tests — also in 9mm Luger chambering.

Eventually the military reconsidered, realizing that plenty of 45-caliber 1911A1 pistols were on hand. In June 1950, the United States became involved in a "police action" in Korea (it was not

called the Korean War until later). The 45-caliber pistols, along with the rest of America's WWII armament, went back into service. Consideration of a 9mm pistol was dropped, at least for the time being.

Colt had already made a decision to market the shorter, lighter version of the Government Model. In early 1950, it was introduced as the Commander Model. Calibers were .45, .38 Super and 9mm. The Colt Commander was a landmark pistol. At 26-1/2 ounces, it was our first big-bore aluminum frame pistol. Often overlooked is the fact that the Commander was the first pistol ever commercially produced in America in the 9mm chambering.

By the end of the 1950s, the position of the 1911 had evolved. Now, almost half a century old, from being a splendid military pistol, it was becoming everyman's pistol.

After the end of WWII, all shooting sports increased in popularity. A joke of the time was that returning servicemen were only interested in two things — and the second one was shooting.

Bullseye pistol shooting benefited from this renewed interest and became very popular. The National Match Course had sections for 22-caliber, Centerfire and 45-caliber pistols. Everyone wanted a .45.

The National Matches, closed during WWII and Korea, resumed in 1953. Military "National Match" pistols were made from .45s on hand beginning in 1955. Most were made at Springfield Armory (thus getting the facility back into providing pistols, if not actually manufacturing them), and were stamped NM. Originally fitted with high fixed sights, they were made with adjustable sights in 1961. Colt furnished parts for such work.

However, the maker of the first, the original pre-war National Match pistol, could hardly have been satisfied without a match pistol of its own. Colt, in 1957, brought out an improved version of its early National Match 45, called the Gold Cup National Match. It was a highly-developed pistol for competition shooting. It became the standard by which .45

target pistols were judged.

Surprisingly, it was not the only newly-made target-oriented .45 auto-loader available. The Spanish Llama pistols (copies of the 1911, but not part-for-part copies), were imported by A. F. Stoeger since 1951. In 1957, the Llama line also introduced a target version in .45 caliber. Before that time, a number of gunsmith shops had begun specializing in "accurizing" .45s for target competition.

As the 1950s went on, then began what has been called "the Golden Age of Surplus." As countries around the world updated their military equipment, they cleaned out their armories. Military equipment, including firearms, was sold on the world market. A large portion of the guns came to the country with the greatest degree of personal freedom — the United States. Some of the pistols that came in as surplus were 1916 and 1927 Argentine .45s. Many were "accurized" and used for target shooting. Norwegian 1914 .45s also made their appearance. Also coming in were a smaller number of the British 455-caliber Colt 1911s. To make the .455s more salable, they were advertised, "Will shoot .45 ACP." (Yes, they would, but not very accurately.)

Traditional Bullseye shooting was not the only pistol sport to gain popularity. A new handgun sport was developing in California. Popularized by the writing of Col. Jeff Cooper, the two-handed action-style pistol shooting was called "practical" shooting. Shooters found it to be fun as well as practical, and the new sport grew. These informal matches grew into the alphabet soup of IPSC, USPSA, PPC and NRA Action shooting of today. Based on the concepts of Accuracy, Power and Speed, the pistol that fit Cooper's ideas best? The 45-caliber Government Model.

The 1960s

The 1960s started as a continuation of the 1950s, but by the end of that decade, things had changed dramatically in the United States firearms scene.

In the early years of the '60s, the popularity of the 1911 got a boost when the Ordnance Department, through the Director of Civilian Marksmanship (DCM) made surplus 1911 and 1911A1 pistols available to members of the National Rifle Association (NRA). The August 1960 issue of *American Rifleman* gave the details. Price was $17, including packing and shipping. Pistols were classed "unserviceable," which meant they may have had minor defects, but were safe to fire. (The Ithaca 1911A1 I got had a cracked slide stop, which cost me a dollar to replace.) The influx of inexpensive .45s was a shot in the arm to the pistol-shooting sports.

Spare parts for the 1911-type pistols were also available. Enterprising small manufacturers made new frames, and gunsmiths assembled new 1911s from the parts.

Those military-surplus 45-caliber pistols sold during the 1960s were the last pistols sold by the U. S. government to civilians. Soon, national tragedy, politics, and the growth of the anti-gun movement would adversely affect the firearms scene.

For those who wanted to buy a .45 and were willing to wade through the onerous restrictions of the Gun Control Act of 1968, Colt had something new. The loose fit of the average military 1911 had given rise to the idea that the 45 was "not accurate." Colt investigated possibilities, and determined that a new barrel bushing, a collet-type with spring-steel "fingers" to position the barrel, would increase accuracy. Without publicity, Colt began fitting pistols with this experimental new system in 1969. About 750 were reportedly made. They can be identified by the letters, "BB," stamped near the correct serial numbers.

The 1970s

The new "accurizer" barrel bushing system worked well, and in 1970, Colt brought it out as a standard item for its 1911 line. New nomenclature then became Colt's Mk. IV / Series '70. The collet-type bushings were used in the Government Model and Gold Cup National Match pistols. The Commander continued to use its original shortened solid bushing.

The next year, 1971, a Combat Commander was added to the Colt line. The same size as the original lightweight Commander, the pistol had a steel frame and weighed 33 ounces. 1971, the Centennial of the National Rifle Association, also saw a special Centennial Gold Cup made to commemorate the anniversary.

In 1973, things took a bad turn for Colt. A strike lasting from April through August took place. With Colt production curtailed for almost half a year, the "lookalike" Llama and Star pistols from Spain (modified copies of the 1911) got more attention. The Spanish pistols listed at ten to twenty dollars less than a Colt Government Model, which sold for $135.

The Colt Commander had provided a more compact 45-caliber handgun, but there was interest in a .45 in an even smaller package.

In 1975, the Spanish firm producing the big Star pistols brought out the Star PD. The new small Star was a shortened and lightened .45 with an aluminum frame. With its 4-inch barrel and weight of 25 ounces, the Star was, for a short time, the smallest .45 available.

In 1976, the year of America's Bicentennial, the 1911 was miniaturized in America by the new firm calling itself Detonics. Originally using Colt parts modified by them, and then manufacturing their own, Detonics brought out a compact steel .45, weighing 31 ounces. It was of innovative design, and had a 3-1/2-inch barrel. The Detonics pistol introduced the cone-barrel positioning system, orienting the short barrel in the slide without a bushing.

Until the 1970s, Colt had been the sole source of newly-made traditional U. S. 1911-style pistols, but during that decade, the market for similar .45s made by other firms grew.

About 1977, the AMT (Arcadia Machine & Tool) Hardballer was introduced. The pistol was essentially of Gold Cup configuaration, a target-grade pistol with adjustable sights. However, the AMT Hardballer was manufactured of stainless steel. It was apparently the first stainless-steel 1911 ever offered.

The AMT line grew, with fixed sight pistols and Commander-size pistols soon offered. Within a short time, they were joined by the striking Long Slide Hardballer, a similar adjustable-sighted pistol, but with a 7-inch barrel and correspondingly longer slide.

As the decade went on, Practical shooting (sometimes called "West Coast Shooting") spread across the country. Practical shooting was joined by other pistol sports, such as Bowling Pin shooting. Reliable quick-shooting pistols using powerful cartridges were in demand.

New companies sprang up across the country. In the closing years of the 1970s, 1911s were made, often in now-trendy stainless steel, by small companies such as Crown City (New York) and Vega (California).

In 1978, M-S Safari Arms began making striking 1911s with some of their own features. Most noticeable was a projection on the front strap of the grip to position the finger below the trigger guard. (M-S Safari was acquired, in 1987, by Olympic Arms, which made 1911s under the Safari and Schuetzen names, and still makes Olympic 1911-style pistols.)

Custom pistolmakers began to thrive. Wilson Combat had opened by 1978 and continues in business.

The 1980s

The growth of new interest in the 1911 that had begun in the '70s had a tremendous increase in the 1980s. In fact, there was a growth of interest in handguns of all types. A category called the "wondernines" gained popularity. They were full-size double-action 9mm pistols with magazine capacities up to 19 rounds,

In 1983, Colt added a firing-pin safety to the 1911 design. This prevented the firing pin from moving until the trigger was pressed. The new variant became the Mark IV / Series '80. In 1985, Colt also added stainless-steel versions of the Series '80 pistols.

During the 1980s, it became very clear that Colt was no longer the only maker of 1911 pistols. By 1981, the ODI (Omega Defensive Industries) Viking pistol, a 1911 fitted with the Seecamp double-action trigger system, was introduced. That same year, Auto-Ordnance, owned then by Numrich Arms, brought out the GI-style Thompson 1911A1 pistol. A number of guns from different companies appeared, based on modified 1911 designs. Representatives of this category were the Coonan, Arminex and Grizzly pistols.

Randall, a company first involved in making replacement stainless magazines for 1911s, in 1983 introduced a line of stainless-steel 1911 pistols. Early stainless autoloaders had developed problems with galling, developed as the stainless slide rubbed across the stainless frame. Randall believed they had solved those problems, and advertised the Randall as "the only stainless steel fit for duty." The most striking Randalls were the left-hand versions, which were completely left-handed—even the rifling turned the opposite way! About 7% of Randall's pistols were left-handed. The Randall Curtis E. LeMay pistol, honoring Air Force General LeMay, was a 4-1/4-inch barrel and a 6-shot finger-rest magazine. After making about 10,000 guns, Randall became overextended and the company failed in 1985.

Faring better was Springfield Armory, a new commercial company that had acquired the name of the former government facility. Springfield began in 1985 with pistols that were essentially recreations of the WWII 1911A1. It continues as one of the major 1911 manufacturers. A few other 1911 pistols, such as the MP Express from Meister Products, were made for a short time and then went out of production. Interarms, the large importer, built over a thousand 45-caliber 1911 pistols on new frames using surplus GI parts. With a sly reference to Colt's Gold Cup, the new pistols were marked and sold as the Interarms Silver Cup.

In 1985, a stir was created by the U. S. military selection of a 9mm service pistol. A version of the Beretta 92, with a 16-round magazine, was chosen. Even in the period of the wondernines, some old-timers were less than enthusiastic about the choice of cartridge. Thinking

of the performance of the .45 during WWII, one remarked, "Now we have the pistol cartridge used by the countries defeated during the war."

1986 arrived, Colt's 150th anniversary. However, the sesquicentennial was not a good period for the company. In 1986, a bitter strike against Colt began and dragged on for four years. The company economized during its time of limited production. Although it was not officially dropped until 1988, no mention of the collet-type "accurizer" bushing apparently was made after 1986.

Although 1986 meant hard times for Colt, other things happened.

The futility of gun-control laws was becoming obvious. In 1986, the

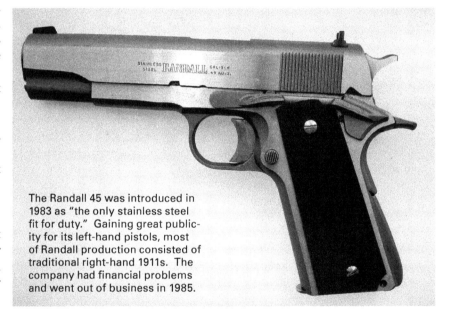

The Randall 45 was introduced in 1983 as "the only stainless steel fit for duty." Gaining great publicity for its left-hand pistols, most of Randall production consisted of traditional right-hand 1911s. The company had financial problems and went out of business in 1985.

Firearms Owners Protection Act was passed. One of the provisions was to allow importation of surplus firearms again, thus reversing one of GCA '68's many restrictions.

In 1986, the Falcon Portsider was introduced, a left-handed pistol made to enter the niche abandoned when Randall went out of business. Falcon made only a small number of pistols, and was gone by 1990.

About 1988, Para-Ordnance, a Canadian company making "non-gun" dye-marking guns, introduced a sideline of large-capacity frames and magazines for the 1911. Standard 1911 parts could be fitted to the frames to create the first

large-capacity 1911-type 45s. Soon, in 1990, the company began making complete pistols. Para-Ordnance, today simply called Para, grew to become a major supplier of 1911 pistols.

Other companies made 1911s before the decade ended. Federal Ordnance made the Ranger, a basic GI-style 1911A1. Michigan Armament (distributed from, of all places, California) made somewhat fancier variants. Custom maker Ed Brown started business in 1988.

In spite of its labor problems, Colt was still active during this time. The 45-caliber Officers ACP was introduced in 1985. The new Colt compact pistol had a 3-1/2-inch barrel, weighed 34 ounces, and had a 6-shot magazine in a shortened frame. The 10mm Delta Elite variant of the full-size Government Model came out in 1987. By the end of the decade, the double-action stainless-steel Colt Double Eagle had become a production item, at least for a few years.

In 1988, Florida enacted a "shall issue" license-to-carry law that became a model for similar laws in other states. The growth of legal concealed carry across the country increased the demand for handguns of various types. The 1911 became even more popular among ordinary citizens for personal protection.

The 1990s

If interest in the 1911 had increased in the 1980s, it can be said to have exploded in the 1990s.

At the beginning of the decade, Colt carried out a plan to get back into the basic 1911 market. Its enhanced offerings had become fancier, and the market for basic "wartime" pistols had grown. By 1991, the Colt 1991 A1 was introduced, actually continuing the serial number range of the company's 1911 A1 pistols of World War II. With a matte finish and simple features, the new Colt was competitive in its niche. Commander (4-1/2-inch) and Compact (3-1/2-inch) variants were offered in 1993.

By 1998, Colt introduced an even smaller pistol with a 3-inch barrel, the Defender. The 23-ounce .45 used a cone-barrel system to orient the barrel in the slide.

Early in the decade, in 1991, a new name, Norinco, was added to the list of 1911 companies. The Chinese entity made a surprisingly good copy of a 1911. The Norinco got good reviews until president William J. Clinton prohibited importation of firearms from China in 1995.

The popularity of the 1911 design grew. Other names were added to the list of companies offering 1911 pistols: McMillan (1992), STI (1993), Rocky Mountain Arms (1993 – trying a third time for the left-hand market), and Mitchell (1994). Because Para-Ordnance high-capacity pistols were gaining popularity, Mitchell's new 45s were offered in double-column configuration — 13+1 — as well as the traditional single-column style. Springfield and Llama also offered large-capacity 13+1 pistols that same year.

1994 was a poor time to offer large-capacity pistols. In that year, the so-called "Assault Weapons Ban" was passed into law.

Among other absurd restrictions, the ban limited magazine capacity of all detachable magazines to 10 rounds or less. High-capacity staggered-column .45 magazines could no longer be made. Obviously, no other pistols of other calibers could have magazines of greater

than 10 rounds, either. The high-capacity "wondernine" magazines, holding up to 19 rounds, were no longer legal to make. Compared to a 10-round 9mm, a traditional 1911 .45 holding seven or eight rounds began to look a much better choice. 45-caliber pistols became more popular. As firearms authority J. B. Wood wryly noted, "If you can't make as many holes, make bigger ones." Interest in the .45, and in particular, the 1911, boomed.

From the midpoint of the 1990s, the demand for, and production of, 1911 pistols grew. In 1995, Ithaca brought out a 50th Anniversary edition of its WWII .45. Even more new names appeared: Brolin (1995), Kimber (1995), BUL and GAL (both imported from Israel in 1996), Armscor (imported from the Philippines by KBI in 1996), Griffon (1997, South Africa), Entreprise Arms (1997), Rock River's first 1911 (1998), Valtro (1998, from Italy), and Shooters Arms Manufacturers, "S.A.M" (1999, from the Philippines). The Charles Daly name, formerly associated with shotguns, was introduced on a pistol for the first time in 1998, when KBI used the name on its 45-caliber 1911.

In 1999, Auto-Ordnance was acquired by Kahr Arms. Kahr rejuvenated the Auto-Ordnance/Thompson 1911 pistol line. Galena industries acquired the right to produce the AMT 1911 line and some other AMT pistols (but sadly went out of production by 2002).

For decades, gunsmiths had been making custom-built pistols based on the 1911. Such guns started as one-of-a-kind handguns. With time, it was realized that many customers wanted similar features. A relatively small number of different customized pistols would satisfy the majority of customers. By the end of the 1990s, this making of "production custom" 1911s was a booming business. Companies such as (alphabetically) Briley, Ed Brown, Les Baer, Nowlin, STI, Strayer-Voigt, Wilson and others had offered such special 1911s.

The New Century

With the flurry of interest in the 1911 that had exploded in the closing

decades at the end of the 20th century, the production of 1911-style pistols had been spread among a large and growing number of different companies Colt was no longer the primary producer. Three relatively new companies — Kimber, Springfield and Para-Ordnance — vied for that position. Kimber advertised their company as "first in the number of 1911 pistols made and sold." Not to be outdone, Springfield claimed "the greatest selection of 1911 pistols." Para-Ordnance introduced features that set its offerings apart.

As the new century began, Colt again fell on hard times. In the year 2000, the company discontinued most of its handgun line. Only the Single Action Army and the 1911 were left. The 1911 was offered in 45 caliber only. Within a few years, however, Colt's fortunes improved.

Not everyone had liked the Series '80 firing pin safety. Colt decided to go back to its roots with new 1911 offerings. The Series '80 continued in the line, but by 2002, Colt had reintroduced its Series '70 pistol, without the firing pin safety. Actually, it could have been considered a "pre '70" Government Model, as it also did not have the fingered barrel bushing. The "new" Series '70 has modern higher sights, and improved barrel ramping.

Reception was good, and in 2003, the original WWI-era Model 1911 was reintroduced. The pistol was a faithful recreation of the .45 as made around the year 1918.

Colt remained a 1911 manufacturer in an increasingly large group of 1911 manufacturers.

New names continued to enter the world of the 1911. New companies appeared to offer their versions of the 1911. In the first few years of the 21st century, one could see new 1911 pistols bearing the names of Dan Wesson (a revolver company making its first autoloaders), High Standard (the resurrected company expanding its product line), Peters Stahl, Rock River, Century, Firestorm, Casull, Pacific Armament, DPMS (prototype only), Bond Arms, Lone Star, Ed Brown, Guncrafter, Uselton and Detonics USA (the latest incarnation of the original Detonics).

In 2003, the familiar old name of Smith & Wesson was also added. Apparently figuring "if you can't beat them, join them," S&W introduced the SW1911, and plunged into an extensive line of 1911-design pistols within a few years. A year later, in 2004, SIGARMS (now SIG-Sauer) also decided to get into the 1911 business. SIG brought out its GSR (Granite State Revolution) line of 1911 pistols, which soon became known by "Revolution."

In 2004, a bright spot appeared for firearms owners: the absurd "Assault Weapons Ban" was allowed to sunset. High-capacity pistols and magazines in all calibers could again be made. Of course, smaller calibers could be made with larger magazine capacities. New high-capacity 9mm pistols were offered. However, the popularity of the 1911 had grown to the point that it was not threatened by new designs.

After the AWB sunset, in the last half of the new century's first decade, firearms developments continued. The pace of 1911 development was breathtaking.

The largest additional entry into the 1911 field was Taurus, in 2005. Billing itself as the "World's Foremost Pistol Maker," Taurus quickly marketed a full line of 1911 pistols. The Brazilian maker joined Smith & Wesson and SIG, all of which had just joined frontrunners Kimber, Springfield and Para as new major players in the 1911 world.

In 2006, the U. S. military called for tests of 45-caliber pistols due to questions of the 9mm's efficacy during the Desert Wars in Iraq and Afghanistan. Exactly 100 years after calling for tests to consider a .45 in 1906, the military wanted to again consider a .45 in 2006. The traditional 1911 was not invited, however; .45s to be considered would be double-action, polymer-frame pistols. As before, the tests were postponed and at the time of this writing have not been resumed. The companies that had been preparing pistols instead offered them to the commercial market, in competition with the 1911.

The 1911 seemed not to notice the new competition. The 2005 introduction of the Taurus 1911 showed that major companies still saw potential in the design.

The Taurus was not the only new entry of this recent period. Just within the last few years, new 1911 pistols with new names were introduced by Double Star, Iver Johnson, Rock Island (RIA),

Smith & Wesson entered the 1911 field in 2003 and markets an extensive line, including variants of the full-size SW1911.

U. S. Fire Arms (1911s with the wide grips of the 1905), Nighthawk, American Classic, Tisas (the first Turkish 1911), EMF (the Cowboy arms company, branching into 1911s), and Legacy Sports (offering their Citadel 1911). Dan Wesson was acquired by CZ-USA, giving the Czech company access to 1911 sales.

Colt remains a major player in the 1911 field, offering new variants as well as traditional models. In 2007, Colt introduced the Concealed Carry model, followed by the New Agent in 2008. Colt decided to cash in on the trend of accessory rails on the front of a 1911 frame, and came out with a gun for that niche in 2009. What to call it? Colt kept it simple: the Colt Rail Gun.

Colt, the original manufacturer, has made the 1911 continuously since its introduction in 1911. The amazing growing interest in the century-old pistol now has, quite literally, dozens of other companies simultaneously making their versions of the same design. These guns are being made in the United States and in a growing number of foreign countries. This situation is unprecedented in the world of firearms.

Conclusion

A complete description of every 1911 made by every maker would be a huge volume of information, beyond the scope of this presentation. What is here presented is the basic history of the development of the 1911 design, and the amazing growth in the popularity of the design with the passing of time.

Now, one hundred years from its beginning, we have no idea where we really are in the story of the 1911. Has the 1911 reached its peak, and will it start a decline? Or, is it about to begin a new phase of popularity?

What words can summarize the amazing story of the 1911 at the event of its centennial, its 100th year?

We can try a few:

The Colt/Browning 1911 design has completed its first century. It has stood the test of time. It has proved itself in military combat, law-enforcement use, target competition of many types, personal protection and recreational shooting.

It has been scaled down, both in size (3-inch barrels) and in caliber (22-caliber). It has been scaled up, both in size (7-inch barrels) and in caliber (50-caliber). Millions upon millions have been made, many of them close to the original specifications, others gussied up with a number of modifications and accessories.

In its early days, the 1911 was so good that it discouraged competition. It was then considered the best pistol ever designed. One hundred years later, there are many who say that it still is.

The Colt Official Police and S&W Military & Police

What were the most popular law enforcement handguns of the twentieth century? The answer might surprise you.

▌ By Paul Scarlata; Photos By James Walter

I want all of you readers under the age of 30 to sit down before we go any further. I want you seated because I don't want anyone getting dizzy and falling down when I tell you that:

There was a time when American police officers DID NOT carry semi-auto pistols!

Yes, children, it's true. From the 1870s until the last decade and a half of the twentieth century, the weapon in the holster of the vast majority of American cops was a revolver. I know some of you are having trouble visualizing this concept, but that's not the end of the story. Not only did the guardians of law and order carry revolvers, but the weapon in question was usually a "plain Jane" blue steel revolver with a barrel of four to six inches, fitted with wooden grips and fixed sights.

I can hear the gasps of disbelief emanating from the readership. "No stainless steel? No adjustable sights? No recoil absorbing, synthetic grips? How could they possibly function with such primitive equipment?" Well, the answer

to that question consists of two words: Damn well!

Those of us who are "experienced" shooters remember when the choice of centerfire handguns available to the public was limited. In fact, until 1954 there was only one (!) American-made, centerfire pistol capable of firing a serious cartridge: the .45-caliber Colt M1911. But even this well-respected icon received little notice from the average civilian

1944. Canadian infantry officers in the Netherlands. They are wearing holstered No. 2 S&W revolvers. (Courtesy of Clive Law)

Two Boston PD officers wearing early bulletproof vests. They are armed with Colt O.P. revolvers. (Courtesy Boston PD Records Center & Archives)

137

shooter or police officer. To us Americans, when the word "handgun" was mentioned, the image that immediately came to mind was the revolver.

During the latter half of the nineteenth century, most American police forces did not issue handguns. Officers were usually supplied with a truncheon and a set of handcuffs, and those desiring to carry firearms were required to buy their own. Standards, when they existed at all, were usually limited to what were acceptable calibers and size. Period photos show these nineteenth-century constables wearing long coats and tall hats but nary a holster in sight. This was because most urban agencies required that the handgun be carried out of sight, which was why small, .32-caliber, top-break designs predominated.

The situation began to change in the 1890s as urban police departments became better trained, organized and armed. One of the first was the NYPD, whose new commissioner, Theodore Roosevelt, equipped all officers with a standard handgun, the Colt .32 New Police revolver – and insisted they receive marksmanship training. This also signified an important technological change as the New Police was a swing-out cylinder revolver. Even then the NYPD was a trendsetting agency and many depart-

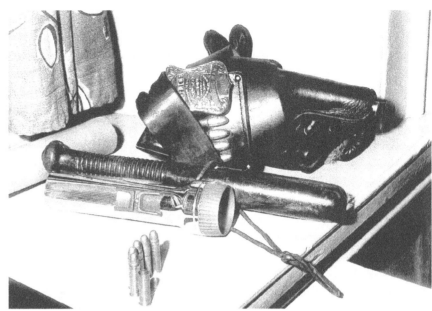

The equipment of a member of the Boston Police Department, circa 1960. (Courtesy Boston PD Records Center & Archives)

ments followed suit and adopted the new Colt.

That same year S&W introduced their first swing-out cylinder revolver, the .32 Hand Ejector Model of 1896, which was taken into service by the Philadelphia PD, among others. The race was now on, as these two titans of the American handgun industry began a non-stop, no holds barred competition to see who could capture the lion's

share of the U.S. police market.

The year 1899 saw S&W's introduction of the .38 Hand Ejector Military & Police revolver. This medium frame (K-frame), swing-out cylinder revolver was their attempt to garner a military contract. And while the government purchased several thousand, Colt's .38-caliber New Model Army & Navy revolvers remained the standard military sidearm.

The next big step occurred during

the first decade of the new century. As is the case today, American police tended to ape the army when it came to side-arms, and the military's acceptance of the .38 Colt revolver convinced many that an upgrading of equipment was called for. While the .32 revolver's popularity with police would continue for a few more decades, the writing was on the wall for all to see: the .38 revolver would be THE next American police handgun of choice. The timing was opportune as the army was getting ready to ditch the .38 wheelgun in favor of one of the new fangled semi-auto pistols. With military sales drying up, Colt began to court police departments and their rivals from Springfield were not far behind!

The S&W M&P

The S&W .38 Hand Ejector – let's just call it the M&P – utilized a swing-out cylinder that was locked into the frame by means of a spring loaded center pin passing through the ejector rod and projecting out of the rear of the cylinder. When the cylinder is closed, the end of the center pin snaps into a recess in the recoil plate, locking the cylinder in place. To open, a thumb latch on the left side of the frame is pushed forward, forcing the center pin out of the locking recess and allowing the cylinder to be swung out to the left. Pushing back on the ejector rod forces out a star-shaped extractor, ejecting all the spent cartridge cases simultaneously.

In 1902 the locking system was strengthened by the addition of a underlug on the barrel with a spring-loaded pin that locked into the front end of ejector rod. This system has proven so practical that it has been used on all subsequent S&W revolvers down to the present day.

But perhaps more historically significant was the new cartridge introduced with the M&P. Known as the .38 S&W Special it consisted of a straight-walled, rimmed case 1.14" in length loaded with a 158-gr. lead round-nosed bullet with a rated velocity of approximately 850 fps. This was an definite improvement over the army's .38 Long Colt and within a

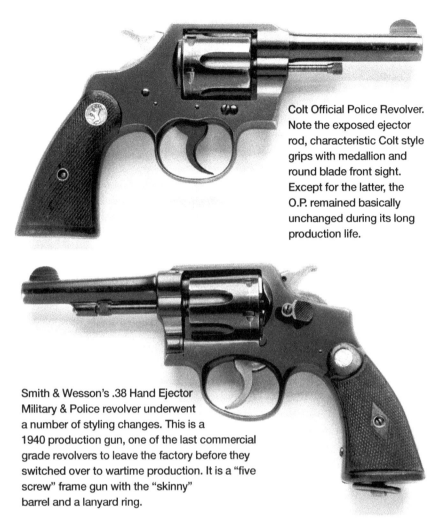

Colt Official Police Revolver. Note the exposed ejector rod, characteristic Colt style grips with medallion and round blade front sight. Except for the latter, the O.P. remained basically unchanged during its long production life.

Smith & Wesson's .38 Hand Ejector Military & Police revolver underwent a number of styling changes. This is a 1940 production gun, one of the last commercial grade revolvers to leave the factory before they switched over to wartime production. It is a "five screw" frame gun with the "skinny" barrel and a lanyard ring.

five years would completely dominate the medium-caliber revolver market to the point where even Colt was chambering revolvers for it.

1908 saw Colt attempt to interest police agencies with a modified New Model Army & Navy revolver: the New Army. They also introduced the smaller .38 Police Positive, which weighed a convenient 22 oz. The Police Positive would prove very popular and it, along with a short-barreled version, the Detective Special, would remain in production until the 1980s. But many agencies wanted a more robust sidearm and to answer this demand, in 1927 the Colt Official Police (O.P.) was released on the market.

The Colt Official Police

The O.P. used the same size of frame (I-frame) as the New Army but the frame and trigger guard were reshaped to make it more comfortable and attrac-

tive. Unlike some of the earlier Colts, cylinder rotation direction was clockwise and cylinder locking was strenghtened by a single peripheral recess for each chamber engaged by a bolt at the rear of the cylinder. Lastly, a pivoting firing pin replaced the fixed protuberance used on its predecessors.

Lockup was via a pin contained in the recoil plate that entered a recess in the center of a rotating ratchet at the rear of the cylinder, locking it securely in place. To unload the O.P., a latch on the left of the frame was pulled to the rear (exactly the opposite of the M&P), allowing the cylinder to be be swung out on a crane to the left. As with the S&W, pushing on the ejector rod activated a star-shaped extractor, extracting the spent cartridge cases simultaneously. Both the O.P. and M&P swing out cylinders permitted fast, fumble-free reloading, although it would be many more decades before the perfection of

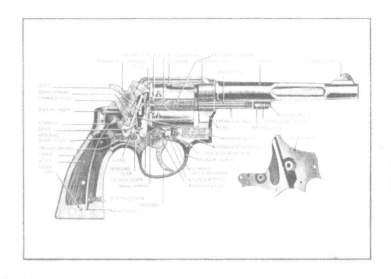

SMITH & WESSON, INC.
SPRINGFIELD, MASS., U.S.A.

A page from a 1940 Colt catalog extolling the virtues of their Official Police Revolver. Note that they refer to its cartridge as the ".38 Colt Special."

Cutaway view of a 1960s vintage M&P revolver. (Courtesy of Michael Jon Littman)

the revolver speedloader really speeded things up.

The O.P. weighed approximately 11 oz. more then the Police Positive and so, depending on what size revolver the customer wanted, Colt had the waterfront covered. In regard to weight, the M&P split the difference between the two Colts.

This entrepreneurial battle royale began with Colt – who traditionally received "better press" – having a distinct advantage. Within a few years, the O.P. was the standard issue sidearm of (among others) the NYPD, LAPD, Chicago, San Francisco, Kansas City, St. Louis, and Portland police departments. The highway patrols of Pennsylvania, New Jersey, Delaware, Maryland and Connecticut (to say nothing of the FBI) soon followed, and sales of the O.P. on the police and civilian markets boomed.

While the O.P. usually outsold the M&P, the S&W was without a doubt the #2 product on the North American police market. Among the more notable agencies adopting it were the police departments of San Antonio, New Orleans, Atlanta, Omaha, Dallas, Philadel-phia, and Charleston. Larger agencies included the Michigan and Virginia State Police and the Provincial Police of British Columbia, Quebec and Ontario. Over the years, many agencies approved the use of both revolvers and it was possible to find Colts and Smiths in service concurrently.

Unlike the O.P., the M&P underwent a number of changes and improvements during its production life, the most notable being:

1902: the addition of a underlug on the barrel with a spring loaded

To load or unload both the M&P and O.P., the cylinders were swung out to the left side. Both were traditional "six shooters."

pin that locked into the front of the ejector rod.

1904: an optional square butt grip frame and larger grips.

1907: the trigger mechanism was modified to provide a lighter DA trigger pull.

1915: the hammer rebound safety was replaced with a spring activated hammer block which was further improved in 1926.

1944: a mechanically activated, positive hammer block

Toth revolvers function identically – except to unlatch the S&W's cylinder, the thumb latch on the left side of the frame is pushed forward....

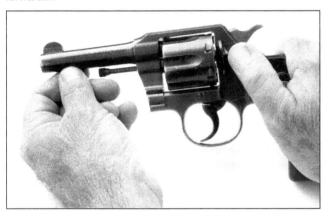

...while that of the Colt is pulled to the rear.

Then their cylinders were swung out to the left and their ejector rods pushed to the rear to extract the spent cases from the cylinder.

safety.

In 1940 Great Britain placed large orders for S&W revolvers to supplement their standard Enfield and Webley revolvers. S&W chambered the M&P for the standard British .380" Mark I cartridge, which was nothing more then the old .38 S&W loaded with a 200-gr. lead bullet (later a 178-gr. FMJ bullet). Deliveries continued until late 1945, with about 600,000 being delivered to British and Commonwealth forces.

In January 1942, to cut costs and speed up production, British production of the M&P was standardized with a Parkerized finish, smooth wooden grips and 5" barrel. S&W referred to this variation as the "Victory Model," and a "V" prefix was added to the serial number.

With the United States' entry into the war, the U.S. Government placed orders for Victory Model revolvers, which differed from the British pattern in that they were chambered for the .38 Special cartridge and were fitted with 2" and 4" barrels. Over 300,000 U.S. Victory Models were issued to the U.S. Navy, Coast Guard, Merchant Marine and security guards at

 SMITH & WESSON

.357 MILITARY & POLICE REVOLVER

MODEL No. 13

PARTS LIST • INSTRUCTIONS FOR USE • MAINTENANCE

SPECIFICATIONS • GUARANTEE

SPECIFICATIONS

Caliber	.357 S&W Special	Sights	Fixed, 1/8 inch serrated ramp front, square notch rear
Number of Shots	6	Frame	Square butt
Barrel	4 inches	Stocks	Checked walnut Service with S&W monograms
Length Over All	With 4-inch barrel 9¼ inches	Finish	S&W Blue
Weight	With 4-inch barrel 34 ounces	Ammunition	.357 S&W Magnum, .38 S&W Special Hi Speed, .38 S&W Special, .38 S&W Special Midrange

SMITH & WESSON

& A BANGOR PUNTA Company

Springfield, Massachusetts, U. S. A.

Instruction manual for a S&W .357 Magnum Model 13 revolver. This model, with a 3" barrel, was adopted by the FBI. (Courtesy of Michael Jon Littman)

government installations. Numbers of them eventually saw combat, mainly in the Pacific theater.

While Colt concentrated on producing other weapons for the war effort, beginning in 1942 a version of the O.P., known as the Colt Commando, was produced with a Parkerized finish, smooth trigger and hammer, plastic grips and 2" or 4" barrel. The government bought approximately 48,000 Commando revolvers, most of which were used by defense plant guards and government security agencies.

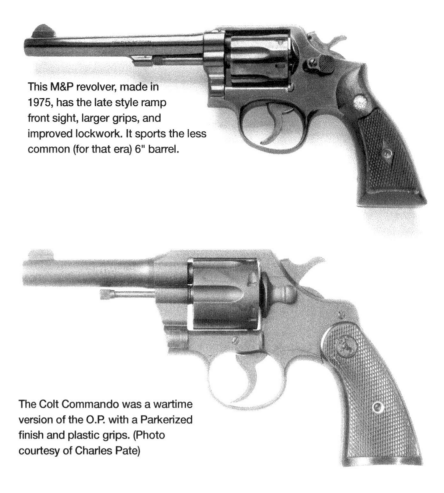

This M&P revolver, made in 1975, has the late style ramp front sight, larger grips, and improved lockwork. It sports the less common (for that era) 6" barrel.

The Colt Commando was a wartime version of the O.P. with a Parkerized finish and plastic grips. (Photo courtesy of Charles Pate)

S&W Takes the Lead

After the war, both companies resumed production of commercial-grade guns for the police and civilian market. As it had been before 1941, the O.P. proved a bigger seller – but the situation was about to change. During the war years, Colt had concentrated on building 1911 pistols and other weaponry, letting their revolver line languish. S&W, on the other hand, had upgraded their manufacturing processes and had a large pool of trained workers. With the war's end, Colt was stuck with outdated equipment and a shortage of skilled labor.

Additionally, Colt revolvers required more hand-fitting and detail work, which significantly increased their price compared to the competition. Lastly, while S&W embarked on a long-term R&D program to improve their revolvers, Colt's management seemed content to live off their reputation and did little to improve equipment, efficiency, their labor force and, most significantly, the product. This recipe for disaster led to S&W's capturing an ever-increasing share of the police and military market.

1948 saw the venerable M&P's designation changed to the Model 10. Seven years later, S&W introduced a K-frame revolver chambered for the .357 Magnum cartridge: the Model 19 Combat Magnum. Police agencies seeking more powerful weapons bought them as fast as they could be produced. Colt attempted to play catchup by re-chambering the O.P. for the .357 cartridge and adding a heavy barrel, adjustable sights

and larger grips. Known as the Colt 357 Magnum, sales were disappointing. The popularity of S&W K-frame revolvers, however, continued to grow as such prestigious agencies as the New York State Police, FBI and Royal Canadian Mounted Police adopted them. S&W also sold large numbers of them to police and military forces in Europe, Latin America and Asia.

The handwriting was now on the wall. Colt went through a series of new owners, none of whom seemed interested in innovation; the product line remained stagnant; and quality control took a hit while a series of labor disputes adversely affected production and the company's reputation.

As is evident from a 1976 survey taken by the New York State Criminal Justice Services, by that time, the police market was S&W's private preserve The sidearms used by the 45 state police agencies responding to the survey broke

down as follows:

S&W revolvers: 30
Colt revolvers: 4
Both: 4
Other: 1 (S&W 9mm pistol)
Revolver brand not indicated: 6

In an attempt to stay solvent, Colt began dropping models and 1969 found the O.P. missing from the catalog. The name was briefly revived with the Mark III Official Police revolver, but sales were so disappointing that production ceased after only three years. Many shooters and collectors found it disturbing that Colt's product line, reputation and popularity had sunk to such low levels.

The S&W Model 10 continued to be the firm's bread and butter product, although with the advent of the troublesome – and more violent – 1970s, .357 K-frame revolvers soon became their most popular law enforcement product. Beginning in the late 1980s, the 9mm (and later .40-caliber) semi-auto pistol became the police sidearm of choice, and today it is rare to see an American police officer with a holstered revolver at his side.

Opinions regarding this change of equipment are varied, with both sides making many good points in favor of their preferred weapon but such discussions – which always threaten to become heated – is beyond the scope of this article.

Which Is the Better-Shooting Revolver?

You knew we were going to get around to burning gunpowder sooner or later, didn't you? Accordingly I obtained samples of each revolver: my brother Vincent provided a very nice M&P made around 1940 while my fellow collector of oddities, John Rasalov,

was able to supply an O.P. Despite its being of 1930 vintage, the latter was in very good condition and as mechanically sound as the day it left the factory.

First, several observations as to each revolver's strong and weak points:

I found the S&W to be the better balanced of the two, making it a more naturally pointing revolver. Double-action trigger pulls are a subjective matter and while some prefer the way the Colt's stroke has a noticeable stage just before

Specifications

Colt Official Police	
Caliber	.38 "Colt Special" (Colt's proprietary .38 Special)
Overall length	9.25"
Barrel length	4"
Weight	33.5 oz.
Capacity	6
Sights	Front, rounded blade; rear, square groove in topstrap
Grips	Checkered walnut

S&W .38 Hand Ejector Military & Police	
Caliber	.38 S&W Special
Overall length	9.2"
Barrel length	4"
Weight	29 oz.
Capacity	6
Sights	Front, rounded blade; rear, U-shaped groove in topstrap
Grips	Checkered walnut or hard rubber

Here is the target Vince produced with the M&P. No complaints there! (Top) While the Colt's grouping was not quite as good as the Smith's, the difference was minimal.

Offhand shooting was performed at a "regulation" seven yards. Note the fumes from the lubricated, lead bullets.

it breaks, I prefer the lighter, stage-free pull of the M&P.

The O.P. was graced with a superior set of sights: a wide, square notch at the rear and the blade of ample proportions up front. While having the same style of sights, the Smith's were smaller and harder to align quickly. In addition, the tip of M&P's hammer spur actually obscured the rear notch until the hammer was slightly cocked. For the life of me I cannot fathom this, and wish someone could explain the reason for it.

When it comes to grips it was a tie. Both were horrible! I do not understand why it took the firearms industry several centuries to figure out that the odds of hitting the target would be greatly improved by a set of hand-filling, ergonomically-correct grips?

In keeping with the proper historical spirit I decided to limit me test firing to the type of ammunition that was most widely used during the era during in which this pair or revolvers had seen service. Black Hills Ammunition kindly supplied a quantity of .38 Special cartridges loaded with the traditional 158-gr. LRN bullets.

While I served as cameraman, my brother Vincent fired a series of six-shot groups with each revolver from a rest at a distance of 15 yards. As can be seen in the photos, both shot to point of aim and produced some very nice six-shot groups. I then set up a pair of USPSA targets at seven yards, and Vince ran two dozen rounds through each revolver, firing them both one-handed and supported.

What can we deduce from this expenditure of ammunition? Inasmuch as my brother Vince did all the shooting, I will quote him:

"I can make several observations," he says. First of all, both revolvers proved capable of excellent accuracy, whether fired from a rest or offhand. And while the Colt's sights were of a more practical design, I shot slightly better with the S&W. Whether or not this was due to the fact that I have much more experience with S&W revolvers, I can't really say. The grips on both revolvers were poorly designed and I believe

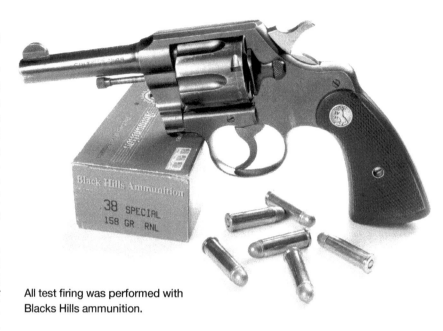

All test firing was performed with Blacks Hills ammunition.

something as simple as the addition of a grip adapter would improve handling to a significant degree. The Tyler-T Grip Adapter was first marketed in the 1930s and I can understand why! As regards recoil control, with its greater weight, I found I could shoot the O.P. faster but, considering the rather sedate ammunition we used, the difference was not all that great."

Vince summed it all up by saying, "I have long been a fan of the fixed-sight, double-action revolver and the performance of this pair only serves to buttress my long-held belief that they are one of the most practical type of handguns ever invented. I contend that for over a century they were proved capable of performing any law enforcement task they were called upon to perform and – despite the present popularity of the semi-auto pistol – still are!"

I then pressed him to choose a "winner." After a few moments of hesitation he said, "The M&P. But then I'm prejudiced."

NOTE: I would like to thank Vincent Scarlata, John Rasalov, Charles Pate, Michael Jon Littman, Donna Wells, Jeff Hoffman and Clive Law for supplying materials used to prepare this report. And I'm indebted to Black Hills Ammunition (PO Box 3090, Rapid City, SD 57709. Tel. 800-568-6625) for their kind cooperation in furnishing ammunition.

Bibliography

Boothroyd, Geoffrey. *The Handgun.* New York: Bonanza Books, Inc., 1967.

Canfield, Bruce N. *America's Military Revolvers.* Fairfax, VA: *American Rifleman*, Volume 145, No. 5. The National Rifle Association. May 1997.

Canfield, Bruce N. *U.S. Infantry Weapons Of World War Ii.* Lincoln, RI: Andrew Mowbray Publishers. 1996.

Ezell, Edward Clinton. *Handguns of the World.* New York: Barnes & Noble Books, 1981.

Haven, Charles T. and Frank A. Belden. *A History of the Colt Revolver.* New York: Bonanza Books, 1940.

Henwood, John. *America's Right Arm - The Smith & Wesson Military and Police Revolver.* Pacifica, CA: John Henwood. 1997.

Hogg, Ian V. & Weeks, John. *Pistols of the World.* Northfield, IL: DBI Books, Inc., 1982.

Jinks, Roy G. *History of Smith & Wesson*, 10th edition. North Hollywood, CA: Beinfeld Publishing, Inc. 1996.

Johnson, George B. and Hans Bert Lockhoven. *International Armament*, Volume 2. Cologne: International Small Arms Publishers. 1965.

Neal, Robert J. & Roy G. Jinks. *Smith & Wesson 1857-1945.* Livonia, NY: R&R Books. 1996.

Pate, Charles W. *U.S. Handguns of World War II.* Lincoln, RI: Andrew Mowbray Publishers.1998.

Wells, Donna. *Boston Police Department.* Portsmouth, NH: Arcadia Publishing, 2003.

Printed in the USA
CPSIA information can be obtained
at www.ICGtesting.com
JSHW060046150824
68134JS00031B/2648